A HEART
—FOR THE—
FUTURE

A HEART
— FOR THE —
FUTURE

WRITINGS ON
THE CHRISTIAN HOPE

EDITED BY
ROBERT BOAK SLOCUM

WIPF & STOCK · Eugene, Oregon

Wipf and Stock Publishers
199 W 8th Ave, Suite 3
Eugene, OR 97401

A New Conversation
Essays on the Future of Theology and the Episcopal Church
By Slocum, Robert Boak
Copyright©1999 by Slocum, Robert Boak
ISBN 13: 978-1-5326-4276-0
Publication date 11/7/2017
Previously published by Church Publishing Incorporated, 1999

Contents

Dedication and
Acknowledgments / ix

1
A Heart for the Future:
Reflections on the Christian Hope
Robert Boak Slocum / 1

2
This Body of Hope
Robert M. Cooper / 31

3
Parousia and Christian Hope
Ralph Del Colle / 48

4
Beneath the Edge of Thought:
Inner Eschatology and the Burden of Hope
Travis Du Priest / 59

5
Jesus and Eschatology
Reginald H. Fuller / 72

6
"I See Your Bridal Chamber Adorned":
An Eastern Orthodox Reflection on the Eschaton
in Light of the "Pattern" of Divine Worship
Hieromonk Alexander Golitzin / 82

7
The Eschatological Eucharist
Charles Hefling / 96

8
The Historic Ought-to-Be and the Spirit of Hope
Robert D. Hughes III / 109

9
Where Lies the Path of Hope in Everyday Life?
Thomas Hughson, S.J. / 121

10
What Shall We Do While Waiting for the End?
Alan Jones / 151

11
"In Times Like These We Need an Anchor": The Quest of a Storm-Tossed Church for a Sure and Certain Hope
Harold T. Lewis / 172

12
Sorting Out Some Synoptic Scenes: The Destruction of Jerusalem and the Second Coming of Jesus
Jeffrey Allen Mackey / 183

13
To Build the New City: An Eschatological and Secular Hope
Jacqueline Schmitt / 193

14
An Augustinian Reflection on the Church and Hope
George H. Tavard / 207

15
Baptismal Living: Steadfast Covenant of Hope
Fredrica Harris Thompsett / 220

16
The Final Reconciliation:
Reflections on a Social Dimension
of the Eschatological Transition
Miroslav Volf / 233

17
The Intolerable Burden of the Past,
the Pure Figment of the Present,
and the Surpassing Worth of the Future
Paul F. M. Zahl / 268

18
Heaven as a State of Mind:
Peter Abelard's "O quanta qualia"
Wanda Zemler-Cizewski / 278

19
Heavenly Hope:
How the Book of Revelation Sings
to My Chronic Pain
John D. Zemler / 287

Contributors / 301

Dedication and Acknowledgments

I want to take this opportunity to thank the editorial staff of Church Publishing Incorporated, especially Frank Tedeschi and Johnny Ross, for their good work to bring this project to completion. I appreciate the professional relationships that have made it possible to publish seven books with Church Hymnal Corporation/Church Publishing Incorporated. Thanks also to John Eagleson, Bob Land, and Amy Davis, who have helped to prepare this book for publication.

I also thank the contributing authors for this volume, especially those who started writing on themes of Christian hope and eschatology before the arrangements for publication were finalized. I hope they will be pleased by the results of their willingness to venture into an unknown publishing future.

I am grateful for the hospitality of the staff and extended community of the DeKoven Center, Racine, Wisconsin, especially the Rev. Dr. Travis T. Du Priest, Director.

I dedicate this book to my children, Claire, Rebecca, and Jacob Slocum, who are the next generation of my family. I also dedicate *A Heart for the Future* to Susanne Sklar, who has shown me a new horizon "in eternity's sunrise."

ROBERT BOAK SLOCUM

Lake Geneva, Wisconsin
January 23, 2004

1

A Heart for the Future

Reflections on the Christian Hope

ROBERT BOAK SLOCUM

WHEN WE SAY the Lord's Prayer, we pray for the coming of God's kingdom on earth as in heaven. We celebrate our expectancy for this completion in the liturgical season of Advent. The *Prayer Book Catechism* concludes with a section dedicated to the Christian hope, which is "to await the coming of Christ in glory, and the completion of God's purpose for the world" (BCP, 861). Austin Farrer warns in the sermon "Always Beginning" that "God has put his infinity in our mind, and if we cannot stretch out for him beyond the little beginnings here allowed us, we must let go of God and loose him wholly."[1] And yet the Christian hope, or eschatology, has been a neglected area in theology and in the life of the church. This neglect can cause the church to be "backward-looking" in its perspectives, more concerned about where we have been than where we are going. Appreciating our destination in terms of the future has everything to say about how we pray, serve, reflect, and decide in the life of the church today. This essay presents a collection of twenty-two reflections —

Thanks are due to Jim Dunkly and Susanne Sklar for helpful suggestions concerning this essay.

1. Austin Farrer, "Always Beginning," in *Austin Farrer: The Essential Sermons*, ed. Leslie Houlden (Cambridge, Mass.: Cowley Publications, 1991), 164.

in their own way topical, even propositional — to consider the future we are called to and how we may welcome it today.

Wrath

I remember attending an Advent service in Wisconsin in the 1980s where the congregation sang "Day of wrath! O day of mourning! See fulfilled the prophets' warning, Heav'n and earth in ashes burning!" (Hymn 468, *The Hymnal 1940*). This was not a hopeful prospect, but it may have given expression to the dread of the future that is present in many of us. The good news is that God will treat us better than we would have expected. It seems that Jesus was constantly scandalizing people in this way. The woman taken in the act of adultery is neither condemned nor stoned to death but told by Jesus to go and sin no more (John 8:3–11). Zacchaeus, the swindling tax collector, is invited to share a meal (Luke 19:1–10). Workmen arriving late in the day get the full day's wage (Matt. 20:1–16). The prodigal son returns home not to harsh punishment for his mistakes but to the welcoming embrace of his father's love and forgiveness; they have a party (Luke 15:11–32).

I'm sure these stories caused difficulties for Jesus' hearers and for Christians throughout the ages. Some may say, "It's not fair! That's not what they deserve!" And the critics are right, of course. It's not what "they" deserve. I remember a parishioner of mine who was concerned about the statement in Eucharistic Prayer D (BCP, 374) that Jesus proclaimed "to prisoners, freedom." He figured that if they were in prison, that's where they belonged, and we shouldn't be praying for anything different! Certainly God our maker knows us — our fallibility, our history, our mistakes. But God also knows who and what we can be in terms of sharing the fullness of divine life and the completion of divine love. That gift is waiting for us, available, and it will become an increasingly present reality as we let go of fear and move into the future of God's love. We can trust that we will be treated better than we deserve.

Acorn and Oak

What is our future in Christ? Answering that question will tell us much about our lives of faith today. There's an old saying that an acorn is only understood in terms of the magnificent oak tree that it can become. Its meaning will elude us if we think only in terms of what the acorn is now as we hold it in the palm of a hand. Under the right conditions, it will become an oak tree and nothing else. Nothing less than becoming an oak tree represents a fulfillment of the acorn's potential. That's its *end* (in Greek, *telos*).

And nothing less than a full union with God represents a fulfillment of our potential. That's *our* end. If we try to understand our lives just in terms of who and what we are now, we'll miss what matters most. We can fail to see beyond ourselves. We're meant for the uninterrupted fullness of sharing God's love. Who we are and how we live today as Christians has everything to do with the future we're meant to enjoy. We may call the uninterrupted fullness of sharing God's love "heaven"; we can describe it as the "beatific vision," or think of it in terms of everlasting life in the kingdom and glory of God. But the completion of Christ's life in us must be located in the future. We may be nearer to salvation than we once were (Rom. 13:11b), but we're not "there" yet. We hope for the completion of what is already begun in our lives, our church, our world. But how do we understand it? How do we prepare that ground? How do we seek it and move toward it? Knowing that an acorn is meant to be an oak can inform how we treat it today, if we really want it to become an oak. We plant it in good soil, where it will get enough water and light. And our lives today — our choices, our actions, our silences — can be shaped and guided in light of our true end in divine love.

Destination

In the poem "Limited," the American poet Carl Sandburg provides an image of an express train hurtling across the prairie with fifteen all-steel coaches and a thousand people. He then warns darkly that "[a]ll the coaches shall be scrap and rust and all the men and women laughing in the diners and sleepers shall pass to ashes." Asked his destination, a passenger replies, with unconscious irony, "Omaha."[2] That destination, in itself, will ultimately lead to scrap and ashes. We need and are meant for something more than Omaha (or Miami or Seattle) as our destination. The apostle Paul urges that we are destined by God for salvation in Christ, not for wrath (1 Thess. 5:9). We need to know where we're called to be and where we're headed, because our sense of destination has much to say about our priorities and choices of direction today.

Diogenes Allen considers the end and the last things of human life relative to "East Coker," the second of T. S. Eliot's *Four Quartets*.[3] Our mortal end is death, the same end faced by our ancestors. Allen calls attention to Eliot's use of the motto attributed to Mary, Queen of Scots, "In my beginning is my end." The dominant theme of the first part of "East Coker" is decay, and the dance of the peasants in this poem is a dance of death. East Coker was Eliot's ancestral village, and "Eliot will become part

---

2. Carl Sandburg, "Limited," in *Complete Poems* (New York: Harcourt, Brace, 1950), 20.
3. T. S. Eliot, "East Coker," in *Four Quartets* (New York: Harcourt, Brace, 1943), 23–32.

of the earth, just like his ancestors." But there's another possibility. When the image of God is understood as a principle of our being, Allen urges, "our life has a different end than the earth." The motto of Mary, Queen of Scots, is reversed by Eliot at the conclusion of "East Coker": "In my end is my beginning."[4] Our end is to realize the image of God. We make a new beginning whenever we discern what we are to become, and when we obey Jesus we "reject a life style that leads to death as our ultimate end and find our rightful place in the ultimate order."[5] As we accept the offer of life in God, our true destination is not one of decay, rust, and ashes. There is always a new beginning and hope for us in the fullness of God's love. That is our future and our true destination.

Grief

People suffer. Sooner or later, we all experience significant loss. This may be the death of a loved one, the loss of a job, a missed opportunity, or the end of a relationship. We may find ourselves missing familiar surroundings after a move, or we may wonder what happened when our familiar surroundings have changed around us. Our situation may change rapidly with a threatening diagnosis from the doctor, or a really bad year for investments, or a phone call that tells us about a tragic event. Or we may notice that our most basic capacities and strengths fade with the passing years. We can no longer count on things or possibilities that were once so important. Eventually, we face grief.

---

4. Ibid., 32.
5. Diogenes Allen, *Quest, The Search for Meaning through Christ*, 2nd ed. (New York: Church Publishing Incorporated, 2000), 24. I discuss Allen's consideration of Eliot's "East Coker" in a book review in the *Sewanee Theological Review*, no. 4 (Michaelmas 2002): 476–78.

St. Paul advises not to be ignorant concerning the dead and not to grieve as those who have no hope (1 Thess. 4:13). Significantly, he does not forbid grieving the loss of a loved one, but he urges that Christian grieving take place with a significant perspective. The loss is real, and it hurts. But the loss is not the last word. Christian hope makes a difference. Life and love continue in Christ. Our lives are changed, not taken away in death. Indeed, love never ends (1 Cor. 13:8).

As he neared the end of his life, the controversial Episcopal priest James DeKoven (1831–79) preached a sermon for the last Sunday of the church year on the miraculous feeding of the five thousand. After the feeding, Jesus commands his disciples to gather up the fragments left over of the five barley loaves and the two fish, "that nothing may be lost" (John 6:12). The sermon was titled "Gathering Up the Fragments," and DeKoven reflected that only in God are the broken fragments and shards of our life gathered up and made whole.

DeKoven was well acquainted with disappointment, loss, and brokenness. He had been nominated and elected as bishop of Illinois, but his election was not ratified by the requisite number of diocesan standing committees in the Episcopal Church because of doubts about his theology. And yet at the end of his life, he articulated a theology of hope so that, as the church year ended and Advent approached, he could look forward to the completion of all things in God. DeKoven urged, "the Gospel for the day tells of something still that can be done, even for a wasted life, saying, 'Gather up the fragments that remain, that nothing be lost.' The fragments of a life, beloved! The broken pieces of a mighty whole — they may be gathered up again."[6]

---

6. James DeKoven, *Sermons Preached on Various Occasions* (New York: D. Appleton, 1880), 315. "Gathering Up the Fragments," was preached at Racine College, Racine, Wisconsin, on the Last Sunday after Trinity, 1878. The Gospel text was John 6:12. The

As we grieve our losses, we are called to remember that all the broken bits of our lives are to be completed in God. We will grieve, but not without hope. As we hear in the psalm (30:5), "weeping may spend the night, but joy comes in the morning." Whatever the darkness of our grief, the joy is ultimately the completion of all our purposes and all our fragments in the future of God's love, who wants nothing to be lost.

The Future in the Present and the Past

Sharing God's love has everything to do with our life today. Knowing God's love isn't just for "heaven" and doesn't require us to "go" somewhere or wait for a special time. God has known us and loved us from the beginning of our existence, as when God "knit me together in my mother's womb" (Ps. 139:12). God has always loved us and our world. Creation was an act of love by God. We are part of that Creation, and our lives are a good gift from a loving God. God's love is part of our past.

Even when humanity sinned and turned away from God, the love of God persisted and was constant to save us. In the times of the Old Covenant, God reached out in love for humanity through law and prophets. Finally, decisively, God's own Son, Jesus, came to humanity for our salvation. Jesus reveals God's love in human terms; his love and ministry are continued in the world by the church, even though the church as a whole and all of us in the church have erred and fallen short of God's glory (Rom. 3:23; see Article XXI of the Articles of Religion, BCP, 872).

---

sermon was preached within four months of DeKoven's death. He is commemorated in the Episcopal Calendar of the Church Year on March 22. See Robert Boak Slocum, "Romantic Religion and the Witness of James DeKoven," in *To Hear Celestial Harmonies: Essays on the Witness of James DeKoven and The DeKoven Center*, ed. Robert Boak Slocum and Travis Talmadge Du Priest (Cincinnati: Forward Movement, 2002), 15–32, 28.

Because we have known God's mighty acts of love in the past, we recognize the importance of our history and tradition. In many ways, the past has made us what we are. Because of the life, death, and resurrection of Jesus of Nazareth, we call ourselves Christians. We revere the sacred record of the scriptures and affirm that the scriptures contain all things necessary for salvation (see Article VI of the Articles of Religion, BCP, 868). We can learn much about ourselves and about God as we recall how God was present to the people of Israel; and how Jesus lived and showed the face of God's love in the world; and how the early church took the first dramatic (if at times faltering) steps to continue Jesus' ministry in the power of the Spirit.

Seeds of Hope

For Christians, the best is always yet to come. For "now I know only in part; then I will know fully, even as I have been fully known" (1 Cor. 13:12b). The past certainly shapes and forms our identity as Christians today. But our past points beyond itself to the future, so that we must not cease from exploration or give up the journey of faith.[7] The beginnings of faith in the world are dramatically recalled and conveyed to us through scripture and tradition, word and sacrament, memory and practice. But the completion of our faith is not yet realized in us, our church, or our world. We stand between the times, between beginning and completion, between start and resolution of the Christian hope. At this time it would be faithless to deny the beginning, and it would be foolish to claim the realization or end.

For now, we have the "seeds" of who and what we are to be. We have the beginning but not the end. The beginning points us

---

7. See Eliot, "Little Gidding," in *Four Quartets*, 59.

in the way of the end and gives us hope. But the fulfillment of the beginning is not found back there in the past; it is not even found here in the present. The Christian hope faces us squarely into the future, where the completion of God's love for us will be found. That orientation toward the future has everything to do with how we live today, in the present.

Surprise

If the seeds of our past and present in Christ are to be fulfilled in the future, how should we live? What can we do to welcome and receive that future, so we may be the people we're meant to be in the fullness of God's love? If we have begun a journey of faith and not yet "arrived" at our destiny or destination, then clearly we are headed for a place or way or time that will be somehow different from what we now experience. Not altogether different, perhaps, because the love of God we now experience will be the same love we hope to know fully. We can expect consistency of purpose and expression between what we already know of God's love and what the future will be. We can rely on God's integrity. But the expression and the experience promise to be quite different! Openness to the graceful and unexpected ways of divine love is essential for us.

As Christians, we need to be ready for discernment and open to surprise. Participating in God's grace to know our destiny in Christ requires discernment. Not everything will be helpful and certainly not everything will be divine. There will be distractions, seductions, and misunderstandings. We will need to "test the spirits" (1 John 4:1), using the gifts of scripture and tradition to provide our compass as we seek to navigate and explore our new world of faith. But we will also need to take some risks. If we hesitate to venture into unfamiliar territory, we may need to recall that the fullness of God's love is to be encountered in ways beyond our current knowing. Even as we hold on to the rudder of divine gifts from the past, we can look forward into a future of faith and life that will surpass our expectations. God promises us "great and hidden things [we] have not known" (Jer. 33:3). The future of God's love is more than we can put into words. It will surprise us! It may also demand more of us than we can imagine, as we find our heart "battered" by God, whose love is relentless. John Donne prays:

> Batter my heart, three person'd God; for, you
> As yet but knocke, breathe, shine, and seeke to mend,
> That I may rise, and stand, o'erthrow me, and bend
> Your force, to breake, blowe, burn and make me new....[8]

God's surprising future for us may be stunning in its beauty and its challenge, as we find ourselves broken, blown, and battered by love.

Patient Impatience

This expectant outlook makes for a paradoxical stance, a kind of "patient impatience." Having a heart for the future is not "otherworldly," as if to deny the importance of the realities in our world today. On the contrary, through today's realities we venture from the present into the future of God's love. Our present reality includes our needs, limitations, hopes, gifts, and desires. Through all of who we are, God engages us and invites us into the future. Therefore we need to consider our current circumstances and conditions with the utmost care and seriousness. Even as we look for something more, beyond the limits of the present visible

---

8. John Donne, "Batter my heart," in *John Donne, Selections from Divine Poems, Sermons, Devotions, and Prayers*, ed. John Booty (New York and Mahwah, N.J.: Paulist Press, 1990), 81.

reality, we also know that the seeds of God's future are here in the present, and only through the present may we begin to discover what the future will reveal. What we do today shapes and forms who we will be in the future and how God's love may be realized and completed in our lives. Farrer urges that "heaven alone gives final meaning to any earthly hopes" and "we have no way to grasp at heavenly hope, than by pursuing hopeful tasks here below."[9]

And yet, at the same time, we may recall that the present does not have the last word. The ultimate resolution of things is outside the things themselves. We should care greatly about the world that surrounds us — but not too much. The issues and styles and trends that touch us deeply and command our attention will give way to other issues, styles, and trends that will be equally compelling. We can put our ultimate hope in none of them.

In the meantime, we can wait, eagerly and patiently, for the further revealing of God's glory to us. We can use what we have received of divine grace to navigate and guide us into an unfolding future. We can be ready for surprise and wonder as we seek to know a fullness of God's love that is beyond our current experience. We can live in trust that God will give us even more and more until we enjoy the incredible fullness and completion of the Christian hope.

The Unknown

Fear of the future can be a kind of faithlessness. God loves us and invites us to share the fullness of divine life. God wants to know us better. That will mean something different from the present, and that "something" will be in the future. We can look ahead with hope and faith. Sometimes it's frightening to imagine how

---

9. Farrer, "The Ultimate Hope," in *The Essential Sermons*, 200.

we will know God if things are different. If things will only stay the same, we assume, then we'll be all right. But things aren't going to stay the same, humanly speaking. That's not possible. Our lives and contexts won't stand still. More importantly, for us to know the completion of what is begun in our lives, we will need to "find and be found by God" in new ways (see The Prayers of the People Form II, BCP, 386). God's love beckons us into the future.

Christian faith has much to do with stepping into the unknown. When Jesus called Peter and Andrew, James and John (Mark 1:16–20), they left their fishing nets and their family fishing business to go and follow him. Where would he lead them? What would happen? They didn't know. They couldn't know. In a moment they left behind an old way of life to follow Jesus into an unknown future. Mary, probably a young girl of middle-school age, was given a startling invitation and choice: to bear "the Son of the Most High" (Luke 1:26–38). At first she was troubled and afraid, and she voiced a very realistic concern: She had no husband, so how could she have a child? There must have been other questions: What would people say? Who would understand the truth of her life or her son? The life she had known before would certainly change, and the future was surrounded with doubts. But she trusted and ventured into the unknown. What if Mary had declined the offer? What if the fishermen had chosen to stay in their boats and keep their jobs? What if we "stay in our boats" and play it safe? Our cooperation is essential if we are to receive the unfolding of God's future in our lives.

Fear

Sometimes I see decals on cars and trucks that boldly proclaim "No Fear," but I don't believe it. I've heard it said that fear and greed are the main competing forces that drive the ups and downs of the stock market. In many ways, we live in a culture of fear in the twenty-first century United States. Many homes and businesses (and churches) are now equipped with expensive security systems. We're afraid of terrorists, afraid of strangers, afraid of our neighbors, even afraid of ourselves. We're afraid of the unknown future.

Before departing from his disciples, Jesus tells them he is going to God the Father and preparing a place for them with God (John 14). He says they know the way to the place where he is going. This is an unexpected future for the disciples; their hearts are troubled, and they are afraid. It's easy to hear the pleading in Thomas's complaint, "Lord, we do not know where you are going. How can we know the way?" Certainly at that moment the disciples are not feeling especially confident about the future. But the future has better things in store for them than they can imagine from that perspective. Jesus promises that he will not leave them comfortless, that God the Father will send them another Advocate at his request, the Spirit of truth, who will teach them everything and remind them of all that Jesus said. In the future they will be found and upheld by God in powerful and unexpected ways. They will receive the Spirit and overcome their fears.

Interestingly, on the day of the Resurrection, the disciples are locked in the house where they met "for fear of the Jews" (John 20:19). Jesus appears to them and says to them, "Peace be with you. As the father has sent me, so I send you." Then he breathes on them and says, "Receive the Holy Spirit" and empowers them for forgiveness of sins. After the disciples receive the Holy Spirit, we never again hear about their locking themselves in for fear of anyone. Similarly, the Episcopal theologian William Porcher

DuBose (1836–1918) points to the "surprising change" in the disciples on the Day of Pentecost (Acts 2:1–11), when their "vague and indefinite emotions" are replaced by "a clear understanding and a definite plan and purpose as to the meaning and the preaching of Christ and the resurrection." DuBose urges that this account cannot be dismissed as "artistic literary fiction." Instead, it reflects the subjective preparation and activity of the Holy Spirit in the lives of the disciples.[10] They are comforted, inspired, and *sent* on a new way — all in the unfolding of God's future for them. Indeed, it is love that casts out fear (1 John 4:18). The disciples' openness to the future is essential for them to share God's life. And our own openness to the future is essential for us, as we welcome the activity of the Spirit who makes Christ present for salvation in the church and our lives.

Flying Backward

Once when my father was in a playful mood, he told the story of the "whiffle-poose," an imaginary bird (unrelated to the more famous creature called a "whiffenpoof"). It was distinguished by flying backward, because — he said with a twinkle in his eye — it was more interested in where it had been than where it was going. Sometimes in the church it seems as if we are more interested in where we have been than where we're going! The past at least seems to be known, and perhaps somewhat manageable. The future seems unknown, dark, and speculative. We're not really open to a future that looks different from the past. We have trouble imagining ourselves and our relationship with God in different terms. What we have known seems to be safer ground than what

---

10. William Porcher DuBose, *The Gospel in the Gospels* (New York: Longmans, Green & Co., 1906), 244–45. See Robert Boak Slocum, *The Theology of William Porcher DuBose: Life, Movement, and Being* (Columbia: University of South Carolina Press, 2000), 82.

we have not yet known or do not yet know fully. It's easy to become suspicious and wary, even scared, of the unknown. It may be easy to recognize God's presence and love in our past and in the history of the church. But somehow we may be less than comfortable with the prospect of being encountered by God in new ways, in a future that may be surprising. A frightened kind of faithlessness may claim our hearts; we find ourselves saying, "We've always done it this way," "The old wine is good," and we have no taste for the new wine of God's future (Luke 5:37–39). In the future our hopes are to be realized. In the future we will know God more clearly, dearly, and nearly than we do now (see Hymn 654, *The Hymnal 1982*).

If we close our eyes to the future, we may miss it. We may overlook the unfolding possibilities of God's future if we refuse to know God in new or unfamiliar ways. God may surprise us if we'll only *see* what's before us. Surprise literally means "overtake," and God will overtake us in new and unexpected ways as we venture into an unknown future.[11] God is not bound by the ways we have known divine love in the past — through law and prophets, through apostles and councils, through reformation and counterreformation, even in the ways we have become accustomed to knowing God in the Episcopal Church. This is not to discount the importance of scripture and tradition or to diminish the significance of God's faithfulness to be present in appointed and promised ways, through word and sacrament, and whenever the church is gathered in Christ's name. But there's more! There's more of God than we've ever been able to describe, express, or present. God's self-disclosure for us and our salvation

---

11. For a further discussion of surprise, see Robert M. Cooper, "The Fantasy of Control," *Saint Luke's Journal of Theology* 33 (September 1990): 259–69, 264–65, 268–69. See also C. S. Lewis, *Surprised by Joy: The Shape of My Early Life* (San Diego and New York: Harcourt Brace & Company, 1955).

is not complete. The fullness of God's love awaits us in the future, along a path that will mean unexpected changes for us as we go.

In too many times and in too many ways, we have failed to claim the adventure of faith. We have failed to see that the God of our past and present is also the God of our future. We can trust that God will be present for us and available to us in that future. We can live the faith with an audacity that welcomes new moments of revelation and new possibilities for being found by God. We can discover new forms and expressions for the faith we have known for a long time, so that the truth of God's love will be more than an object of memory. Fear can hold us captive to the well-worn and familiar, but we may find that our eyes have been closed to possibilities that are still beyond us in God's future. The Christian hope is about having our eyes open, willing to see what God will show us and what we can discern, even when the light "surprises" us in the middle of our song to discover a new world of possibilities (Hymn 667, *The Hymnal 1982*).

The Spirit

Openness to the future has much to do with openness to the Holy Spirit, who will guide us into all truth (John 16:13). The wind blows where it chooses (John 3:8). Despite our doubts, the promise about guidance into truth tells us much about ourselves, God, and the future. To sin against the Holy Spirit, therefore, may be understood as sinning against (blocking) hope and the future. Michael Ramsey describes this as " 'an *aeonian* sin' — a sin relating to the aeon to come."[12] We stand on the frontier of

---

12. Michael Ramsey, *Holy Spirit: A Biblical Study* (Cambridge: Cowley Publications, 1992), 30 [first published, 1977]. Ramsey considers Mark 3:28–30 and Matt. 12:31–32. See Robert Boak Slocum, "Zacchaean Effects and Ethics of the Spirit," in *Engaging the Spirit: Essays on the Life and Theology of the Holy Spirit*, ed. Robert Boak Slocum (New York: Church Publishing Incorporated, 2001), 215–23, 220.

the coming kingdom of God as we welcome the activity of the Holy Spirit in our lives.

To be guided into all truth means we're not yet there. We haven't *arrived,* which is painfully evident to many of us most of the time. We know ourselves to be anything but perfect. But we have potential; we have capacity for truth that we haven't achieved. We can be guided to this blessed condition, which will have to happen in the future if it is going to happen at all for us. Finally, most importantly, our faith isn't in either ourselves or even the future as unrealized potential. We have a promised guide, the Holy Spirit, who will be with us as we move from present to future, from partial to complete in God's truth. But for this to be a reality, we need to be willing to travel and let ourselves be guided to experience an unknown future.[13] We don't travel alone. By the Spirit, Christ is present with us, even if Christ seems a "Traveler unknown" appearing unexpectedly when we are lost in darkness (Hymns 638–39, *The Hymnal 1982*). With his help we can recover our bearings and direction. We can discern and follow the way of God's future. The Spirit will guide us into all truth.

Letting Go

Having faith in the future has nothing to do with an expectation that the future will be easy or that everything will turn out

---

13. With respect to the connection between travel and knowing by experience, Edward Schillebeeckx states that "the basic meaning of the Dutch word for experience is travelling through the country and thus — through exploration — being taken up into a process of learning. Experience means learning through 'direct' contact with people and things. It is the ability to assimilate perceptions." Edward Schillebeeckx, *Christ: The Experience of Jesus as Lord,* trans. John Bowden (New York: Crossroad, 1983), 31. Schillebeeckx adds in a footnote that "in Old Dutch, *varen* means simply to travel," and this meaning was only later "restricted to travels by sea or on inland waterways." Drawing out the connection with experience, he states that "*ervaren* means to get to know something, not by hearsay but by seeing it oneself: by sight and living contact" (854, n. 2).

as we planned or wanted. That would be naive. After Peter correctly identifies Jesus to be the Messiah (Mark 8:27–33), Jesus proceeds to explain what his identity and mission will mean in the future. It is an ugly picture from Peter's perspective, involving Jesus' suffering, rejection, and death. Peter attempts to deny that future for Jesus, but the future that will unfold from Jesus' identity as messiah has everything to do with suffering and death. The promise of the future is not about a fantasyland where everything goes right and no one gets hurt. The promise is that God will be with us, even as we face our crosses, and that God's love will prevail. We can know a fullness of divine love that we have not yet encountered.

Hope in God's future for us will sometimes mean letting go of any particular hope we have for the present. Sometimes we must wait without hope because, as T. S. Eliot says, "hope would be hope for the wrong thing."[14] Sometimes we may be confronted with things that are good in themselves, but bad for us in our present situation. When Jesus is hungry, Satan tempts him with the possibility of having bread (Matt. 4:1–4). In itself, bread would have been good for a very hungry person to eat. But for Jesus, at that moment, it becomes an object of temptation, a good thing whose meaning and purpose can be twisted into something destructive. Accepting Satan's suggestion would be a kind of idolatry, giving reverence due to God to something or someone less than God.[15] At that moment, it is better for Jesus to refrain from

---

14. Eliot, "East Coker," 15.
15. For further discussions of the idols of temptation relative to the temptation of Christ in the wilderness, see William Stringfellow, *Free in Obedience* (New York: Seabury, 1964), 69; William Stringfellow, *Instead of Death*, 2nd ed. (New York: Seabury, 1976), 109–10; William Stringfellow, *Count It All Joy* (Grand Rapids, Mich.: Eerdmans, 1967), 86–88; James E. Griffiss, *A Silent Path to God* (Philadelphia: Fortress, 1980), 87–108; Robert Boak Slocum, "William Stringfellow and the Christian Witness against Death," in *Prophet of Justice, Prophet of Life: Essays on William Stringfellow*, ed. Robert Boak Slocum (New York: Church Publishing Incorporated, 1997), 26–28.

eating. He must not put his hope in bread, or the immediate satisfaction of his need, or the one suggesting an immediate "solution" for his problem. It is better to wait in hope, even when waiting means an urgent, unrelieved hunger.

Beyond Us

Christian hope is not optimism; it is not a facile assumption that things just naturally get better and better. On the contrary, Christian hope is rooted in a supernatural understanding of what everything is and is to be in God. The immediate circumstances around us may do anything but improve. The Christian hope, for example, does not have any specific predictions or advice to offer about what to expect in the coming years for the American economy, or the stock market, or the next presidential election. Things may get better — or worse. It is that way in our individual lives as well. Will we get sick? Will we recover? Will we get a wonderful new job? Will we lose the job we have? Who knows? But the Christian hope reminds us that we are meant for divine love and called to fulfillment in God. Our victories and defeats, our joys and heartaches can all be the occasion for deepening our relationship with God. We can find God's love in the present through these moments (be they good, bad, or seemingly indifferent) and be led more fully into the future of our completion in God's love.

Real growth often cannot begin until a person has hit bottom and faced despair, along with acknowledging personal limitations and helplessness. This becomes the first step in a process of recovery. Sometimes it is necessary to acknowledge — with St. Ignatius of Loyola — the alternation of times of consolation and desolation in life. In this way, the focus of our life in God's love and future will not be obscured by either the elation of good times or the frustration of bad times. The Christian hope, the eschatological future, is beyond us. It is *for* us, but it is not *about* us, as if we were the source of hope or even the rightful center of attention. And if we are centered on ourselves — whether we are experiencing things getting better or worse — we can miss God's future for us. We need to be expectant, eager, watching, and ready to receive. God's future, like divine love, comes to us from beyond our present limits.

A Foretaste

The future is not otherworldly. It is not remote or disconnected from the realities of life. The future is constantly breaking into our lives in the present. That's why our orientation to the future is so important for our lives and faith today. The Prayer Book describes the Eucharist as "the foretaste of the heavenly banquet" (BCP, 860) and notes that the sacraments "sustain our present hope and anticipate its future fulfillment" (BCP, 861). If, say, a host is getting ready for a banquet on the night before the guests arrive, the host may take a sip of the wine that will be served at the banquet. The wine will be the same wine when the celebration is complete. It will taste the same. But certainly no one would confuse the preparatory sip with the full celebration on the next day.

The life and love of God we know today — through word and sacrament, friends and family, ministry and service — is the real item. We don't have to wait until we go to heaven or anywhere else to receive God's love. Indeed, "heaven is God."[16] We already know it, but not yet in its fullness. That comes later, in the future. For now, we see "through a glass, darkly" (1 Cor. 13:12a, KJV). But we do see, even if imperfectly. Turning toward the future

---

16. Farrer, "The Ultimate Hope," in *The Essential Sermons*, 203.

means we want to see better. Turning toward the future means we want to enjoy the full banquet, relative to which all we have known of God's love may prove to be just a sip or a nibble. Turning to the future means we want our present turned to God, so that God's promise will become a reality in our lives.

All Things

If ever we find ourselves tempted to assume that the promised end is just for human beings — or even disembodied spirits — we're reminded by St. Paul that "the creation waits with eager longing for the revealing of the children of God." We are to share the "hope that the creation itself will be set free from its bondage to decay and will obtain the freedom of the glory of the children of God" (Rom. 8:19-21). Thomas Aquinas speaks of all creation proceeding from God and returning to God (*"exitus et reditus"*).[17] Similarly, Jürgen Moltmann states that "with the rebirth of Christ from death to eternal life we also expect the rebirth of the whole cosmos. Nothing that God has created is lost. Everything returns in transfigured form."[18] Completion in God is the intended end of all things, all creation — including humanity but not *only* humanity.[19] Julian of Norwich proclaims the divine

---

17. God is "the productive cause of all things" and "the end of all things." Thomas Aquinas, *Summa Contra Gentiles, Book Three: Providence, Part I*, trans. Vernon J. Bourke (Notre Dame, Ind.: University of Notre Dame Press, 1975), 73 (3:17 [8]). See *Summa Contra Gentiles, Book Three: Providence, Part I*, 74 (3:18 [3]). Jan Aertsen notes that Aquinas's "scheme of *exitus et reditus* is derived from Neoplatonism and plays a fundamental role in Aquinas's thought. The origin and end of things are one and the same. The dynamics of reality is a circular motion (*circulatio*)." Jan A. Aertsen, "Aquinas' Philosophy in Its Historical Setting," in *The Cambridge Companion to Aquinas*, ed. Norman Kretzmann and Eleonore Stump (Cambridge: Cambridge University Press, 1993), 16.

18. Jürgen Moltmann, *The Source of Life: The Holy Spirit and the Theology of Life*, trans. Margaret Kohl (Minneapolis: Fortress, 1997), 123.

19. In this regard, an interesting perspective is provided by Stephen H. Webb, who considers the affectionate relationship that can be shared by a person and a dog. The dog in this relationship is a gift, not just a property to be owned and exploited. And the relationship can draw out the human and the dog in ways that enrich both lives. It is possible to love and be loved by a being who is different from yourself. This relationship

revelation that "All shall be well," and she explains that "the fullness of joy is to see God in everything; for by the same power, wisdom, and love with which he made all things, our good Lord is continually leading all things to the same end and he himself shall bring this about; and when the time comes we shall see it."[20] Our hope is the fulfillment of all things in God — not just all righteous souls, or even all humanity, but *all*.

When we recognize that all things have an intended place in the kingdom of God, we may reconsider our own behavior relative to all things. As William Blake says, "Every thing that lives is holy!"[21] Indeed, the new Jerusalem will include "even Tree, Metal, Earth & Stone."[22] If we see that the air and waters of the earth, and the earth itself, are meant for inclusion in the kingdom of God, we may see them as more than things fit to be consumed by our needs. We may use different parts of creation for our own lives and survival, but we may also find a new respect for what we see in the world around us. Stated more bluntly, we won't be so glad to abuse or pollute the things in our world if we understand their origin and destiny and their sacredness in the kingdom of God. The Christian hope can draw us to an unexpected ecology.

---

anticipates the harmony of all beings in the end times of God's peaceable kingdom, and petting a dog can be "an eschatological statement about who we want to be." Stephen H. Webb, *On God and Dogs: A Christian Theology of Compassion for Animals* (New York and Oxford: Oxford University Press, 1998), 106. This commentary is drawn from my review of Webb's book in the *Anglican Theological Review* 81, no. 3 (Summer 1999): 513, 515–16.

20. Julian of Norwich, *Revelations of Divine Love (Short Text and Long Text)*, trans. Elizabeth Spearing (London: Penguin, 1998), 89 [The Long Text, chaps. 34–35]. Julian (c. 1342–c. 1413) experienced fifteen showings on May 8, 1373, a sixteenth "on the following night," and a supplementary showing about 1388. A. C. Spearing, "Introduction," in *Revelations of Divine Love*, vii–xxxiii, vii–viii. The promise of Julian's revelation is echoed in Eliot's "Little Gidding" at the conclusion of *Four Quartets:* "And all shall be well and/ all manner of thing shall be well...." Eliot, "Little Gidding," 59.

21. William Blake, "Visions of the Daughters of Albion," in *The Complete Poetry and Prose of William Blake,* newly revised edition, ed. David V. Erdman (Berkeley and Los Angeles: University of California Press, 1982), 51. This statement also appears in Blake's "The Marriage of Heaven and Hell" and "America," *The Complete Poetry and Prose of William Blake,* 45, 54.

22. Blake, *Jerusalem,* in *The Complete Poetry and Prose of William Blake,* 258.

Sabbath

On Saturdays at Morning Prayer we ask that we may be "duly prepared" for the service of God's sanctuary on Sunday, and that "our rest here upon earth may be a preparation for the eternal rest promised to your people in heaven" (BCP, 99). That prayer has seemed ironic to me at the beginning of Saturdays that promised to be anything but restful. If we are to live in the future hope, we need to suspend the overwork and frantic pace that can characterize daily life. If we insist that we want it now (whatever "it" is), we may discount the value of what we can't have now. Our busy-ness can blind us. Sabbath-keeping means we are willing to wait and see what is yet to come. Sabbath-keeping means we have trust for the future, and that we don't have to squeeze dry the present day. Sabbath-keeping means we see value in rest, in letting the ground lie fallow so it can bear fruit in the future. It means we realize that, if we will not keep Sabbath, our rest may be thrust upon us by exhaustion or illness. Sabbath-keeping means we acknowledge that the timetable of our wants and objectives doesn't and shouldn't drive everything in this world. Sabbath-keeping means we believe there is more to come, more than we have known, and that we need to be rested and watchful to see what God is bringing into our lives. As we pray at Compline on Saturday night that "our joy may abound in the morning," we can rest in hope for joy (BCP, 134).

Life Together

"The end" — the fulfillment of the Christian hope, the parousia, the eschaton, the second coming of Christ — has often been envisioned in terms of military triumph, with Christ returning in power and glory like a conquering Caesar returning to Rome.

In Revelation (19:11–14), the armies of heaven, dressed in white and pure linen, ride out on white horses behind the one whose name is the Word of God. This perspective on the Christian hope has perhaps been strengthened in some places by the celebration of "Christ the King Sunday" at the end of the church year.

But the image of the triumphal returning hero has its limitations for the end. The only reported triumphal entry by Jesus was his entry to Jerusalem, which we celebrate on Palm Sunday (see Matt. 21:1–9; Mark 11:1–10; Luke 19:28–40; John 12:12–19). However, as a triumphal entry, this scene is ironic. Jesus rides into Jerusalem on an ass or an ass's colt, which would seem to be improbable transportation for a conquering hero on his day of triumph. And the notion of "final conquest" seems to leave out some important aspects of our hope for the future in Christ, whose life proceeded from a manger to the cross.

A different and more helpful image for the end would be that of realized community. In the Nicene Creed, we affirm our belief in the "one holy catholic and apostolic Church" (BCP, 359). At present, we must admit that we cannot yet see the completion or fullness of any of these four traits (or "notes") of the church from the creed. John Macquarrie states that "in the actual historical Church these notes may be more or less visible, according as the essence of the Church is emerging more or less purely."[23] "More or less" is probably the best way to describe the church's present achievement of the creedal notes. For example, the present divisions in Christendom and even in the Episcopal Church make apparent that we have not yet become "one" in any way that is visible and completed on earth. But we do already participate in these attributes to some degree and look forward to their realization and

---

23. John Macquarrie, *Principles of Christian Theology*, 2nd ed. (New York: Charles Scribner's Sons, 1977), 402. Macquarrie provides a discussion of "The Notes of the Church and Their Embodiment" in *Principles of Christian Theology* (401–13).

completion, as we pray in the Lord's Prayer for God's kingdom to come and God's will to be done "on earth as in heaven" (BCP, 364).

We look forward to a community of love on earth in which the unity of the church is realized and completed. This unity will not mean the obliteration of differences, or the dissolving of ourselves into a homogenized sameness. As God's own trinitarian life is a dynamic community of love, with the distinctness of persons uncompromised by their unity, our hope is to share a common unity with distinct others in God. The life of the church will then be truly trinitarian, so that the complementarity of our differences can be seen and celebrated.

Brothers and Sisters

For now, we can be guided in direction by our destination. If we understand an inclusive community of love in God to be our future hope, we can seek to live out of that future in the present by welcoming all kinds of people into our church. This may not seem controversial, but it contradicts much of the "like attracts like" marketing strategy for church growth. Do we really welcome persons who are elderly, or single, or disabled in some way, or poor with the same enthusiasm as, say, an affluent young couple with children? Do we want to draw "the right kind of people," people who remind us of ourselves or the way we wish we were? Do we seek to serve the needs of everyone who comes to us, or are we really seeking to use others to serve our own needs?

Evangelism means we are sharing not only our present and past but also our future and our hope with others. Our life is the life of the communion of saints, which is "the whole family of God, the living and the dead" (BCP, 862). From this perspective, our inclusion of others is not just a question of tolerance or open-mindedness. When we pray the "Our Father," we stand together as children of the same parent, brothers and sisters who share the one life of the whole family of God. The love of God is relational, drawing us into a community that is for all, including all, seeking all. We scandalize that community when we turn others away, whether our making-unwelcome is done in direct or subtle ways.

Celebration

Another good image for the end in Christ is a festive meal or party. Jesus' first miracle was to change water into wine at a wedding celebration (John 2:1–11). His life and teaching are filled with banquets, parties, and special meals. In many respects, hospitality stands at the opposite extreme from guilt, sin, and whatever separates us from God. For example, when the prodigal son has squandered his share of the family wealth and returns home, his father greets him with a loving embrace instead of reproaches to make him feel even more guilty (Luke 15:11–32). The father gives his newly returned son the best robe and throws a special party in his honor. That's hospitality! In this parable, the father's hospitality provides the context for the son's forgiveness, and it is the expression of the son's reconciliation.

Zacchaeus, a dishonest tax collector, has a change of heart when Jesus comes to his town. He climbs a tree to see Jesus better, and Jesus tells Zacchaeus that he will stay at Zacchaeus's house that day. Zacchaeus promises to give half his goods to the poor and to restore fourfold whatever he has wrongly taken from anyone. Jesus' visit, a time of hospitality, is the occasion for Zacchaeus's forgiveness and restoration to be celebrated (Luke 19:1–10).[24]

---

24. See Robert B. Slocum, "Zacchaean Effects and Ethics of the Spirit," in *Engaging the Spirit: Essays on the Life and Theology of the Holy Spirit*, ed. Robert Boak Slocum (New York: Church Publishing Incorporated, 2001), 215–23.

Jesus urges all who are heavy laden with burdens to draw near to him. He promises rest and refreshment (Matt. 11:28–30). These are comfortable words of assurance for even the most distressed.[25] Refreshment and hospitality go together. We can experience the healing that Jesus offers each one of us in terms of lightening our burdens and uplifting our souls, and we may well experience all of this in terms of hospitality. At its most basic level, that's what we do every Sunday and at other times as the church: we eat bread and drink wine together; we have a meal. We share hospitality.

And so we can envision the end in terms of a heavenly banquet where sin is forgiven, guilt is acquitted, divisions are reconciled, and the complications of love are undone. Sharing the means of life in food and drink takes the form of a celebration of life that is our hope. There is one life, one banquet, and it is to be shared by all.

Glory

As we pray for the future time when we may see Christ's glory, our prayer is really for our own discernment, that we may see in a complete and full way. Clearly, nothing needs to be added to Christ's glory as the Son of God, the second person of the Trinity. When Jesus stands on the Mount of the Transfiguration (Mark 9:2–8), his appearance is dazzling white. His glory is revealed in a wonderful and memorable way. But he is just as much the Son of God when he walks up the holy mountain as when his appearance is transfigured and visibly glorious. This is a moment of revelation, not a moment of change for Jesus. It gives Peter and

---

25. These verses may be used after the absolution and before the peace in a Rite I Eucharist (BCP, 332).

James and John (and through them, us) a momentary glimpse of Jesus' glory that is always true. It is a reminder for them and for us not to lose heart during the challenging times that are to come until Christ's glory is triumphant in all the earth. But the glory of Christ seen briefly on the mountaintop is the one and only glory that will be revealed fully in the future.

I once visited friends who lived near Mount Hood in Oregon. For days the weather was overcast and cloudy in that part of the Pacific Northwest, and I had to take my hosts' word that there was an enormous mountain nearby. Then finally one day the weather cleared, and there was the majestic mountain rising up as if in my friends' backyard. Of course, the mountain had been there all along, but something had obscured my vision.

Christ's glory has always been the glory of God's own Son. We look for that glory to be revealed, and we hope that we may *see* Christ's glory in its fullness. We pray for a future when we may see better than now and discern more clearly the glory that is Christ's always. His glory will transform us. As St. Paul writes to the Colossians, "when Christ who is your life is revealed, then you also will be revealed with him in glory" (Col. 4:3). The only way we can talk about "adding" to Christ's glory is in terms of adding *us* — so that our lives are transfigured and filled with Christ's glory, and so that Christ's life radiates out and is known through our lives. We will fully see divine glory when we can fully *be* God's glory, and that is the end and future of our hope. In the meantime, we can seek for Christ's glory to be increasingly seen and reflected in our own lives, helping others to resist captivity to sorrow and sin, so "the earth may be filled with the glory of God as the waters cover the sea" (Hymn 534, *The Hymnal 1982*).

Joy

The Christian hope is joyful. In Advent we pray that "we may without shame or fear rejoice to behold [Christ's] appearing."[26] We understand "heaven" as "eternal life in our enjoyment of God" and "hell" as the opposite of this — "eternal death in our rejection of God." Everlasting life is likewise shared in union with all the people of God "in the joy of fully knowing and loving God and each other" (BCP, 862). It is joy, not guilt, that is to be at the heart of our Christian experience. The overstrong emphasis on the advent of the kingdom of God as Judgment Day has perhaps driven this attention to guilt: Who will be embraced? Who will be punished? Who is really righteous? Who is really guilty? Who's in? Who's out? With this view of the kingdom of God, it's no surprise that there is so much about guilt in many Christian churches. The ultimate question would seem to concern who is worthy of punishment, and how much. The embodiment of this faith is a church preoccupied by judgments — quick to exclude, and ready to punish, condemn, and disagree. This can be a rather joyless faith, or perhaps a faith in which the only joy would be that of the few righteous true believers who remain when everyone else has been sent away in shame.

True joy reflects divine love that eagerly welcomes us into relationship and saves us. The net of God's love travels gently through the waters and picks up many unlikely and unusual fish. This is the love that completes us and fulfills us, because, as Augustine says, our hearts are restless until they rest in God.[27] Nothing less will do. In God's love we find the true rest and joy that we are meant to know. God's benediction for our hearts is not a "thing" that we receive or an award we are given; it is a life of love that we

---

26. Preface for Advent (for use at a Rite II Eucharist), BCP, 378.
27. See Augustine, *Confessions,* trans. R. S. Pine-Coffin (Harmondsworth, England: Penguin, 1961), 21 (I, 1).

are to share. We look forward to a complete and uninterrupted enjoyment of God's love. With this faith, we can seek to embody our faith in a church that *enjoys* what we share with God and each other. We can enjoy exploring the possibilities for relationship that we encounter in our world, our church, our lives. We can make people welcome — really welcome — even when we don't agree with them, or when they are different from us, or when they seem difficult. If we listen carefully and patiently to others, we may discover God's love present in surprising ways. Instead of rejecting, dismissing, or passing over others, we can rejoice to discover in them the same light that is in us and saves us. That is our hope.

After the Crucifixion, when Jesus appeared to his disciples on the evening of the first day of the week, the day of Resurrection, they "rejoiced when they saw the Lord" (John 20:20). They had been separated from him, and they had seen terrible things. They had witnessed Jesus' arrest and his gruesome execution. But then he was alive and with them again. Their worst fears were overcome; their broken hearts were mended. They must have been very, very happy when they saw Jesus with them again. They rejoiced when they saw the Lord.

Sometimes it can seem that God is remote from us and that we are very much alone as we struggle day to day. But we can find God in our world — in our daily lives — as we look forward to the completion of God's love in us. We can have a heart for the future and rejoice as the Lord's glory appears.

2

This Body of Hope

ROBERT M. COOPER

We are born hungry
We are born helpless
We think we know these things
The cut umbilicus severs
Each from one world into another
We think we know this too
Yet we are still born
Hungry still born helpless
But we are born hopeful

IT CAN BE COLD in south central Arkansas in late November. It is cold today, made even colder and more disagreeable by the rain that is falling steadily and by the gusting wind that is moving the scalloped edges of the undertakers' canopy which, from time to time, flaps in the wind and allows large accumulated drops to blow in on us who are "inside" it. This is reminding us yet again of our own vulnerability, of our fragility. And — yes — it is reminding us as well of our tenderness and of our own loveliness. "Rest in Peace" Cemetery is in receivership. From where we are, we can see two other open graves. This cemetery is located on land that some of the people around here say "ain't fit to grow nothin' but pine trees." The soil is clayey and the remaining tufts of grass provide only a barely secure footing for the twenty-five or so of us who have come to bury the thirty-seven-year-old man who has finally — and mercifully — died of renal failure. The coffin is open, as the family had wanted it to be. His mother is seated in the front row of us mourners. In a voice that is almost a keening one, but yet is more of a steady, high-pitched moan she laments, "For the last time!" "Darrell, this is the last time I'll see you!" "This is the last time!" again and again till she collapses in her chair and into the arms of the others around her. The only other words that work here on this morning are those of the Committal from the Book of Common Prayer (501):

> My heart, therefore, is glad, and my spirit rejoices;
> My body also shall rest in hope.

And further:

> In sure and certain hope of the resurrection to eternal life through our Lord Jesus Christ, we commend to Almighty God our brother Darrell, and we commit his body to the ground; earth to earth, ashes to ashes, dust to dust. . . .

The priest makes a rough sign of the cross on the coffin with the wet earth — call it "mud" — blesses the mourners with the sign of the cross, as some of us bless ourselves. It is an action that I have performed thousands of times before, touching fingers to the skin of my forehead and then across my body — the only body I have, the only body I am. And how many times have I professed that "I believe in the resurrection of the body . . . "? What can this mean? What is the resurrection of the body? What is it for us to hope for the resurrection of the body? And how am I to think about the resurrection of the body? It is not only this habitual making of the sign of the cross that has sharpened my concern for this inevitable future of us all. It is also, doubtless, because of the fact that the longer I live the older I get, and with that fact comes more frequently to mind the refrain from the poem of the Scots poet William Dunbar, "Lament of the Makers" (c. 1508): *timor mortis conturbat me* (freely translated, "the fear of death hangs like a cloud over me").

Succinctly put, I shall be claiming that the resurrection of the body recapitulates the creation of our bodies in God's Creation of the bodies of Adam and Eve, the bodies of the man/woman.

For me, "thinking" about bodies, death, and resurrection takes the form of imagining (I prefer the term "image-ing"). How are we to image what a resurrected body could be? My image-ing will be metaphor-laden and reliant upon myth and upon the poetic. Balancing the rather dark view of Dunbar, I think often too of Alfred North Whitehead's claim, in his 1929 "essay in cosmology," *Process and Reality,* that "God is the poet of the world, with tender patience leading it by his vision of truth, beauty, and goodness." I hope, therefore, that my reader treats what is written here as more meditation than discourse and as more speculative than strictly exegetical, as more poetic than prosaic.

Mindful of Dunbar and Whitehead, I have particularly in mind also the words of the author of 1 Peter, who urged the Christians for whom he wrote to "be ready always to give an answer (a defense, *apologian*) to every man that asketh you a reason (*logon... aitiounti*) of the hope (*elpidos*) that is in you, with meekness (*prautetos*) and fear (*phobou*)..." (KJV, 3:15) What follows, as I have already indicated, is more poesia that apologia, more mythos than logos, yet nevertheless serves as an "answer" and a "reason." Call it a "reply."

There are several related themes to be addressed. First, our own bodies, from the womb-time of each of us, from infancy through early childhood and into not just adolescence but on to so-called adulthood and then into decline, these bodies that we are always are surprising to us and they continue to surprise us, provided that the others around (mostly the adults) our growing have not tried to squelch or even kill our surprise and our pleasure. Anyone who has experienced an infant discovering the manifold shapes that her skin takes — her hands, fingers, and toes — knows what I am talking about. This early surprise goes on and on in the discovery of menstruation; the pleasures around our mucous membranes; the erectile properties of nipples, clitorises, and penises; the ejaculation of semen. It goes on variously for us in our lifetimes, in the delights of dance or athletic performances, these mysteries of our bodies, that these bodies that we have, that we are, can be disciplined into art or sport. Apart from the possibility of surprise there is no hope. That is why Dante warns those entering the *Inferno* to "abandon every hope" because there can be no surprises in hell. Virgil, because he has seen it before, is not surprised, nor are those who "belong" there surprised. Only Dante who does not "belong" there is surprised. Nothing changes there and nothing will change there. (Only in Dante's *Purgatorio* is there any possibility of change, change with its concomitant prospect of surprise; there is no surprise in Dante's *Paradiso* either.)

Surprise, when it is twinned to delight, issues into joy. Surprise, then, is the key to what I shall have to say about the resurrection of the body and our "sure and certain hope" in it, for as I have claimed, we all already have, for all of our lives, the experience of surprise in the discovery of our individual bodied being and in the bodied beings of others who touch us and whom we touch. We only learn that we are bodied by being with another bodied one, by being among other bodied ones; there is no other way than by bodies that we can mutually confer human being on each other. Hence, this meditative pursuit of surprise shortly leads us to consider God's own surprise and delight and — yes — also God's heartbrokenness in what God sees in this creation, and especially what God sees in us women and men who are even now continuing to be made in the image and likeness of that one who is our Creator, for as Nicolas Berdyaev has taught us, we are even now in "the eighth day of creation."

Charles Sanders Pierce, moreover, has claimed that "there is a degree of baseness in denying our birthright as children of God and in shamefacedly slinking away from anthropomorphic conceptions of the universal" (*Collected Papers,* 1:316). As I am taking my cue from Pierce, I am aware that some find the views that I am beginning to develop repugnant. Some will wonder, "Hasn't Cooper slipped dangerously close to, if indeed he hasn't fallen into, the dread third-century heresy of Patripassionism (or Sabellianism)? Is he also ignorant of that proposition from another world and time, viz., Article I of the Articles of Religion which avers that 'God is without body, parts or passions'?" This latter is an assertion that has long inclined me to say, "More's the pity!" Yet evidently it is a thought that "long ago," indeed, occurred to God and, further even, a thought upon which God acted: We have, some of us say, a founding faith in God's incarnation in our skin, our flesh and bones and blood. In short, God craves and continues to crave having a body. God craves being embodied. This is a claim wonderfully and further elaborated in the articulated faith of Paul the apostle, namely, concerning the one we call "the second Person of the Trinity" (not, of course, Paul's way of putting it). It is an expression hardly less abstract and theoretical-sounding than Pierce's "universal" mentioned above. Not only did this second Person empty himself, but further, it is averred by Paul, that not only was that one found in human form, but that "being found" in such a condition, further took upon himself "the form of a slave." Another misunderstanding of orthodox Trinitarian dogma, a confusion of the Persons of the Trinity? No. But if it must be called something other than misunderstanding, then call it "poetic license."

If calling it "poetic license" is still too great a reach, then call this way of meditating and image-ing something theological. Call it by an antique term. Think of it as the *circumincessio* (the Cappadocian Fathers and later in the seventh century, John of Damascus) of the three Persons of the Trinity, that is, the interrelatedness of the three Persons among themselves, their mutual "interpenetration." God has — and isn't this what drives the development, the alteration, of the church's doctrine of the Trinity, its doctrine of God? — a perfect life of God's own, a life that, while it may be perfect, is not whole, "perfect but not whole." If we are to remain alive, and as long as there is human being, the doctrine of God (i.e., our *teachings* about God) is never either filled up or finished. (No systematic theology can be achieved as long as anyone continues to live, because the writers cannot encompass their own deaths in their so-called systems. This is something we learn from Kierkegaard.) God has an inner life, an inner-personal and an interpersonal life of God's own. The greatest mystery is that God was not content with that (apparently) self-sufficient life, and craved a life of embodiment, craved being flesh. Can there be anything more pertinent here, more vivid or more poignant, than what can be seen in Michelangelo's (1475–1564) painting in the Sistine Chapel? It has become perhaps the best-known *portion* of a work of Western art, "The Creation of Adam." A languid Adam's forefinger of his left hand is almost — not yet — touching the forefinger of God's right hand. God and Adam are at this point just out of reach of each other; they are tantalizingly close. (Recall the Greek mythological figure Tantalus, who, for his offenses against Zeus, is being tortured by that god by — among other things — eternally reaching out for the grapes hanging forever inaccessible above him.) In this scant, this bare, separation of God and Adam, I can hear in my heart the pathetic words of Christopher Marlowe's "The Tragical History of Doctor Faustus": "O, I'll leap up to my God! — [Who pulls me down? —]." Mythology and poetry both must have their place here, for nothing else will do.

Further along I hypothesize that the Incarnate one was struck again and again with surprise in the exigencies of being *in carne,* surprised at being flesh, bone, blood, and skin. To Thomas, "Touch me. Stick your hand into me, into my wound (into my pleural cavity)!" To Mary in the garden of tombs, "Don't touch me." To the woman in the crowd who surreptitiously touched him, "Who touched me?" All of these — and there are more — are holy instances of the primacy of our skin [and for the Hebrew male there is the mark in his skin made by the mohel, the scar of circumcision], the skin that mediates our own individual worlds and the individual worlds of all who are around us. Incarnation, indeed!

I now offer two biblical images and one extrabiblical image in an effort to flesh out this connection of surprise and delight with our being embodied creatures. The Creator becomes creature, a creature of flesh and blood, bone and skin. I have already spoken of the surprise occasioned in God in discovering the events which unfold in that man/woman made after the very image and likeness of God. That surprise of God is mirrored then in the surprise of the man/woman so created. There is the delightful vignette from the older of the two Creation myths of Genesis. Here it is in Everett Fox's translation:

> ...but for the human there could be found no helper corresponding to him.
> So YHWH, God, caused a deep slumber to fall upon the human, so that he slept,
> he took one of the ribs and closed up the flesh in its place.

> YHWH, God, built the rib that he had taken from the
>   human into a woman
> and brought her to the human.
> The human said,
>   this-time, she-is-it!
>   Bone from my bones;
>   flesh from my flesh! (Genesis 2:21b–23)

We recall that Adam/the human, accompanied by YHWH, had just been, before this wonderful episode, about the divine business of naming all of the other creatures in that Eden, in that paradise; while he could indeed name them, he alone remained incomplete, remained not whole. "[T]his-time, she-is-it!" Enchantment, surprise, and delight have kissed each other! Whether or not this passage was in the heart of Joseph Brackett Jr. (1797–1882) when he wrote, " 'Tis the gift to be simple," I have no idea, but yet how very right it is to use these two lines from that song in the present context:

> and when we find ourselves in the place just right,
> 'Twill be in the valley of love and delight.

And isn't it fitting to believe that, while these words might not have been also on the lips of Eve, that they were at least in her heart: (this-time), he-is-it!? Although he is writing about Ulysses and Penelope in his fine 1952 poem "The World as Meditation," Wallace Stevens has these lines, which we could well give to Eve:

> Companion to his self for her, which she imagined,
> Two in deep-founded sheltering, friend and dear friend.
> . . . .
> . . . . His arms would be her necklace
> And her belt, the final fortune of their desire.

Desire too will find its "final fortune" "in the valley of love and delight."

We only begin truly to discover ourselves in otherness, in the other. Adam and Eve, we may believe, are surprised by each other, surprised at each other, and surprised at the otherness of each other continuing in their oneness. In *circumincessio* the three Persons of the Trinity continually engage in mutual discovery, and because of the mutual discovery there is an "ever" deepening self-discovery on the part of each Person. But even so, there is no body, no flesh, and this three-personed God craves union with a body, union with the man/woman creation. For us, this may yield a new and enriching dimension to John Donne's words, from his *Holy Sonnets:*

> Batter my heart three-person'd God; for you
> As yet but knock, breathe, shine, and seek to mend.
> (XIX. i. 1)

Taking great liberties here with Donne's poem, it indeed, does batter our hearts to find that God's craving human flesh is "mended" in the creation of woman/man. And surely it boggles the mind of the earnest systematician.

As Everett Fox's translation puts it, "there could be found no helper corresponding to him." Finding the other, God finds Godself. "The human" (Fox) finds himself only in finding and in being found by the other, and it is not really until that point that finally there is human being at all. This essential dialectic of otherness has neither beginning nor end, for like myth it has neither beginning nor end but is, rather, eternally true. Being found and finding are at the same moment a being-found-out and a finding-out. This brings us now to the second biblical image, an image already alluded to above, an image (image-ing) that I am continuing to use poetically and meditatively in order to feel our way further along in our quest to grasp an image-ing of the resurrection of the body.

Here are some of the well-known words of Paul the apostle — in Philippians 2:6–11 — which have become a principal fount for exegesis, for theology, and, for me, of speculative meditation: "Christ Jesus"

> made himself of no reputation and took upon himself the form of a servant and was made in the likeness of men: And being found in fashion as a man, he humbled himself and became obedient unto death, even the death of the cross. (KJV, vv. 7, 8)

The New American Bible, a Roman Catholic translation, prints 2:6–11 in poetic form inasmuch as this famous kenotic passage has been widely thought to be an early Christian hymn, or a portion of one. The KJV rendering is actually more poetic than the version printed here in "poetic form." The latter translation of verses 7b and 8a is this: "being born in the likeness of men/He was known to be of human estate...." The difficulty of adequately rendering this passage, this extraordinary claim about God and God's becoming human, is readily evident in the contrasting renditions of the King James Version and the New American Bible. The former has "being found in fashion as a man," while the latter has "He was known to be of human estate." Of these two, the KJV is the more faithful to the Greek text, and the difference between the two translations is neither trivial nor inconsequential.

"[B]eing found in fashion as a man" and "being born in the likeness (the Greek word here is *schemati,* virtually our English word "schema") of men" both are efforts at rendering into coherent English the Greek *euretheis* (the first aorist passive participle of the verb *eurisko* [recall Archimedes' exultant cry, "Eureka!"]).

The translation of *eurisko* by "known" is not at a large remove from the more accurate rendering of the Greek verb as "found." (I prescind here from arguing for a plausible linguistic relation of "known" and "found," although it is no great stretch to make interesting connections of the two words.) A deeper question, however, has troubled and intrigued me: *being found (or known) by whom?* Well, presumably those among and by whom he, having emptied himself of (triune) divinity, was found or known. That seems obvious, and it is the commonly held understanding of Paul's claim. In the light, however, of the assertion made earlier and based in the account in Genesis 2, and flowing further from my hypothesis — namely, that God, on the one hand, is surprised at finding God-likeness in Adam and Eve, and that, on the other hand, my furthering of that hypothesis by claiming that Adam was surprised at finding his own flesh — and rib — othered from himself, while *pari passu* Eve is similarly surprised at finding herself, and moreover, at finding her very own other (Wallace Stevens's poem).

I further hypothesize, in that same earlier spirit, that Jesus was found also by himself (I am aware that Greek has a perfectly good use of the reflexive and that the reflexive does not appear in our Greek text.). I am, thus, claiming here that Jesus, having found himself in the *schemati* (in "the fashion") of a man, did at least two things. The first thing that he found out was that not only was he in the fashion of a man, but that, moreover, presumably, from our human point of view, he further finds himself as having chosen that *morphē* of a slave. If we think of the Incarnation as an othering of the inner life of the Trinity, think of it as an outering of the inwardness of the interpenetration of the three Persons, then that Christ Jesus finds out not only what it is to be a human being, but more amazingly, what it is to do so in "the form of a slave." The second thing that he did was to find out that only in such a form could God find out what it is, indeed, to be(come) "the human," as Everett Fox put it. Inasmuch as Incarnation continues (Berdyaev's "eighth day of creation") even today, not only is God continuing to create, but is at the same moment continuing to find out the insides, the innerness, of "the human." The Creator, the Artist, becomes his creation. Speculative? Yes. I am not, however, finding myself alone on a hitherto untrodden path, for some readers will already have seen a certain Franciscan note in what has been said earlier — that is, some will have detected a certain bias in this writer not so much against the Thomistic emphasis on mind or intellect but rather a certain bias for the Franciscan emphasis on love and will above mind and intellect. So, we turn now and in conclusion to such a Franciscan writer; this is my third, the extrabiblical, witness.

The important Franciscan theologian, known as "the subtle doctor," John Duns Scotus (c. 1265–1308?), years ago funded my imagination, my image-ing, with an idea not strange among Franciscans — namely, that there would have been an Incarnation even had there been no sin in the world, even had there been no "original sin" entering into the garden through the agency of Adam/Eve. My dwelling on this amazing and gracious conception of incarnation as not having been occasioned by the notorious *felix culpa,* "the happy fault," has led me to a formulation altogether consonant, I believe, with the reading, the image-ing, I have offered regarding Genesis 2 and Philippians 2. I have already, virtually, given my reasons for this. (1) The Trinity outers its own inwardness, its *circumincessio,* into the "this-is-it" (Everett Fox) of Adam/Eve. Thus (2) God, the Creator, finds out what it is to be a creature. And (3) Paul's Christ Jesus finds himself "in the fashion of a man." My reading of Scotus is that God would be incarnate for the sheer joy and delight of being "the human." I find this view of Scotus, in principle, immensely freeing, and if not altogether freeing us from, at least lightening and lifting the gravity of, "the bonds of sin and death." That the Incarnation itself is salvific would have come as no news at all to St. Irenaeus (c. 130–200).

Everyone recalls that sin first occurs in a garden paradise, "originally" a place of love and delight. An ugly showing on this theme is found in a manner both wonderfully transfixing and simultaneously horrifying in the painting done by Hieronymous Bosch (a contemporary of Luther and Dürer, Erasmus, etc.) in the years 1510–15, the *Garden of Earthly Delights*. I find this picture to be not only exquisitely painted but at the same time to be an imaginative and terrifying rendering of the hypertrophy of late medieval concepts of human sin (parodied in our own recent past by Mencken as "the paralyzing fear that someone somewhere may be happy," which he said about Puritanism) divine punishment, and hell.

It is astonishing to recall here with my reference to Bosch that Sandro Botticelli (1444/45–1510) was also Bosch's contemporary. Botticelli painted his *Primavera* (Spring, and see also his *Birth of Venus*) between 1479 and 1481. This painting and Bosch's *Garden of Earthly Delights* are light-years apart both in theme and mood. In Botticelli's scene, the young woman Flora and the goddess Venus (and these two can be "read" iconographically as types of Eve, of the eternal woman as sexual love and, perhaps, also as courtesan) are at the center, surrounded by another god, Mercury, by a zephyr grasping a nymph, and other wondrous beings in a sylvan, a garden setting. (Is it an orange grove, bearing further sexual connotations?) Thank God that this was not one of Botticelli's works that he destroyed under the influence of the zealous preaching of another of his contemporaries, the Dominican Girolamo Savonarola.

With these two paintings we are again in a garden, in the paradise of Eden perhaps. Now, finally, let us believe that we, as in John Brackett Jr.'s hymn, have "come round right." Let us believe that Ezekiel's "valley of dry bones" has become Brackett's "valley of love and delight." We can continue to prophesy to the dry bones, understanding as we do so that they will be raised up at the last day, even as Adam's rib was raised up into Eve on a primordially earlier day by the Creator of "the human." No, this (God bless us all!) is not "the last time I'll see you."

The wound in the side of Jesus brings forth still the continuing activation of "the bellows of life" (the phrase is that of Dr. Ann Hedge-Carruthers), echoing the words of the Fourth Gospel that "without him was not anything made that was made." This is but one of the many ways that the church has understood that Christ is the second Adam from whose "wounded" side the taken rib is built by YHWH, God, into (a) woman, the "she-is-it!" And ever since that primordial occurrence, all of us — Darrell, his mother and his father, you and I — have come forth from cavities, from the wombs of our own mothers.

Yes, resurrection, our second birthing into new bodies, will stun us all, and as that being stunned settles into, and smoothes out into, the eternal possibility of surprise, our own surprise will forever embrace and kiss those twins, delight and joy, even as they enfold us always. Always.

"Power follows hope," declared Walter Rauschenbusch (1861–1918), who is best known for his articulation and espousal of "the Social Gospel." What we hope for sways, and may largely determine, the whole direction of both our individual and our corporate lives. Further, wherever and whenever there is hope, there desire will be found also. We desire that for which we hope, unless, I suppose, language means whatever I say it means, as was the case with Alice (in Wonderland), or we are insane. In what follows here, I am interested in pursuing this vital notion of the relation of power as following the direction of hope, and in how, ineluctably, that directing hope is twinned to desire. To put some important concepts in a hierarchy, I would place "desire" at the top, "want" below it, and "need" at the bottom, noting that it is common to find want and need equivocated. I distinguish insistently "desire" from "want." I stipulate here that, for me, desire carries with it the component of organized affect, that it is not merely organically determined, for that would be to speak of a basic human drive (what Freud called *Trieb*) and too easily lead to reducing human being to a varying congeries of organic forces. Desire is conscious and intentional, and it may be either loving or hateful and so on. My wants (needs) — at the organic, biological level — for food, sleep, and so on, must be satisfied or I will perish. Yes, I had rather be "Socrates dissatisfied than a pig satisfied." So, at the least, hope and desire energize the lives of each of us even as we live them. The American philosopher Josiah Royce taught us more than a hundred years ago that we live both in and between a "community of memory" on the one hand and a "community of hope" on the other hand. We, all of us, thus live in more than one community, one world, at a time. This claim becomes quite evident when I turn to a discussion of myth.

Myth is the eternal and ubiquitous realm of the eternally true; myth shows us that what Mircea Eliade taught us to call an *illud tempus* (a "that time," a "once-upon-a-time") lives in us. He has shown that we thus live *in illo tempore* (in that time) in what may be called the eternal now. More about myth and its power in our lives is offered later.

I am essentially interested in this essay in emphasizing the bodied aspect of ourselves, and in arguing that the power that enlivens and moves our bodies leads us readily to claim that our bodies are bodies of hope, that we are, indeed, hopeful bodies.

Paul certainly did tell the Roman church that ours are "bodies of death." Would that he had also called them "bodies of hope" as, indeed, he very nearly did! In this very important sense, each of us is (em-)bodied hope; the very power of our natures can, therefore, be called hope. To be human is to be hopeful. Dorothy Soelle in the late twentieth century offered us, in a study of suffering, the wonderful heuristic question, "Is this [whatever it may be that 'this' is] the best that can be hoped for?" I write on the assumption that most of us — I do not say "all of us" — will answer no to her question, even though there are millions and millions of us on this fragile earth, those who have been referred to by Frantz Fanon as "the wretched of the earth," for whom the question may never even arise, but were it to arise these presumably would answer yes.

When the proposal first came to write an essay for this volume, the proposal suggested that the essays be devoted to "eschatology." Now eschatology, of course, concerns doctrines and ideas concerning "the last things," the four last things, traditionally understood to be death, judgment, heaven, and hell. Even without much thought about this old, old topic, my immediate second thought was a question: "But what are the first things?" This is a crucial matter to have in mind inasmuch as we, all of us, live through our days between those first and last things whatever they may be, just as we live also in both memory and in hope. There is, of course, another well-known way to think of these matters. The concept of "realized eschatology" is a vital and fruitful one. There is scarcely a better example of what I mean by "realized eschatology" than the encounter of Jesus with the Samaritan woman at the well, in John's Gospel where timelessness is interjected stunningly into her clock-time day. That event and the concept drawn from it show that we live always in an "eternal now," whether she or we are aware of it. All of our moments are chairotic moments.

This Body of Hope

One of the apostle Paul's ways of putting this — and it was fundamental both to his thinking and to his preaching — was to declare to the Corinthian church that they [we] are "those upon whom the ends of the world have come." Hence, for Paul we always are living in the *chairos* (let us call this "God's time") even as we note the passage of hours and days by "clock time" *(chronos)*. We live in two times at once. Paul also put this in another way: We live in "this age" and in "the age to come." I can affirm all of this Pauline expression, yet that is not enough for me.

I want to consider that neither the (temporally) first things nor the (temporally) last things are perspicuous to human reason. That is, we are unable to think them through, subject them to reason's ways, but we can imagine them and we can enter yet again into the myths that invest them. First and last things are, indeed, *aporias,* that is, they are things unknown to us and thus must remain undecideable by us; they are literally matters beyond the pale of discursive reason's reach. They must, therefore, at a minimum, be matters of faith, matters for faith. We recall that it is not for nothing that Paul so closely among the three things that abide — remain or stay put — links faith, hope, and agape love. But there must be more to be said on this matter. Notice that if agape never ends, then hope never ends either; nor, indeed, does faith (I think here of Immanuel Kant's three postulates — "postulates" because they cannot be proven to or by reason: freedom, immortality, and God). While many things are beyond discursive reason's reach, there are yet other vast and hope-filled resources. I have in mind four of them: metaphor, myth, imagination, and poetry.

3

Parousia and Christian Hope

RALPH DEL COLLE

"CHRIST HAS DIED, Christ is risen, Christ will come again." This memorial acclamation in the eucharistic canon of the Roman Rite, revised following the Second Vatican Council, represents the liturgical integration of the paschal mystery of Christ's saving death and resurrection with the eschatological hope of his Second Advent. Although this eschatological note is represented in nearly all of the renewed eucharistic liturgies of the past generation in the Western church, one still wonders to what extent the hope for the coming of the Lord Jesus informs the faith and lives of the faithful. The Second Coming, at least in the popular imagination, seems to be reserved to that strain of evangelical Christianity whose focus on the rapture and the end-time fulfillment of Bible prophecy seems quite alien to the majority of Christians.[1] Does this mean that the "blessed hope" (Titus 2:13) cannot be as central to Christian faith for those Christians who are members of the historic or "mainline" churches as are

---

1. Eschatological views among evangelicals is in fact quite varied, ranging from dispensationalism to all forms of millennialism although premillennialism, dispensational or otherwise, seems to have gained the ascendancy among contemporary evangelicals. For some helpful sources for these views, see the following: Stanley J. Grenz, *Millennial Maze: Sorting Out Evangelical Opinions* (Downers Grove, Ill.: InterVarsity, 1992); Robert G. Clouse, ed. *The Meaning of the Millennium: Four Views* (Downers Grove, Ill.: InterVarsity, 1977); Craig A. Blaising and Darrell L. Bock, *Progressive Dispensationalism: An Up-to-Date Handbook of Contemporary Dispensational Thought* (Wheaton, Ill.: Bridgepoint, 1993).

other Christian doctrines? Conceivably one might ask whether any Christian doctrine can be adequately understood without an eschatological dimension? Even the more recent emphasis on justice as constitutive of the gospel, and its importance for Christian witness, is not a little motivated by a new appreciation of eschatology.[2]

All of this is to say that eschatology as a theological theme has not been wanting in the work of theologians in the last century and has certainly informed ecclesial documents whether Catholic, Orthodox, Anglican, or Protestant. It is fair to say that eschatology as the doctrine of the "last things" (heaven, hell, judgment, eternal life) has successfully emerged from its isolation at the end of the dogmatic loci to permeate thinking about christology, soteriology, ecclesiology, and nearly the entire spectrum of Christian doctrine, as indeed it should. To take one obvious example, Jürgen Moltmann in his *Theology of Hope* was correct when he stated: "[E]schatology cannot really be only a part of Christian doctrine. Rather, the eschatological outlook is characteristic of all Christian proclamation, of every Christian existence and of the whole Church."[3] It is now the rare theologian who would disagree with this proposition. But again I ask if this sentiment would characterize the consciousness of most Christians. Hope, yes; but hope in the coming of the Lord? I am not so sure. Then where is the glitch, so to speak?

---

2. See especially the 1971 Synodal Document, *Justice in the World*. Its statement — "Action on behalf of justice and participation in the transformation of the world fully appear to us a constitutive dimension of the preaching of the Gospel" — appearing at the beginning of the document is consonant with the concluding "Word of Hope" with its strong eschatological flavor: "Let Christians therefore be convinced that they will yet find the fruits of their own nature and effort cleansed of all impurities in the new earth which God is now preparing for them, and in which there will be the kingdom of justice and love, a kingdom which will be fully perfected when the Lord will come himself." St. Paul Editions (Boston: Daughters of St. Paul, 1971), 4, 24.

3. Jürgen Moltmann, *Theology of Hope* (New York: Harper & Row, 1967), 16.

Perhaps it is the so-called delay of the parousia along with those imminent expectations that have always proved wrong in history when dates were prophesied and predicted. The mark of fanaticism associated with these claims is also something to be avoided. Meanwhile, on the scholarly front, the opinion that Jesus or Paul were wrong in their expectations of the end has been displaced by various attempts to interpret the theological import of the apocalyptic conceptuality they employed. This may have the danger of deflating the shock such language might possess for modern or postmodern ears even as it is appropriated at the level of mythological or symbolic discourse that may still bear religious meaning for those who no longer have such a worldview. In all of this, however, we are still compelled to ask about the dogmatic truth and spiritual implications of the church's confession and hope that Christ will come again.

We might draw wisdom from some basic catechesis both scriptural and doctrinal, and from the lived internalization of the church's liturgical observance, specifically the unfolding of the liturgical year. The two combined can instantiate the hope of the parousia in the day-to-day life of the ordinary Christian. Continued theological reflection on the matter can help support and further interpret for the church this fundamental Christian hope.

The creedal affirmations that Christ will come again constitute the obvious confession from any prayerful reception of the Word of God in the New Testament scriptures, a natural link as well with the Old Testament prophetic expectations that conclude the arrangement of books in the Christian canon of the Hebrew scriptures. From the apocalyptic passages in the synoptic Gospels (Matt. 24; Mark 13; Luke 21), the Apocalypse itself (the book of Revelation), and the Pauline exhortations on the Second Coming (1 Thess. 4:13–18; 2 Thess. 2:1–11; 1 Cor. 15:50–58) it is clear why the creed confesses the parousia: "He will come again to judge the living and the dead" — Apostles' Creed; "He will come again in glory to judge the living and the dead, and his kingdom will have no end" — Niceno-Constantinopolitan Creed. The association of the parousia with judgment is self-evident in the creed with no further elaboration of what is entailed in the Second Coming apart from final judgment and the arrival of Christ's everlasting kingdom. In the New Testament, however, more is said in the emergence of two major themes repeated throughout the scope of the canon.

First, the theme of judgment is not restricted to the living and dead on the threshold of eternity, although that too is mentioned (Matt. 25; Acts 17:31; Rom. 14:10-12; 2 Cor. 5:10). A time of trial, judgment, deception, and tribulation presages the eschatological event even as it forms a part of it (2 Thess. 1:5-10). "These are the beginning of the labor pains" (Mark 13:8). And, "when you see these things happening, know that he is near, at the gates" (Mark 13:30). Second, the exhortation to perseverance and holiness becomes even more pronounced for he comes to be "glorified among his holy ones" (2 Thess. 1:10) since Christians are called by the gospel "to possess the glory of our Lord Jesus Christ" (2 Thess. 2:14). Watchfulness and steadfastness ought to characterize believers during this difficult time, when persecution will increase amid deception and the love of many growing cold. "But the one who perseveres to the end will be saved" (Matt. 24:11-14).

It is interesting that this biblical apocalyptic scenario, so often employed by evangelicals of *The Late Great Planet Earth* variety,[4]

---

[4]. The book of that title by Hal Lindsey with C. C. Carlson (Grand Rapids, Mich.: Zondervan, 1970) has been so strongly influential as a popular form of dispensationalism with a focus on the rapture, i.e., in this case the pretribulational extraction of true believers from earth, and Israel as a locus for the fulfillment of prophecy (the "signs of the times"), and the arena of catastrophic judgment on the nations at the apocalyptic battle of Armageddon.

is referred to in the *Catechism of the Catholic Church* (CCC). There the reign of Christ is affirmed as having begun in his ascension, and "is already present in his Church" while awaiting its fulfillment " 'with power and great glory' by the king's return to earth" (671).[5] Even though the church has entered the last days with the exaltation of Christ and the outpouring of the Holy Spirit (732), she now exists between the times as a pilgrim community, waiting and watching for the "glorious advent of Christ," which will be preceded by "distress" and the "final trial" (672–75). Gleaning in the New Testament we find religious deception and the Antichrist mentioned, the latter manifested in any pseudo-messianism in which humanity glorifies itself "in place of God and of his Messiah in the flesh" (675). This may even include secular versions thereof, as in the instance of Pope Pius XI's charge against Communism in his 1937 encyclical *Divini Redemptoris (On Atheistic Communism)* footnoted in the *Catechism*.

In addition to the "Church's ultimate trial" as an event prior to Christ's Second Advent, the parousia is also linked to the identification of Christ as the "hope of Israel." The CCC goes so far as to suggest that the "Glorious Messiah's Coming is suspended at every moment of history until his recognition by 'all Israel' " (674). Similar to many evangelical expectations this requires the "full inclusion" of Jews in the Messiah's salvation" (674). However, no timetable is given. The *Catechism* simply states that this "eschatological coming could be accomplished at any moment, even if both it and the final trial that will precede it are 'delayed' " (673).

I rehearse this catechetical instruction because I believe it is fair to say that most Catholics are unaware of these specifics associated with the hope of Christ's coming. Apocalyptic movements

---

5. The references are to the numbered paragraphs of the *Catechism of the Catholic Church*, henceforth CCC. The English translation used is New York: Doubleday, 1997.

in church history have remained at the fringe of Catholic life and have never permeated Catholic teaching and sensibility. The same could be said for most of the historic churches. The question therefore still remains about the import of the parousia for Christian faith if these specifics are to have some meaning beyond an outstanding future event that lies outside the scope of history. In order to address this we must first consider the relationship between the theology of history and eschatology, between salvation history and the parousia. We turn, therefore, to the liturgical expression of these themes.

The premise for any theology of history is the biblical narrative of salvation history with its culmination and focus in the Christ event. Salvific action and divine promise shape the form of this history, eliciting the human response of faith, witness, and the establishment of the covenant community. Eschatology is vital to the structure of salvation history. The arrival of God's salvation points to greater and fuller dimensions of divine presence and action. The formal structure of promissory narrative in the Deuteronomistic history and prophetic writings anticipate, especially in the latter, that the fulfillment of God's promise will transform the creaturely and sinful limitations of the covenant people with consequences even for history, nature, and the cosmos (Isa. 2:2–4). The more apocalyptic strain of eschatology expands this beyond the restraints imposed by death and the reign of evil in the present age. All of these are taken up in Jesus' proclamation of the kingdom and the early church's expectation of Christ's parousia.

In the ministry of Jesus the signs of the coming kingdom are present in his words and deeds. In answer to John the Baptist's query as to whether Jesus was the one to come, Jesus responds by enumerating the signs that are seen and heard: "the blind regain their sight, the lame walk, lepers are cleansed, the deaf hear, the dead are raised, and the poor have the good news preached to them" (Matt. 11:5). These signs of the kingdom bear a strong pneumatological stamp — "if it is by the Spirit of God that I drive out demons, then the kingdom of God has come upon you" (Matt. 12:28). The early church likewise recognized that such signs would continue as confirmation of the gospel (Mark 16:19-20) and apostolic evangelization (Rom. 15:18-19).

The mighty deeds that accompany the reception of the Spirit (Gal. 3:5), however, do not obviate the eschatological advent of the parousia and the fullness of the kingdom of God. Paul in particular battled enthusiasts in Corinth and insisted that eschatological correspondence between the resurrection of Christ and the resurrection of the dead needed to be maintained in order to uphold the truth of the gospel (1 Cor. 15). The present gift of the Holy Spirit is but a harbinger of what is to come. The Spirit as firstfruits (Rom. 8:23) and down payment (2 Cor. 1:22; Eph. 1:13-14) is a guarantee of the fullness of salvation that will arrive with the eschaton. So too, Christ is the firstfruits of the resurrection (1 Cor. 15:23), and Christians are the firstfruits of salvation through sanctification by the Spirit (2 Thess. 2:13). In this sense the future already transforms the present, but the present still yearns for future consummation.

The baptized have been enlightened through the Holy Spirit and now taste the heavenly gift, the word of God and the powers of the age to come (Heb. 6:4-5). Christian hope emerges from this pneumatological reality that constitutes Christian existence. This existence lies not in eschatological fulfillment but between the times, the already and not-yet of the work of God in Christ. For the disciple this entails a cruciform existence, both through the initiation of Christian life in proclamation (1 Cor. 1:18-25) and baptism (Rom. 6:3-4), and in the ongoing apostolic life of the church in mission (2 Cor. 4:10-11).

It is within the above framework that we need to consider the importance of the parousia for Christian life today. If the gospel and Christian life possess this eschatological (even apocalyptic) structure, then we cannot dismiss the relevancy of the parousia.[6] Nor, as J. Christian Beker has observed, can the parousia as an apocalyptic event be reduced to "purely existentialist terms (e.g., Bultmann)" or to a "nonchronological promissory language (e.g., Moltmann) that, notwithstanding its emphasis on anticipation and anticipatory realization, does not address itself to either the material or the temporal aspect of the concrete incursion of the kingdom of God into our world."[7] Or, to put in a query as old as the primitive church, "Where is the promise of his coming?" (2 Pet. 3:4).

Beker's own answer is to emphasize the imminence of Paul's apocalyptic gospel under the aspects of its necessity, incalculability, and the dialectic between patience and impatience.[8] The latter two prevent the necessity of the parousia's imminence from degenerating into the literalist neo-apocalypticism of the *Late Great Planet Earth* variety that has more to do with prediction and divine determinism than with the gospel.[9] The incalculability of the time of Christ's coming is itself a dominical imperative (Mark 13:32), and the dialectic between patience and impatience ensures the integrity of Christian discipleship. We wait patiently for the coming of the Lord who is at hand (James 5:7-8) even as the integrity of Christian life — "leading lives of holiness and godliness" — hasten that same day (2 Pet. 3:11-12).

---

6. This is the substance of J. Christian Beker's argument in his excellent book *Paul's Apocalyptic Gospel: The Coming Triumph of God* (Philadelphia: Fortress, 1982). He prefers the term "apocalyptic," because it keeps the focus on "a definitive closure/completion-event in time and space, rather than simply a continuous, open-ended process" (50). My sympathies with his position are evident in the remainder of the essay.

7. Ibid., 117.

8. Ibid., 44-53. For Beker, imminence is but one aspect of this apocalyptic structure along with vindication, universalism, and dualism (30-44).

9. Ibid., 24.

We cannot uphold the imminence of the parousia, however, without taking seriously Beker's challenge that "some form of chronological expectation" must be a "concomitant aspect" of the "actualization of... hope."[10] Although the imminence of the parousia is indeed incalculable, nevertheless the presence and action of divine energy and power in the Holy Spirit signifies the *novum* that is salvation here and now as well as then and there in the kingdom. Each new advent and movement of the Spirit, every refreshment from above (Acts 3:20), the bestowal of charisms and the emergence of new ecclesial movements, all point to the Lord who is coming to make all things new. Two examples in the history of theology, one medieval and one contemporary, are instructive.

When St. Bonaventure became minister general of the Franciscan Order, he was faced with the eschatological enthusiasm of the Franciscan Spiritualists. They anticipated a third age of the Spirit headed by a new order of contemplatives, a *novus ordo* as an eschatological *ordo futurus*. Bonaventure countered these Joachimite tendencies when he interposed an eschatological reserve into these sensibilities. He could not concede to the Spiritualists that Christ could be surpassed in a third pneumatological age. Nevertheless, he could and did acknowledge that St. Francis did possess an eschatological role and that the Franciscans along with the Dominicans heralded a deeper understanding and praxis of the truth of Jesus Christ.[11]

More recently, Pope John Paul II in his 1994 Apostolic Letter *Tertio Millennio Adveniente* anticipated a "new springtime of Christian life" at the turn of the third millennium (#18). In his 2001 Apostolic Letter *Novo Millennio Ineunte* he spoke of the

---

10. Ibid., 116.
11. Here I am following the analysis of Joseph Ratzinger in his *The Theology of History in St. Bonaventure* (Chicago: Franciscan Herald Press, 1971, 1989).

Jubilee that celebrated the new millennium "not only as a memory of the past, but also as a prophecy of the future" (#3). Both exhortations were intended to open up the future and encourage the spiritual integrity needed in this new time for the church and the world.

Bonaventure and John Paul II engaged in a spiritual discernment of how the present work of the Spirit is presently "building up the body of Christ, until all of us come to the unity of the faith and of the knowledge of the Son of God, to maturity, to the measure of the full stature of Christ" (Eph. 4:13). Eschatological hope makes for the possibilities of movement, growth, and maturation. This is not necessarily a linearly progressive process. Until the advent of the Lord it will also embrace the mystery of the cross. However, the parousia of Christ evokes the obedience of faith (Rom. 1:5, 15:18) by which the church reveals the Lord and contributes to the transformation of the human condition that will be purified and transfigured in the kingdom of God.[12]

Finally, as I earlier hinted, the enactment of Christian hope in the liturgy is not incidental to the eschatological structure of the Christian life. Not only does this pervade every eucharistic celebration as the congregation is gathered into the sacramental time of eschatological anticipation and the present transformation of the elements, the ecclesial body, and eventually the cosmos itself, it is also enacted in the repetition of the cycle of the liturgical year. It is no accident that the readings in the latter part of November following All Saints and All Souls — certainly a meditation on the last things! — draw from the books of Daniel and Revelation.

---

12. This eschatological theme in its relationship to human development greatly informs the Pastoral Constitution on the Church in the Modern World (*Gaudium et Spes*) of the Second Vatican Council, especially chaps. 3 and 4 of Part I. As one example, consider the following: "Hence, while earthly progress must be carefully distinguished from the growth of Christ's Kingdom, to the extent that the former can contribute to the better ordering of human society, it is of vital concern to the Kingdom of God" (#39).

These apocalyptic readings culminate in the feast of Christ the King, the last Sunday of the liturgical year, when the consummation of the kingdom is celebrated. Then at the beginning of Advent these apocalyptic readings along with those in the synoptic Gospels gradually yield to the prophetic eschatology of Isaiah. It is as if to say that the longing for the coming of the Lord expected under the conditions of the present age in the modality of apocalyptic irruption calls the church to prophetic engagement as it embodies its response to the imminent advent of Christ through the obedience of faith. In the latter part of Advent the focus shifts to Christ's coming as the Incarnate One, Emmanuel, in Bethlehem.[13] Thus apocalyptic hope leads to the eschatological praxis of those who long for a new heaven and a new earth where God's justice is at home (2 Pet. 3:13). This in turn immerses the church in the world, living a fully incarnate existence where all things human are taken up in Christ.[14] The Maranatha cry of the Spirit and the Bride — "Amen. Come, Lord Jesus!" (Rev. 22:17, 20) — is the prayer of those who share the "distress, the kingdom, and the endurance we have in Jesus" (Rev. 1:9).

---

13. This is liturgically noted in a new preface (Advent II) for the eucharistic prayer and the use of the "Emmanuel" antiphons in the Liturgy of the Hours and as the gospel acclamation in the eucharistic liturgy, both of which begin on December 17.

14. See the first encyclical of John Paul II's pontificate, *Redemptor Hominis:* "Man in the full truth of his existence, of his personal being and also of his community and social being... is the primary and fundamental way for the Church, the way traced out by Christ himself, the way that leads invariably through the mystery of the Incarnation and Redemption" (#14).

4

Beneath the Edge of Thought
Inner Eschatology and the Burden of Hope

TRAVIS DU PRIEST

The Wellspring of Hope

> "*Hope springs eternal
> in the human breast....*"
> — Alexander Pope[1]

WE CAN TRY through various means available to us — holy scripture, prayer, spiritual direction, intentional waiting — to discern a vocation, a plan, a direction in life, what we might call God's will for us; but ultimately it is a human decision to act, to decide, to set forth on a particular quest in life. We do so based on reason, on weighing sides, often with intuitive insight and a sense that the inner world and outward signs have convened to point us correctly.

If we are open and honest with ourselves, however, we are never precisely sure that we are following God's plan, God's will, God's appointed direction for our lives. It does not fall to us to know exactly, but rather to apprehend from a distance, as "in a mirror dimly" (1 Cor. 13:12).[2] Christians make these decisions,

---

1. Alexander Pope, "An Essay on Man," in *The Norton Anthology of Poetry*, ed. Arthur M. Eastman et al. (New York: W. W. Norton, 1970), 449.
2. All scriptural quotations are from *The New Oxford Annotated Bible*, ed. Herbert G. May and Bruce M. Metzger (New York: Oxford University Press, 1973).

these plans, "in hope" — in the hope that God wills the best for us, no matter which path we end up on.

This virtue we call hope, like all good things, comes from God. Indeed it is a virtue of God's, not of ours. Likewise, hope's concomitants: faith and trust. These too are virtues of God's, not of ours. Hence, we make life choices and decisions against the backdrop of God's faith in us, God's trust in us, God's hope for us.

We do not so much have faith in God as God has faith in us, in humanity. God puts trust in us, in the created order — in the world, in human beings — and God has hope for us. God's hope charges the grandeur of the universe, to paraphrase Gerard Manley Hopkins.[3] Hope is not ours to have; rather, we live in and out of the traces of divine hope.

Christian hope is the belief that the ever-expanding cosmos, our universe, our planet, all creatures on earth, the human race, and each of us as individuals came into being in allegiance with a loving creator. We Western Christians in particular hold that the universe and our own lives are evolving toward a purposeful end, that even the fullness of what we call "salvation" is awaiting us in the future.

The hope that wells up from the divine and springs eternal in the human breast posits a future existence that is in some way an improvement over the present state of things, individually or collectively. This tug from the future, pulling us forward, in thought and imagery, permeates Western consciousness, thought, and theology. In fact, the theologian Jürgen Moltmann "erects a theology of hope teaching that all forces are to be concentrated on the final apocalyptic goal of history."[4] We see history, even

---

3. Gerard Manley Hopkins, "God's Grandeur," *Poetry of the Victorian Period*, ed. George Benjamin Woods and Jerome Hamilton Buckley (Chicago: Scott, Foresman, 1953), 775.

4. Walter Schmithals, "Eschatology," *Dictionary of the History of Ideas*, vol. 2 (New York: Charles Scribner's Sons, 1973), 157. Schmithals discusses Walter Pannenberg's prolepsis of final events and Moltmann's theology of hope, as well as Rudolf Bultmann,

what is sometimes called "salvation history," as a linear, chronological phenomenon, with a beginning and an end, unlike Eastern philosophies, which assume a cyclical pattern of life, death, and rebirth.[5]

These are comforting, reassuring thoughts, given that we humans often "do those things which we ought not to have done" and neglect those things that we have left undone."[6] Since we do commit human errors; do fall short of our own goals, as well as those of religious and cultural norms; and on occasion perpetrate acts of horrifying brutality, there is solace in thinking that God loves us in a broader, wider sense, that God created us and accepts us but also loves us in our becoming: God sees us not only for who we have been, or even for who we are, but also — and perhaps most poignantly — for who we desire to become.[7]

Jesus eats with sinners (Luke 7:36ff), but he often charges those with whom he converses, as in the case of the rich young man, with future transformation (Matt. 19:21ff). He plants seeds of change, through prayer, in Matthew 21:22. Christ heals, teaches, and himself gives new directions in life: "Go and do not sin again," he says to the woman caught in adultery (John 8:11). Even Jesus' emotional outburst anticipates transformation in the cleansing of the Temple (Matt. 21:13).

Heidegger, and Luther on the concept of the present moment as eschatological time, citing Bultmann's *History and Eschatology* (New York: Harper Torchbook, 1962), Walter Pannenberg's *Offenbarung als Geschichte* (Göttingen: Vandenhoeck & Ruprecht, 1961), and J. Moltmann's *Theologie der Hoffnung* (Munich: C. Kaiser, 1964).

5. See Mircea Eliade, *Cosmos and History: The Myth of the Eternal Return* (New York: Harper Torchbook, 1959). See also Mircea Eliade, *Essential Sacred Writings from around the World* (San Francisco: HarperSanFrancisco, 1992). For a Westerner's poetic conceptualization of cyclical time, see T. S. Eliot, *The Four Quartets* in *Collected Poems 1909-1962* (New York: Harcourt, Brace & World, 1963).

6. Confession of Sin, Holy Eucharist I, The Book of Common Prayer (New York: Church Hymnal Corporation, 1979), 331.

7. This concept is most fully discussed by the anonymous author of *The Cloud of Unknowing*, trans. Ira Progoff (New York: Dell Publishing Co., 1983).

Each of us is in process, and all of our relationships are in process. Indeed, spiritual writer Henri Nouwen speaks of the kingdom of God itself as process.[8] When we inspect our lives carefully, we notice how we are forever creating each other anew in each encounter, in each dynamic exchange of ideas and feelings. With friends we are always in the process of forming relationships; we are practicing how to be friends. Even with spouses, we are, as the poet Rainer Rilke puts it, "learning how to love."[9] A seemingly insignificant conversation makes us and the other person different, newer. We are our own advent, always coming to ourselves, just as the thoughts which we say "have come to us." Like the Prodigal Son in Luke 15:17, who "came to himself," we too are living projects, practicing being human, in the process of "coming to our senses, coming to ourselves." We wait, as it were, for the fullness of the Spirit of Truth who will inform us about what is to come (John 16:1–6).

And in some dire situations — slaves on the Middle Passage or under a tyrannical master; hostages of war in unspeakable squalor; those experiencing extreme brutality, abuse, torture, or starvation — hope in a better life or at least justice for our persecutors can become the reason for living, or more realistically, the best comfort in our dying. Often in life, we make it through horrific obstacles, as the African American slaves did on escape routes northward, only by holding a future vision in mind. Moreover, in recent decades, Western cultures have begun to recover what was perhaps always known in the ancient and tribal cultures of the world: that hope itself is medicinal, a curative for diseases.

---

8. Henri Nouwen, *Reaching Out: The Three Movements of the Spiritual Life* (Garden City, N.Y.: Doubleday, 1986). For a theological discussion of the kingdom within and eschatology, focusing on Augustine, Luther, Kierkegaard, Barth, and Bultmann, see Schmithals, *Dictionary of the History of Ideas*, 2"160–61.

9. Rainer Maria Rilke, "Learning to Love," in Helen Caswell, *Whom God Has Joined Together* (Nashville: Dimensions, 1997), unpaginated.

The Burden of Hope

> *"One world at a time."*
> —Henry David Thoreau[10]

Westerners, however, are all but obsessed with the concepts of progress and a linear time line, believing not only that the future will be better, but that the future, once achieved, will be a curative for what ails us in the present: The right new medicine will take away our ills, the next academic degree will assure us a better job, the perfect partner will make life happier, the stylish automobile or club membership will enhance our image in the eyes of others.

The vast majority of human beings seem not to be able to live without hope, but to do so is burdensome on our souls and can be dangerous to a life of faith and trust, for at least two reasons: To hope is to leave the present and the grace available to us in the present moment; and to put all our hope in hope, as it were, can be to set ourselves — our minds and hearts and spirits — up for potential disappointment.

Living in, or dwelling on, the future radically wrenches us away from the present, away from what is, from what many spiritual mentors call "direct experience" and the grace of this present moment,[11] that is, clear and intense looking (or hearing, touching, smelling, tasting) at our existing environment. Our thoughts, our mental imagery, and our daydreams separate us from the hope inherent in our life right now, from the hope that undergirds the assumption that all is well — right here, right now. And that I am loved and accepted just as I am, just as we are, just as the world

---

10. Henry David Thoreau, when asked about the hereafter, in David Schiller, *The Little Zen Companion* (New York: Workman Publishing, 1994), 293.
11. See Toni Packer, *The Work of This Moment* (Boston: Shambhala, 1990). See also Toni Packer, *The Light of Discovery* (Boston: Charles E. Tuttle Co., 1995), and Jean-Pierre de Caussade, *The Sacrament of the Present Moment,* trans. Kitty Muggeride (Glasgow, Scotland: Collins Son and Co., 1981).

is.[12] We sorely neglect what might be called "present hope,"[13] thereby negating authentic hope, God's providence and presence.

Moreover, by negating present hope and by focusing on future hope, we can do great harm to ourselves, physically and spiritually. Future hope raises expectations. Even on the simplest, most mundane levels of our lives, we can see this detriment:

> I hope this evening is the best ever /
> I expected that meal to be better
>
> I hope we will all get along /
> I expected her to react more affirmatively
>
> I hope my company will reward my hard work /
> I expected I would get a raise
>
> I hope the committee understands my position /
> I expected to be treated with more respect.

Hope / expectations. Hope / expectations. Expectations lead almost inevitably to disappointment. Disappointment almost inevitably leads to anger and frustration; and repeated scenarios of unmet expectations, anger, and frustration lead almost inevitably to some form of despondency and ultimately to despair.

The church also tells us that we are not adequate as we are, but that change is necessary in order to gain future rewards. Sometimes we need to change to fit in the local church; we need to repent, we are told, in order to become acceptable and have one's name "enrolled in the book" in heaven. It is hard, if not nearly impossible, for any of us to accept that anyone — parents, society at

---

12. See Graham Dowell, *Enjoying the World: The Rediscovery of Thomas Traherne* (London: Mowbray, 1990).
13. This is a term used by Philip Chard, columnist for the *Milwaukee Journal Sentinel*, in a seminar attended by Dorothea Midgett, member of The Milwaukee Mindfulness Center, Milwaukee, who suggested its use to me.

large, even God — loves and accepts us as we are.[14] After all, true acceptance depends upon our becoming someone or something different from who or what we currently are.

Most of us feed off of, even nurse, past events, wounds, or pleasures; or we project ourselves forward into a future that has not arrived, and may never arrive. Hence, we live in hope — in hope that one more replay of the memory-tape in our mind or one more fantasy trip into the future will make things right.

The more we long for this or that, the more heightened our expectations become; our expectations are rarely, if ever, completely met or fulfilled. So long as hope leads to expectation, hope becomes a burden. And those expectations can block the deepest hope available to us, and we "miss the coming of the Son of God because [we] are so tied to [our] own desires and expectations."[15]

Hope breeds eternal in the human breast — breeds desire, and desire can be the cause of much of the anxiety and disappointment in our lives. Hope-become-expectation is a major stumbling block not only to happiness but also to a lived, human confidence in the goodness of life, of the purposefulness of our own lives and actions, the practice of a life-affirming, grounded spirituality.

Present Hope

> *"All that we see without is already available to us within."*
> — Sir Thomas Browne[16]

Each of us has an inner eschatology, or end-time, which parallels the cosmic eschatology recorded in the Revelation of John, an

---

14. For a discussion of this idea, see Desmond Tutu, "What Do We Have That Is Not Gift?" *Trinity News* (Summer 2002): 14–17.
15. Susan Ruehle, Sermon for the Seventh Sunday after Pentecost (Cycle A), Atonement Lutheran Church, Racine, Wis., July 7, 2002, 2.
16. Sir Thomas Browne, quoted in *100 Small Comforts* (Philadelphia: Lawrence Teacher Books, 2001), 101.

end-time when we will have become all we can be, perhaps not all we had hoped we would be, but all there was time for us to become in this life. Awareness of our inner eschatology, of our becoming who we are in relation to God, generates our desire for union with God through worship, prayer, and contemplation — not necessarily to improve ourselves or the world, but rather to find fulfillment or what some call "completion" through intimate communion with God. In other words, we yearn to be, to become more than we are; or as the mystics might put it, less than we are and more of what God is in us. The cliché "God isn't finished with me yet" captures the gist of this idea.

Yet when we yield deeply to quietness, stillness, and intentional solitude, we discover present within us what some theologians call "realized eschatology,"[17] a future already here. We discover that the very moment we are experiencing is eternal and that what we hope for in the future is here in all confidence hidden beneath our conscious thoughts and prayers. William Blake said it succinctly in "Auguries of Innocence":

> To see a World in a grain of sand,
> And a Heaven in a wild flower,
> Hold Infinity in the palm of your hand,
> And Eternity in an hour."[18]

Follow me, our Lord says, and instead we worship him. Listen to me, and instead we sing hymns about him. Look at the lilies of the field, and instead we daydream about future fields. Say nothing and come away with me to a quiet place, and instead we argue, debate, and blabber on about God and religion and try to work, or, if I may use it as a verb, "faith" our way into Heaven.

---

17. See Schmithals, "Renewal of New Testament Eschatology," 160–61.
18. William Blake, "Auguries of Innocence," *The Norton Anthology of Poetry* (New York: W. W. Norton, 1970), 533.

Sadly, the practices of a reflective life are shunned, overlooked by our churches: "To reflect on this inner life rationally is a skill no longer taught, though successful introspection, if it can make us at peace with ourselves, is sanity itself."[19]

When we engage in effective introspection, we discover that what Joseph Campbell calls "inner space" is as expansive and worthy of exploration as outer space: "outer space is within us inasmuch as the laws of space are within us; outer and inner space are the same."[20] If we sit with our inner world and explore it in what the Prayer Book calls "rest and quietness,"[21] or sit still in some form of mental or contemplative prayer, or allow sacred literature to slowly seep inside through Lectio Divina or Holy Reading,[22] or when we animate our imaginations with guided meditation — we become more keenly aware of what Eastern spiritual traditions call "direct experience."

We are no longer looking on, or observing, or reading about or studying about prayer and meditation, we are practicing first-hand. But we are not simply practicing a form of reading or praying or meditating, we are actually practicing, participating in, "direct experience," we are part of the present moment — "in" the moment, not removed from it.

Practicing direct experience — looking directly, seeing clearly what is, being present to each moment as it unfolds before us, staying radically in the present — requires of us a state of being, not a state of doing. To be rather than to do does not mean we

---

19. Guy Davenport, "Montaigne," *Every Force Evolves a Form: Twenty Essays* (San Francisco: North Point Press, 1987), 41.
20. Joseph Campbell, *The Inner Reaches of Outer Space: Metaphor as Myth and as Religion* (New York: Alfred Van Der Marck Editions, 1986), 28. For a discussion of the psychology of introspection, see James Hillman, "Introspection," *Healing Fiction* (Barrytown, N.Y.: Station Hill Press, 1983), 57–63.
21. Prayer 59: "For Quiet Confidence," The Book of Common Prayer, 832.
22. For a contemporary example of Lectio Divina, see Robert J. Miller, *Fire in the Deep: Lectio Divina Series, Cycle A* (Chicago: Sheed & Ward, 2001). For a historical examination of meditative reading from the Christian Tradition, see Brian Stock, *After Augustine: The Meditative Reader* (Philadelphia: University of Pennsylvania Press, 2001).

don't act or take action; rather, it means we are awake, as Jesuit Anthony de Mello puts it in his book *Awareness*.[23] Awake as Christ was to people, to wounds, to the nuances of relationships, to life itself, and to God. We are conscious of what is happening at that moment, not nursing past memories or obsessing over future plans.

The journey within is no less rocky than the journey without, and several scenarios are possible during such inward journeys of prayer and meditation. One, we rewind the inner videotape and replay past hurts and wounds, hoping against hope that one more replay will yield a different outcome. Or, two, we fast-forward the inner tape to a land of milk and honey that momentarily releases us from present angst. Or, three, our minds send up endless and seemingly unrelated streams of thoughts.

Yet a fourth possibility exists if we allow the tapes to rewind to the beginning or fast-forward completely to the end. They stop and there emerges direct experience of the Holy Spirit in the kingdom within (Luke 17:21).

Direct experience is not something we can induce or bring about on our own, though we can seek a quiet and lonely place, we can attend to the lilies of the field, we can sit still. This too is a gift, like the gift of time to sit, the gift of silence and solitude, the gift of holy space, the gift of a lively mind, the gift of prayer itself. To paraphrase Anthony de Mello on happiness: happiness is already here; we don't need to add anything; we only need to drop that which hinders our awareness.[24] Likewise, direct experience. Often what we name "distraction" might not be distracting us at all but calling us to attention; we might have a romantic

---

23. Anthony de Mello, *Awareness: The Perils and Opportunities of Reality* (New York: Doubleday, 1992).
24. Ibid., 56ff. On the theme of the illusion of rewards, see 42ff.

notion of what an experience of God is and miss the experience right at hand.

On these rare occasions when we are aware of what is, we see that we are not practicing a posture or a method of prayer, but are actually practicing the presence of God, to draw from Brother Lawrence of the Resurrection's lexicon.[25] A common thread of both the Christian and Eastern mystical traditions is that self-knowledge leads to contemplation of God. Moreover, "If one does not study himself through direct experience, he will be dependent all the time on the opinions of others."[26] Can we not broaden the Eastern mystic's dictum? If one does not study God through direct experience, she will be dependent all the time on the opinions of others — in other words, dependent upon secondary sources, rather than the text of oneself, a text Christians believe was originally "written" by God.

The practice of the presence releases us, at least for a time, from fretting over the waves of the mental ocean, from too harshly judging the replayed inner tapes or the fast-forwards to the greener pastures of imagination. In this present presence, we do not need healing from the past, do not need the rewards of the future, because all is already well, and we can relax and enjoy our own minds. As T. S. Eliot writes in "East Coker": "the faith and the love and the hope are all in the waiting."[27] We are living into — and out of, at the same time — an unseen confidence that is the heart and core of hope itself: "Even last night at my saddest, I felt this confidence like a hammock rocking me just below the edge of thought. I'm not sure it's the same thing as trust, but I wonder if accepting what is may not be the seedbed

---

25. See Brother Lawrence of the Resurrection, *The Practice of the Presence of God*, trans. John J. Delaney (New York: Doubleday, 1977).
26. Swami Rama, "Self-Training," *The Himalayan Institute* (Spring 1987): 6. Christian writers in the Cistercian tradition are equally strong in this same tradition of self-study.
27. Eliot, "East Coker," *Collected Poems*, 186.

for trust, maybe the 'root' that trust grows from?"²⁸ What some call "present hope" is the lifeblood of human existence, of the human will to live.

As we see clearly what is happening in the moment, we become aware, at least intuitively, of an inherent hope — a kind of quiet confidence that is even stronger than future hope, that is "realized hope" already within us, one of the many fruits of direct experience.

Living in Unresolved Paradox

> *"If preachers are going to talk about hope,
> let them talk as honestly as Saint Paul did
> about hopelessness."*
> — Frederick Buechner[29]

The practice of direct experience opens us to our own realized interior eschatology, to present hope, to hope present in us, to God's hope for us to live our own human lives fully and abundantly without rewards, but completely from the kingdom within, its own "reward." Carter Heyward puts it this way in "The Spark Is God": "I, yet not I, am responsible for whatever good I, yet not I, have done. The dynamic tension is critical and it is here to stay, not to be resolved."[30] The realization that this place of dynamic tension is to be sought, not escaped and lived out of, not ignored, is beautifully expressed in this poem by a thirty-year professed member of a religious community:

---

28. Katherine Greer Clark, unpublished letter on spiritual direction, June 9, 2002.
29. Frederick Buechner, "Preaching on Hope," www.pulpit.org/articles/preaching_on_hope.asp (July 1, 2002). This sermon was first called to my attention by Susan Ruehle, the bishop's assistant for Southeast Wisconsin in the Lutheran Synod of Milwaukee.
30. Carter Heyward, "The Spark Is God," in *Speaking of Christ: A Lesbian Feminist Voice*, ed. Ellen C. Davis (New York: Pilgrim Press, 1989). "The Spark Is God" is a revised sermon preached at Episcopal Divinity School in 1982.

> Where is the space of choiceless passion
> passionate detachment,
> detached zeal,
> zealous surrender,
> surrendered commitment?[31]

Wherever this time and space, it is the personal eschaton of the mature individual Christian. In "Ash Wednesday," T. S. Eliot writes, "teach us to care and not to care...."[32] Here the poet captures the essential paradox in which people of faith live, and it is this same unresolved paradox that Christians have when they live in hope. Caring and not caring is the essential dynamic that spirited people live between: heartfelt yet detached concern.

In "East Coker," another of the *Four Quartets,* Eliot writes, "I said to my soul, be still and wait without hope/For hope would be hope for the wrong thing...."[33] Indeed, hope itself may be "the wrong thing." Almost anything can become a substitute for God, and hope is no exception. Many mystics over the years, including Thomas Merton in the twentieth century, have observed that even prayer can be a hindrance; hence, the dictum, Don't pray, go directly to God. So it is with hope: Hope for a better future can become an end in itself, can indeed be a substitute for God.[34]

We live, then, with hope and without hope. Linked to the heartfelt hope of God, detached from the human hope with expectation: Not caring in order that caring might be genuine; not hoping, in order that hope might be valid, in order that God might be fully present to us.

---

31. Sister Dorcas Baker, C.S.M., "Hold that space!" Unpublished poem.
32. Eliot, "Ash Wednesday," *Collected Poems,* 86.
33. Eliot, "East Coker," 186.
34. I wish to thank Sister Brigit-Carol Lay, S.D., of Vigeat Radix Hermitage, Santa Anna, Tex., for reading this paper in manuscript and in particular for clarifying the concept of substitution.

5

Jesus and Eschatology

REGINALD H. FULLER

IN SEVERAL different quarters the end of the Weiss-Schweitzer[1] consensus on eschatology is being confidently proclaimed. It is no longer obvious to everybody that Jesus announced the imminent end of the present world and the coming of the kingdom of God, resulting in a new heaven and a new earth.

Actually there never was really a consensus on this question. One of my own teachers, C. H. Dodd,[2] argued back in the 1930s for what he called a "realized eschatology." For Dodd, the kingdom of God was already fully present through the appearance, proclamation, and activity of Jesus. Dodd based his view primarily on his interpretation of Mark 1:15 together with his understanding of the parables of the kingdom. Dodd argues that *eggiken* in Mark 1:15 should be translated "has come," and that *ephthasen* in Luke 11:20 (Q) had lost its sense of anticipation, and had come to mean "it is here." There was some point in this argument. There is certainly a present element in Jesus' view of the kingdom, an element that Weiss and Schweitzer ignored. The present element is in fact crucial for Jesus' implicit christology. Jesus was more than a prophet announcing God's

---

1. Johannes Weiss, *Jesus' Proclamation of the Kingdom of God* (Philadelphia: Fortress, 1971). German original, 1892. Weiss's views were popularized by Albert Schweitzer, *The Quest of the Historical Jesus* (London: Black, 1910). German original, 1906.
2. C. H. Dodd, *The Parables of the Kingdom* (London: Nisbet, 1935).

future action. He was enacting proleptically the kingdom whose future coming he was announcing. It is clear, however, from other sayings, especially the second petition of the Lord's Prayer, "thy kingdom come," from the Beatitudes, and the eschatological saying at the Last Supper (Mark 14:25) that the future element in Jesus' view of the kingdom was equally important. If there ever was a consensus, it is the view that held the ground between about 1950 and 1980 that there was a combination of "already" and "not yet" in Jesus' view of the kingdom. In some sense the reign of God was at present operative in Jesus, and yet its full realization lay at some point in the future. Such a view was represented by leading European scholars, notably Oscar Cullmann,[3] Werner Georg Kümmel,[4] and Joachim Jeremias.[5] Jeremias coined the phrase *"sich realisierende Eschatologie"* (eschatology in the process of realizing itself). In my first published work,[6] I proposed the term "proleptic eschatology," thus emphasizing both the present element of Jesus' view of the kingdom and his anticipation of its decisive consummation in the future. The post-Bultmannian New Questers, while following Bultmann in designating Jesus' eschatology as one of "reduced apocalyptic," nevertheless recognized a present element which permitted them to speak of an implicit or indirect christology in Jesus' self-understanding. Thus they justified their revival of the quest of the historical Jesus. The purpose of the quest was to demonstrate the continuity between the pre-Easter Jesus and the kerygma. True, the post-Bultmannian New Questers were concerned to demythologize the present element in Jesus' eschatology by means

---

3. Oscar Cullmann, *Christ and Time* (London: SCM, 1951).
4. Werner Georg Kümmel, *Promise and Fulfillment* (SBT 22; London: SCM, 1957).
5. Joachim Jeremias, *The Parables of Jesus*, rev. ed. (New York: Scribner's, 1962).
6. Reginald H. Fuller, *The Mission and Achievement of Jesus* (London: SCM, 1954).

of an existential interpretation,[7] but that does not alter the fact that they agreed with the then-prevailing view of the "already" and the "not yet" as characteristic of Jesus' eschatology.

It appears that this presumed consensus has broken down, at least in English-speaking scholarship. Here two divergent alternatives have emerged. On the one hand the North American Jesus Seminar and some of its associates are trumpeting the (re-)discovery of the "non-eschatological Jesus."[8] This elimination of eschatology from the proclamation and teaching of Jesus is supported by two main arguments. First, it is held that the eschatological elements in the Jesus tradition are secondary and of post-Easter origin. Thus the eschatological elements in Q are relegated to a hypothetical secondary redaction, designated Q^2, leaving only Q^1 consisting of sapiential (wisdom) material.[9] This reconstruction of the Q tradition is supported by the Gospel of Thomas whose sayings are notably sapiential in character. Second, the eschatological elements in Mark are similarly classed as secondary, post-Easter in origin, notably the Marcan summary of Jesus' proclamation in Mark 1:15. This view, however, ignores the presence of the same saying, "the Kingdom of God has come

---

7. Ernst Käsemann, "The Problem of the Historical Jesus," in *Essays on New Testament Themes* (London: SCM, 1964), 15–47.

8. In a series of works, beginning with the book that emerged from his doctoral dissertation, *Conflict, Holiness, and Politics in the Teachings of Jesus* (New York: Mellen, 1984), Marcus Borg has put forward what he calls "A Temperate Case for a Non-Eschatological Jesus." Significantly, Borg wrote his dissertation at Oxford under George Caird, who in turn had studied at Cambridge under C. H. Dodd. It seems that realized eschatology can eventually end up in no eschatology!

9. This (completely speculative) reconstruction of the traditional history of Q originates with J. S. Kloppenborg, *The Formation of Q: Trajectories in Ancient Wisdom Collections* (Philadelphia: Fortress, 1987). Kloppenborg's work was inspired by the earlier work of James M. Robinson on the history of Wisdom tradition. On the history of the Q material, too little attention has been paid to Heinz Schürmann's proposal that collections of Jesus' sayings had a pre-Easter *Sitz im Leben*. They were made by the disciples for use on their missions in Galilee (Mark 6:7–13; Luke 10:1–12 [Q]). See his essay "Die vorchristlichen Anfänge der Logientradition," in Helmut Ristow and Karl Matthiae, eds., *Der historische Jesus und der Kerygmatische Christus* (Berlin: Evangelische Verlagsanstalt), 342–70. I am grateful to Professor Schuyler Brown for reminding me of this article.

near to you," in the Q material (Luke 10:9 [Q]). Thus this crucial saying, even if Mark 1:15 as a whole is Marcan redaction, must be derived from pre-Marcan tradition, and given its double attestation (Mark and Q), it passes one of the recognized criteria of authenticity.

Next, the Jesus Seminar and its followers interpret the parables of the kingdom not in an eschatological but in a spiritualizing or sociopolitical sense, thus reviving the liberal Protestant interpretation of earlier times, prior to Weiss and Schweitzer. Jesus is then reconstructed as a cynic-like sage, a "spirit person," or a social rather than eschatological prophet.[10]

My intention here is not to offer a detailed refutation of this attempt to eliminate apocalyptic eschatology from the authentic, pre-Easter Jesus tradition. A convincing attempt along these lines has recently been offered by my friend and former student, Arland Hultgren.[11] Let me just say this: The assumed incompatibility between the sapiential and the apocalyptic is entirely without justification. Many years ago my late colleague Raymond E. Brown observed in discussion that apocalyptic writers from the book of Daniel on make regular use of Wisdom motifs. There is every reason to suppose that Jesus, precisely as an eschatological prophet, would have drawn on Wisdom tradition in order to demonstrate the kind of behavior expected of those who responded positively to his eschatological message. This is particularly obvious in the Great Sermon (Sermon on the Plain in Luke, Sermon on the Mount in Matthew) with which the Q material properly begins.[12]

---

10. For a recent presentation of these portraits of Jesus, see Marcus J. Borg and N. T. Wright, *The Meaning of Jesus: Two Visions* (San Francisco: HarperSanFrancisco, 1998), 53–76.

11. Arland J. Hultgren, "Eschatology in the New Testament: The Current Debate," in Carl E. Braaten and Robert W. Jenson, eds., *The Last Things: Biblical and Theological Perspectives on Eschatology* (Grand Rapids, Mich.: Eerdmans, 2002).

12. It is commonly thought that Q began with narrative material concerning John the Baptist, the Baptism of Jesus (?), and the Temptation. Because there are signs of a similar sequence in Mark and John, I am inclined to regard this complex of material as a separate

Other scholars have put forward a very different treatment of Jesus' eschatology. Quite independently of one another, two scholars, one British and Anglican, and the other American and Roman Catholic, namely, N. T. (Tom) Wright[13] and John P. Meier,[14] are coming independently to very much the same conclusion. Both agree (against the Jesus Seminar and its adherents) that Jesus' central message was eschatological. But both agree that it was an eschatology not in the Weiss-Schweitzer sense of the end of history and the coming of a new heaven and a new earth, but in the sense of a new order within history. N. T. Wright states the argument as follows:

> If Jesus or the early church used the relevant [apocalyptic] language in the same way as their contemporaries, it is highly unlikely that they would have been referring to the actual end of the world, and highly likely that they would have been referring to events within space-time history which they interpreted as the coming of the kingdom.[15]

John P. Meier states the same position:

> By end time or eschatology one should not mean some phantasmagoric destruction of heaven and earth or the complete end of human history in the manner of Jewish apocalypses such as 4 Ezra [note the divergence of Wright and Meier on this point]. Rather, Jesus was announcing only the end of

---

collection, rather than a part of Q. On this view, Q would begin with the Beatitudes — a natural opening for a collection of sayings announcing the nearness of the eschatological kingdom and spelling out in Wisdom style the ethical consequences of accepting that message.

13. N. T. Wright, *Christian Origins and the Question of God*, vol. 1: *The New Testament and the People of God* (Minneapolis: Fortress, 1992); vol. 2: *Jesus and the Victory of God* (Minneapolis: Fortress, 1996).

14. John P. Meier, *A Marginal Jew: Rethinking the Historical Jesus*, vol. 1: *The Roots of the Problem and the Person* (New York: Doubleday, 1991); vol. 2: *Mentor, Message, and Miracle* (New York: Doubleday, 1994); vol. 3: *Companions and Competitors* (New York: Doubleday, 2001).

15. Wright, *Jesus and the Victory of God*, 2:321.

the present state of things, the end of sacred history as Israel had known it up to now, and the definitive beginning of a new, permanent state of affairs.[16]

It is remarkable how for all the differences in their starting points (Wright sets up a hypothesis and tests it by the evidence; Meier builds up his case by a careful analysis of the evidence), the two scholars end up close together. Both agree on the nature of this historical-eschatological realization: It involves the restoration of Israel within history, the fulfillment of the promise of Israel's return after the exile.

There are, of course, differences of emphasis. Wright in particular insists that the apocalyptic imagery used to describe the "end" events, such as we find in Mark's Little Apocalypse (Mark 13:24–25), is not to be interpreted literally but symbolically,[17] and in particular those passages that speak of the Son of man "coming on the clouds of heaven," such as Mark 13:26 and 14:62, refer not to the second coming from heaven to earth, but to the exaltation of Christ to heaven after the Resurrection.[18] Wright also assumes that the Little Apocalypse, interpreted in this way as referring to events *within* history, is authentic Jesus tradition.[19] This view is hardly likely to commend itself to most New Testament scholars.

The general critical view of the Little Apocalypse is that while it may include some authentic Jesus sayings, it is in its present form a composition of the post-Easter community, edited by Mark. Verses 5–23 of Mark 13 describe events within history leading up to the end, while verses 24–25 are symbolic language based

---

16. Meier, *Companions and Competitors*, 3:624.
17. Wright, *Jesus and the Victory of God*, 2:226–43.
18. Ibid., 2:361.
19. Ibid., 3:339–65, assumes without question that the Little Apocalypse goes back to Jesus. Wright's neglect of detailed discussions of authenticity is a major weakness of his work, compared with that of Meier.

on Old Testament prophetic imagery such as Isaiah 13:10 about the end-point of history. Whether such imagery goes back to Jesus himself is difficult to decide, and is much debated among scholars. Given the state of the question it would be hazardous to base any conclusion about Jesus' eschatology upon the parousia sayings. It is perhaps more likely that direct echoes of Daniel 7:13-14 are creations of the post-Easter community. It is more likely, as Ferdinand Hahn argued many years ago,[20] that those sayings which appear to distinguish between the earthly Jesus and the future Son of man, such as Luke 12:8-9 (Q) and Mark 8:38 (note the double attestation) are authentic to Jesus. In that case we would have a clear indication that Jesus envisaged a last judgment which would mark the end of history and the inauguration of metahistory in a new heaven and a new earth.

In a later work,[21] written in a more popular style, in debate with Marcus Borg, Wright allows that the post-Easter church, unlike Jesus himself, believed that Christ would come again at the end to judge the world and establish the kingdom of God in a new heaven and a new earth. In other words, it held a metahistorical eschatology. This discontinuity between Jesus and the post-Easter church was the result not of the teaching of the earthly Jesus himself, but mainly from the Easter experience.

I would assess the role of Easter in the development of apocalyptic eschatology somewhat differently from Wright. The Easter experience was a surprise, not because Jesus rose from the dead, but because no one else did. In Jewish apocalyptic eschatology, what was expected was a general resurrection of all Israel or in some cases of humanity beyond Israel. Instead, one resurrection occurred, that of Jesus himself. The effect was to create a sense of

---

20. Ferdinand Hahn, *Christologische Hoheitstitel: Ihre Geschichte im frühen Christentum* (Göttingen: Vandenhoeck & Ruprecht, 1963), 32-42.
21. Borg and Wright, *The Meaning of Jesus*, 202.

"not-yet-ness." What had happened in the case of Jesus was the resurrection of the "first fruits" (1 Cor. 15:20), the first instance of what as a consequence was to follow later. This would suggest that Jesus himself had encouraged his disciples to look for a general resurrection. Such an expectation would not have been unusual, given the fact that the Pharisees and the Essenes looked for a similar end of history.

Here it may be objected that Jesus did in fact look for his own resurrection as an individual event, which would be the case with the Marcan passion predictions.[22] These predictions are widely regarded as prophecies after the event. It may be argued elsewhere, however, that an earlier stratum in these predictions is much more general in character, and reflecting the language of Isaiah 53: "the Son of man will be handed over to men" (Mark 9:31), "be rejected" (8:31), and perhaps including "suffer many things" (ibid.). This layer in the predictions would be thoroughly consistent with Jesus' self-understanding as eschatological prophet, the one in whom Israel's rejection of God's emissaries reached its culmination. Those scholars who are prepared to acknowledge an authentic stratum in the passion predictions usually add that they also envisaged God's vindication of his final prophet, but without specifying how this could be expressed.[23] Clearly, the mention of resurrection would belong to the later post-Easter stratum. How then did Jesus speak of his vindication? I would suggest that it was expressed by the term "will be lifted up," as found in the Johannine Son of man sayings (John 3:14; 12:34; cf. 8:28; 12:32). If this argument is tenable, it would leave open the possibility that Jesus anticipated a general resurrection as part of his eschatology. This general resurrection would be his own vindication.

---

22. Mark 8:31; 9:31; 10:33–34.
23. See, e.g., Edward Schillebeeckx, *Jesus* (New York: Seabury, 1979), 294–306.

Support for this proposed understanding of the "lifting up" of the Son of man may be found in Jesus' language about the messianic banquet. In the eschatological saying at the Last Supper, mentioned above, Jesus clearly implied that he would participate (with the disciples, as Matthew correctly notes) in that festive meal. It will also be shared with Abraham, Isaac, and Jacob (Luke 13:28–29 [Q]). Clearly the messianic banquet implies a general resurrection and therefore a metahistorical eschatology.

We turn now to the episode known as "the Sadducees' question" (Mark 12:18–27, and parallels). John Meier has argued thoroughly and convincingly for the authenticity of this tradition.[24] Jesus accepted the Pharisaic view, rejected by the Sadducees, of a general resurrection at the end. First, Jesus argued from scripture that the very nature of God, as the God of Abraham, Isaac, and Jacob, is that he is the God of the *living*. Second, Jesus argues that in the resurrection life there will be a completely transformed mode of existence, in which men and women will no longer be married. It will be a life like that of the angels. As the book of Daniel put it, they will shine "like the stars" (Dan. 12:3), or, as Paul said, they will have a "spiritual body" (1 Cor. 15:44). Sadly, Meier never relates this tradition of the Sadducees' question and the insight it provides into Jesus' eschatological views to his overall reconstruction of Jesus' eschatological message. Jesus could hardly have envisioned an end merely of "history as we know it." Rather, he contemplated an end of history as such, a resurrection life in which there is no marrying or being given in marriage, and therefore no conception or birth, no succession of generations. In other words, Jesus' eschatology, while clearly expecting a restoration of Israel within history, goes beyond that and anticipates a general resurrection and a subsequent metahistory.

---

24. Meier, *Companions and Competitors*, 3:416–44.

Jesus' eschatology was both proleptic and metahistorical. Therefore, the Christian task is to anticipate here and now the ultimate goal of the universe. We set out signs for this future by our efforts for justice and peace, even though our efforts in this world will never be perfect. The goal will be fulfilled when Christ comes again, and there will be the new heaven and new earth.

6

"I See Your Bridal Chamber Adorned"

An Eastern Orthodox Reflection on the Eschaton in Light of the "Pattern" of Divine Worship

HIEROMONK ALEXANDER GOLITZIN

WHEN I WAS THIRTEEN or fourteen years old, I chanced on a book whose title and author I no longer remember, but which left an impression on me. It was not a profound book, but rather one of that genre which offers a Cooke's Tour of different varieties of Christianity. Its chapters thus included one on the Orthodox Church that focused, quite properly, on Orthodox worship. What struck me at the time were the author's criticisms. He was troubled that the Eastern Christian liturgy he attended was much too exclusively focused on beauty and joy. It had no place, he thought, for moral exhortation, did not foster repentance for sin, nor leave the believers attending it with a sense of dissatisfaction regarding their shortcomings. I remember that I was puzzled by this complaint, wondering how the Divine Liturgy should be anything other than beautiful. Perhaps I had already read, or heard somewhere, of the legendary report of Great Prince Vladimir's envoys to golden Byzantium in the tenth century, who came back to tell their sovereign that never had they seen "such beauty" as in the Church of the Holy Wisdom at the heart of the imperial capital, beauty so great, they said, that "We knew not whether we were in heaven or on earth."[1] Naturally, at least according to the terms of the legend, the prince chose for his nation the faith that had so impressed his ambassadors.

The Second Rome no longer stands, nor the Third. Christian Constantinople became Muslim Istanbul centuries ago, while whatever was left of "Holy Russia" at the turn of the twentieth century disappeared forever beneath the bloody tides of the October Revolution. Yet, battered and scarred to be sure, the Orthodox Church did not disappear, nor has its liturgy changed significantly — at least in its emphasis on beauty — since Vladimir's representatives were ushered into Hagia Sophia. Orthodox Christians have clung to their form of worship over the course of the intervening thousand years, a millennium that has seen a succession of catastrophes, invasions, and mass slaughters — from the Turkish conquest of Asia Minor and the Balkans, to the violent incursion of the Crusaders, to Genghis Khan, Tamerlane, and, greatest of all, the unrelenting horrors of the twentieth century: the genocide of Armenians and Greeks at the hands of Young Turks and Kemalists, of Serbs under the rule of the Ustashi in Satellite Croatia, the German invasion of the Soviet Union bringing with it twenty million dead, and a roughly equal number slain by the Bolshevik Terror and Stalin's Gulag, not to mention the somewhat milder versions of the latter set in place by the Red Army in the ever-suffering Balkans. Throughout this sequence of misery, destruction, and enslavement, the liturgy has been a light, a beacon, and a promise. Its beauty has sustained the Orthodox world with what is, in sum, its enduring image of the eschaton.

---

1. Quoted from the *Russian Primary Chronicle* by Kallistos Ware, *The Orthodox Church* (Baltimore: Penguin, 1964), 269.

One does not in America normally associate "the end" with worship in a neighborhood church. Popular imagination, especially in the Bible Belt, fixates rather on what we might call the "special effects" of the last things: the rise and fall of kingdoms of evil, the melting earth, celestial rearrangements of a cataclysmic nature, lakes of fire, heavenly ascents (the "rapture"), and a descending, cubical city fifteen hundred miles on a side, equipped with flora ("trees of life"), fauna ("the Lamb" and "the living creatures" of the Throne), and waterworks ("the river of life"). Calculations of an exact kind, based on Daniel (a mistake never again repeated in apocalyptic literature), abound, coupled in past decades with a distinct, Cold War accent that I recall listening to with astonishment while driving across the Colorado plains a couple of years ago. Apparently, the evaporation of the Soviet Union ten years before had not yet put to rest the desire of this radio preacher to cast Russia in the role of Ezekiel's Gog and Magog. Perhaps — and I hope — another ten years will suffice to still this particular expression of American xenophobia. But if this feature of, say, Hal Lindsay's *Late Great Planet Earth* subsides together with the geopolitical circumstances that provoked its rise, we may be assured that other villains will be found to replace the unfortunate Russians (the Ayatollahs, perhaps?), and that a preoccupation with eschatological pyrotechnics will continue indefinitely.

A flatly literalist reading of biblical symbols is certainly not confined to these shores, nor more generally to the Christian West. The invasions and catastrophes I sketched above have stimulated apocalyptic speculations of a similar kind in the Christian East. Nor was calamity necessarily required, as in the preoccupation with "interpreting" the Revelation that we find in, for example, nineteenth-century Russia, at least to judge from my admittedly hazy recollections of a few passages from Dostoyevsky's novels. There was also that old Greek monk, a visitor to the monastery where I was staying twenty-five years ago, who regaled a number of the fathers and me with a detailed account of the *eschata,* featuring conflict over oil in the Gulf, the overthrow of America (described with relish), Russian invasions (again! but then, they were still Communists), Turkish downfalls, and the emergence — complete with Chalice — of the last priest to celebrate liturgy at Hagia Sophia from out of the latter's walls in order to complete his interrupted service in the presence of a newly triumphant, six-fingered Byzantine Emperor. (Take that, Mr. Lindsay!) A few days later, however, the abbot of the monastery summoned those of us who had been enjoying the old man's tales in order to forbid us to listen to him and his fellows. "They're good old men," said the abbot, "pure and simple-hearted. But if you listen to them, you'll either believe them, which is bad, or you'll laugh at them, which is worse!" So we were instructed instead to smile, nod, and excuse ourselves as quickly and politely as possible.

Yet this same abbot speaks elsewhere of the "essential eschatological dimension of our Church life," that the eschaton is "identical" with the Orthodox faith. It is, he writes, "the air we breathe."[2] His understanding of it, however, is markedly more sober and theologically informed than that of the garrulous old monk, whose elaborate skein of myth, folklore, contemporary geopolitics, and biblical imagery annoyingly mirrors — though with an appropriately different assignment of white hats and black — his counterparts among the Bible-beaters on our side of the Atlantic. It also matches, unfortunately, the typically modern misunderstanding of eschatology generally, and of the biblical and

---

2. Archimandrite Aimilianos, "To Walk in Newness of Life," in idem, *Spiritual Instructions and Discourses,* vol. 1: *The Authentic Seal* (Ormylia, Halkidiki, Greece: Ormylia Publishing, 1999), 371.

extracanonical apocalypses in particular. Up until a generation ago, this approach was also pretty much the standard scholarly reading of apocalyptic literature — that is, that it was typically written under the cover of an ancient name from Israel's past, and was notable chiefly for *ex eventu* prophecy, the woes of the end-times, and the assignment of divine rewards to the righteous (identified with the writer's group or sect) and spectacular punishments to the reprobate (the group or sect's enemies). More recent studies, however, have begun to rediscover other elements at work in these ancient documents, and include a certain opening to the possibility that these may be testimonies to visionary experience; to a gospel of transformation and commerce with the things of heaven or, more precisely, with the liturgy of heaven; and, in view of the last, that their imagery is more often than not saturated with motifs taken from the cult and lore of the Jerusalem Temple.[3] John the Seer's cubical New Jerusalem (Rev. 21:16), for example, is unmistakably derived from the dimensions of the Holy of Holies (cf. 1 Kgs. 6:20). That point on earth where, as in the vision of Isaiah (Isa. 6:1–6), heaven and earth coalesce becomes in the Revelation the new creation itself, where God and the Lamb are to be immediately and everywhere present. Likewise, the flora of the city to come, the trees of life, and its waterworks, the river of life (Rev. 22:1–2), deliberately recall the Tree in Eden and the rivers that flow from the Garden to water the earth. Creation begins as a temple with Adam its priest in the book of Genesis, and it is therefore a perfect and conscious symmetry that the new creation should also be depicted as temple

---

3. See, for example, C. Rowland, *The Open Heaven: A Study of Apocalyptic in Judaism and Early Christianity* (New York: Crossroad, 1982), for a renewed interest in mysticism in the apocalypses, and, on temple motifs, M. Himmelfarb, *Ascent to Heaven in Jewish and Christian Apocalypses* (Oxford: Oxford University Press, 1993), 9–46; together with Margaret Barker, *On Earth as It Is in Heaven: Temple Symbolism in the New Testament* (Edinburgh: T. & T. Clark, 1995).

or, indeed, as innermost sanctuary, with the Lamb its great High Priest and unique oblation.⁴ It is surely no accident that John has his vision on "the Lord's day" (Rev. 1:9), the day of the Eucharist.

Thus my Greek abbot again, here speaking about the liturgy of the church in a sermon recorded several years ago and recently published:

> The most splendid likeness of the beauty itself of God's court on high is the daily worship that we have in our churches [lit., "temples," *vaoi*]. We are talking today about the heavenly court of Christ, but the exact impression of our worship is also that same court. There is a single living and moving image of the glory of Christ which becomes present in our worship. It becomes our life, bread, light, river of life, voices as of cataracts [cf. Ps. 42:9; Ezek. 1:24], just as above in heaven. He who sits enthroned there is also here, upon the cherubim, with fire and radiance of light.⁵

In the phrase "exact impression," the abbot is likely echoing a much earlier writer, the anonymous Syrian monk who wrote under the pseudonym Dionysius the Areopagite at the turn of the sixth century. This was the inventor of the word "hierarchy," by which he did not mean simply the ecclesiastical chain of command, but rather and preeminently the liturgy itself, which he, too, called the "exact image" (*akribēs eikōn*) of heavenly things, and elsewhere "the image of the divine beauty."⁶ One could justly

---

4. See again Barker, *On Earth as It Is in Heaven,* 26–39; and, specifically on the Jerusalem Temple tradition and its links with the Genesis creation narratives: J. Levenson, *Sinai and Zion: An Entry into the Jewish Bible* (San Francisco: Harper & Row, 1987), 142–45; together with, again, M. Barker, *The Gate of Heaven: The History and Symbolism of the Temple in Jerusalem* (London: SPCK, 1991), 57–103.

5. Archimandrite Aimilianos, "The Throne of God," in idem, *Spiritual Instructions and Discourses,* vol. 2: *Life in the Spirit* (Ormylia, Halkidiki, Greece: Ormylia Publishing, 1998), 380 (in Greek).

6. Dionysius Areopagita, *Ecclesiastical Hierarchy* II.2.6; *Patrologia Graeca* III:401C; and for "image of divine beauty": *Celestial Hierarchy* III.2; 165B. The translation here is my own, but for a handy (if theologically flawed) English translation of Dionysius, see

render the intended thrust of these two phrases as meaning "the exact image of the eschaton," a point that I take Dionysius as confirming when, at the end of his labors and by way of conclusion, he addresses a brief letter to the author of the Revelation ("To John at Patmos"), and — *inter alia* — makes the claim that he is "carrying on" the apostle's work.[7]

As the last remark suggests, the concluding book of the Christian Bible was read as liturgical in its fundamental orientation and imagery. I think it very likely that this was also the primary reason for the Revelation's inclusion in the canon of scripture (though not without some resistance, especially in the East). The "exact image" to which Dionysius refers, as well as my abbot long afterward, also looks toward the opposition between "image" (*eikōn*) and "shadow" (*skia*) drawn by Hebrews 10:1, where the latter's author has just finished his account of Jesus' entry into the sanctuary "not made with hands" as fulfillment of the type of the High Priest's ministry on Yom Kippur, portrayed in Leviticus 16. Once again, therefore, we have a reference to the liturgy of the Temple. I would also suggest that the ultimate biblical referent for the "exact image," and the opposition between "image" and "shadow," is the "pattern" that God shows to Moses on Sinai in Exodus 25:9ff: "In accordance with all that I show you concerning the pattern of the tabernacle ... so you shall make it." Now, while what the original writer meant by this "pattern" may be debated among scholars, the evidence is indisputable that already some centuries before Christ it was understood as signifying the heavenly prototype of Israel's wilderness shrine, and later on of its temple (cf. 1 Chron. 28:11, 19), hence the citing of John's vision

---

Pseudo-Dionysius: The Complete Works, trans. C. Liubheid, ed. P. E. Rorem (New York: Paulist Press, 1987).

7. Dionysius Areopagita, *Epistle X; Patrologia Graeca* III:1120A.

in Revelation 4ff., and hence, too, the understanding of Christian worship as image and anticipation of the eschaton that is arguably adumbrated in the New Testament, and evident as early as Ignatius of Antioch in the early second century, and which continues on through Dionysius down the centuries to my Athonite abbot.[8]

There is also another aspect to this image or "pattern" that we find highlighted in Eastern Christian ascetic tradition: It is not inert, but rather (as in my abbot's remarks) "living and moving," and shaping the soul. As a late fourth-century ascetic writes regarding the form of the liturgy, "We receive the manifest arrangement and administration of the Church as a pattern [*hypodeigma*] for what is at work in the soul by grace."[9] Dionysius expands on this same idea, defining the goal or purpose of "hierarchy" — which is to say, of the liturgy — as:

> ... shaping [lit., "stamping," *apotypoun*] ... and perfecting its celebrants as divine images, recipients of the primordial light and divine ray, who, once filled in sacred manner with this radiance, unselfishly reflect it to those who come after them.[10]

He is also writing here, of course, about the famous (or infamous) Eastern Christian soteriology of deification: that, in Christ, we are called to become participants in God, reflections — as in my quotation — of the divine Glory given us through incorporation into the Lord's risen body. Put another way, and one in more obvious consonance with this essay and volume, each Christian is called to become, in Christ and by the operation of his Spirit, an

---

8. For texts and analysis, see A. Golitzin, "Liturgy and Mysticism: The Experience of God in Eastern Orthodox Christianity," *Pro Ecclesia* 7, no. 2 (1999): 159-86.
9. Homily 52.2.1, in *Makarios/Symeon: Reden und Briefe. Die Sammlung I des Vaticanus Graecus 694 (B)* (Berlin: Akademie Verlag, 1973), 2:140.
10. *Celestial Hierarchy* III.2; *Patrologia Graeca* III:165A.

embodiment of the eschaton. Another anonymous Syrian ascetic, this time from the second century, places this idea in the mouth of the Lord Jesus himself:

> When you make the two one, and when you make the inside like the outside, and the outside like the inside, and the above like the below... then you will enter [the Kingdom].[11]

Eight hundred years later at the turn of the second millennium, a Greek abbot echoes much the same thought at greater length:

> Grace... is seen and revealed to those who with faith and in fear and trembling do the commandments and give evidence of a worthy repentance. The same grace of itself incontestably brings the future judgement to pass in them. Rather, indeed, it becomes itself the Day of divine judgement by which he who is purified is continually illumined, sees himself as he is in truth and in every detail... and becomes wholly immaculate, a son of the light and of the day.... The Day of the Lord will never come upon them [as judgement] because they are already in it forever and continually.[12]

More than any other single idea, what links these several witnesses together, who range from second-century Syria to twentieth-century Greece, is the common understanding of the eschatological temple, the dwelling-place of the divine Glory that "all flesh shall see" (cf. Isa. 40:5), and which will be the reality of the world to come. In the New Testament, that temple is first and foremost the body of the risen Lord Jesus, who "tabernacled among us" (John 1:14; cf. 2:19–21). Through his resurrection and

---

11. *Gospel of Thomas* 22, from *The Nag Hammadi Library*, ed. J. M. Robinson, rev. ed. (New York: HarperCollins Publishers, 1990), 129.
12. Discourse X, "On the Fearful Day of the Lord," in *St. Symeon the New Theologian on the Mystical Life: The Ethical Discourses*, vol. 1: *The Church and the Last Things*, trans. A. Golitzin (Crestwood, N.Y.: St. Vladimir's Seminary Press, 1995), 145–46.

the consequent gift of the Spirit, the believers are incorporated into that body, such that the assembly of the faithful becomes itself the temple of the new creation (cf. Eph. 2:14–22; 1 Pet. 2:4–9). By extension, each Christian is also a temple (1 Cor. 6:19–20), so that all of us, as St. Paul puts it, "are being transformed into the same image [of Christ] from glory to glory" (2 Cor. 3:18). It is with that temple of the end-times that the Revelation of John is likewise fundamentally concerned, as I intimated above when touching on the shape and contents of the New Jerusalem in Revelation 21–22. He is also, at least arguably, rooted in the liturgy, and what is not arguable at all but rather incontestable is the witness of subsequent generations of Eastern Christian writers to an assumed linkage between the eschaton, Christian worship, and the transfiguration of the believer who is called to conformity with the "the body of Christ's glory" (cf. Phil. 3:21).[13] This transformation begins now, however hiddenly, and is to be completed on that day when — to recall the second-century Syrian quoted above — the eschatological outside matches the transfigured inside. To cite once more from my fourth-century source:

> Just as when our Lord ascended the mountain [cf. Mark 9:2ff.], he was transfigured into his divine glory, so are there souls which even in the present life are illumined and glorified with him, while on the last day their bodies as well will be glorified and flashing with light.[14]

Note here the "flashing with light," and then recall my contemporary Greek abbot on Christ's presence in the liturgy "with fire and radiance of light." Both sources, separated though they be by sixteen centuries, and together with them the Orthodox

---

13. Golitzin, "The Experience of God in Orthodox Christianity"; and more recently, idem, "Spirituality: Eastern Christian," in W. M. Johnston, ed., *Encyclopedia of Monasticism* (Chicago/London: Fitzroy Dearborn, 2000), 2:1185–92.
14. *Makarios/Symeon: Reden und Briefe*, homily 18.7.3, 1:207.

Church as a whole, see the transfigured saint and the Glory present in the liturgy as belonging to the same "pattern": that which was revealed to Moses on Sinai, fulfilled in the priesthood of Jesus Messiah, made available to us in the church's worship, and realized partially even now in the saints and wholly at the eschaton.

Turning back to that author of forgotten name with whom I began, I think it fair to say that he missed the point. The beauty of Orthodox worship is neither extraneous ornament nor, worse, a wallowing in things pleasing to the senses. It is instead, consciously and emphatically, both theological and eschatological in orientation, a deliberate artifice that seeks, in obedience to the "pattern" of divinely revealed worship, to mirror heaven, the world to come. But what of that author's related complaint, that all this beauty dims any sense of sorrow for sin? There, too, I think him wrong. I would point out, first of all, that all the sources I have quoted are ascetic or monastic writers, people whose entire lives were and are given to the cultivation of repentance. Second, we might recall the words of my turn-of-the-second-millennium Greek abbot, that the "Day of the Lord" abides in "those who, with faith and in fear and trembling, do the commandments and give evidence of a worthy repentance." Obviously, he does not think that sorrow for sin and deeds of loving-kindness are optional, nor surely do his fellows. Here I might add that both Orthodox spirituality and worship have been hugely influenced by the monks. Together with the martyrs and ascetics before them, they have always been considered the models of the Christian life. Quite simply, Orthodox spirituality (to use a word I do not much like) is monastic spirituality. This is in turn, third, reflected in the texts of the services, in particular in the offices that are still celebrated in parish churches, if in more abbreviated form than in the monasteries. Thus, for example, during the Sunday Matins service of Lent, we sing the following hymn while facing the altar behind the closed gates of the icon-screen:

> Giver of life, open to me the gates of repentance; for early in the morning my spirit seeks your holy temple, bearing the temple of my body all defiled. But in your compassion, by your loving-kindness and your mercy, make it clean.[15]

Note here the parallel assumed between the "gates of repentance" and the gates, or "royal doors," of the icon-screen, with perhaps the added echo of Psalm 24:7-10; and then the more explicit assumption of a second set of temples: God's temple on high and the worshiper's own body. There is also the plea for the Lord to make clean what the speaker cannot. Last, and perhaps most significantly, there is an effective equation here between the state of repentance and the divine presence in that the "gates of repentance" open onto the One who dwells in the holy place.

The note of the eschaton is at least implicit in this hymn, just as it is implicit in the Christian notion itself of repentance — thus the first recorded words of the Lord Jesus as he begins his public ministry: "Repent, for the reign of God is at hand" (cf. Mark 1:15). That same note is elsewhere sharply accentuated in Orthodox services, as in the following from the Matins services of Holy Week:

> My Savior, I see your bridal chamber adorned, but I have no wedding garment that I may enter there. Giver of light, make bright the vestment of my soul, and save me.[16]

Here we recall, first, the Matthean parables of the wedding feast (Matt. 22:2-14) and the ten virgins (25:1-13), both of them parables of the kingdom. Second, there is the note of the divine

---

15. *The Lenten Triodion*, trans. Mother Mary and Archimandrite Kallistos Ware (London/Boston: Faber and Faber, 1978), 101.
16. Ibid., 514.

bridegroom, here and in the parables equated with Christ, and in the prophets (e.g., Hos. 2:2ff.) with YHWH God of Israel. Third, the bridal chamber itself, that place where YHWH consummates his marriage with Israel, is at least in the rabbinic tradition associated with the Holy of Holies in the Temple on Zion.[17] I would myself discern an echo of this tradition in my hymn, which is sung once again while looking toward the church sanctuary, which in its turn is frequently — or even normatively — understood as a type of the eschaton.[18] A fourth point concerns the "vestment of the soul" that Christ is asked to "make bright." Here the referent is surely the ancient Jewish and Christian motif of the "robe of light": that with which Adam was clothed, which was lost with the Fall, and which Christ restores. It is also the robe of heavenly priesthood, based on the white linen vestments worn by the High Priest on Yom Kippur (Lev. 16:4, 23), and as early as Ezekiel (cf. Ezek. 9:2, 11; 10:2ff.) also clothing the angels as heavenly priests, whence the motif appears everywhere in the later apocalypses, as in the white vesture of both the Elect and the angelic host in the Revelation (cf. Rev. 7:9, 19:14).[19] The message of the hymn is thus the entry of the believer, as at once bride and priest, into the holy place — the *debir* — of the eschatological presence, an entry effected through repentance and by grace of Christ.

---

17. See R. Patai, *Man and Temple in Ancient Jewish Myth and Ritual*, 2nd enlarged ed. (New York: Ktav, 1967), 88-94.

18. On the Jerusalem Temple in this regard, see M. Barker, *The Gate of Heaven*, 104-77, and, on the Christian side, Maximus Confessor (+682), *The Mystagogy* 2, 15, and 23; in *Patrologia Graeca* XCI: 668C-69D, 693BC (where the sanctuary is expressly identified with "the bridal chamber of Christ"), and 701BC; and in English: G. Berthold, trans., *Maximus Confessor: Selected Works* (New York: Paulist Press, 1985), 188-89, 201, and 204-6.

19. See again Himmelfarb, *Ascent to Heaven*, 9-46; and S. N. Lindemann, "From Figleaves to Fingernails: Some Notes on the Garments of Adam and Eve in the Hebrew Bible and Select Early Postbiblical Jewish Writings," in *A Walk in the Garden: Biblical, Iconographical, and Literary Images of Eden*, ed. P. Morris and D. Sawyer (Sheffield: JSOT, 1992), 74-90; and, with regard to later Christian literature: S. Brock, "Clothing Metaphors as a Means of Theological Expression in Syriac Tradition," in *Typus, Symbol, Allegorie bei den östlichen Vätern und ihren Parallelen im Mittelalter*, ed. M. Schmidt and F. C. Geyer (Regensburg: Pustet, 1982), 11-38.

So I have a bone to pick with the nameless author from my youth, and as well with both the radio preacher who startled me on the high plains and the folklore of the garrulous old monk. To the first I answer, again, that the liturgy I grew up with is an image of the last things and a call to repentance. Its beauty is meant to prick the heart, and it has done that down the generations, just as it has supported and sustained the life of the church in frequently dreadful circumstances. To the other two, the second of whom is after all one of my own, I say that the Christian hope, the end of ends and the beginning of the new creation, is not to be sought by way of interpreting the geopolitics of a perishing world, nor through calculations and other esoterica, but first of all, as our Lord himself makes clear at the end of his eschatological discourse in Mark 13 — where he also expressly forbids calculations (cf. v. 32) — through the sober watchfulness over one's own proper work and calling (vv. 34–37). Second, and here I conclude with the words of my Greek abbot from a thousand years ago, I reply that the Christian hope is right here in front of us:

> The eternal good things "which no eye has seen nor ear heard" [cf. 1 Cor. 2:9]... are not protected by heights, nor enclosed in some secret place, nor hidden in the depths, nor kept at the ends of the earth or sea. They are right in front of you, before your very eyes. So, what are they? Together with the good things stored up in heaven, these are the body and blood of our Lord Jesus Christ which we see every day, and eat and drink. These, we avow, are those good things. Outside of these, you will not find one of the things spoken of, even if you were to travel the whole creation.[20]

---

20. Discourse III, "On the Ineffable Words Which Paul Heard," in *St. Symeon the New Theologian on the Mystical Life*, 1:130–31.

7

The Eschatological Eucharist

CHARLES HEFLING

IT IS NEARLY SIXTY YEARS NOW since Gregory Dix announced disconcertingly that the whole Western church was living in the Middle Ages, so far as its eucharistic worship was concerned. Protestants as well as Catholics — and, either way, Anglicans — were still clinging to the notion that the Eucharist is *historical*. On all sides it was taken for granted that the essence of this sacrament lies in its relation to a single, datable event in the past, namely, the crucifixion of Jesus. The relation itself was a matter of sharp disagreement, but as to whether everything turns on it there was no disagreement at all. Dix held that the Eucharist is not historical but *eschatological*. This was the primitive and patristic understanding. Gradually, however, it had been obscured by a "translation of the meaning of the Eucharist from eschatology to history," which the Reformers, despite their veneration for the early church, did nothing to reverse.[1] Thus Cranmer's final Prayer Book has a eucharistic rite which, in its exclusive emphasis on Christ's passion and death, stands just as squarely within the devotional and theological tradition of the Middle Ages as the Latin Mass it was meant to replace.

---

1. Gregory Dix, *The Shape of the Liturgy* (London: Dacre Press, Adam & Charles Black, 1945), 622.

By and large, Dix's views have been vindicated. Not only have liturgical scholars confirmed and strengthened his thesis about the eschatological character of the early Eucharist, but the new rites that proliferated in all the liturgical churches in the 1960s and 1970s are very evidently modeled on patristic liturgies. If what the Eucharist meant originally is what it should mean now, the recovery of premedieval form and phrasing would seem to have ensured a recovery of meaning that was lost in the "translation from eschatology to history."

What meaning?

By derivation, eschatology is some kind of discourse about *ta eschata*, the last things, what comes at the end of some sequence or series. Not just any sequence, of course. A blizzard is a sequence of events, but knowing which snowflake is the last one to fall makes no difference for the way we think about the whole storm. In a narrative sequence, on the other hand, what comes last does matter. It matters, that is, insofar as it belongs to a series of events which is just *that* series, the series it is, because the events within it involve intentions and decisions, agency and purpose, deliberate action as contrasted with mindless motion. Such a series is narrative, and the last things in it constitute an end in both of the senses which that English word can have. On the one hand, "end" may mean simply the completion or finish, the item in a series after which there is no further item and the series stops. Example: the end of an explosion. On the other hand, *end* may mean a goal or aim or purpose on the part of an agent who affects or influences the sequence. Example: means to an end. These two meanings coincide inasmuch as the end (the last thing) discloses the end (what was meant), and this conjunction is what distinguishes a narrative from a meteorological report. Suppose, for example, that you decide to carry out some course of action. Your decision will not be evident to anyone — perhaps not even to yourself—until you have finished doing what you meant to do. Once you have done it, the completed deed expresses the purpose you have carried out and the end for which you were aiming. An account of your course of action would be a small narrative. The same principle applies to more complex sequences. To understand a journey (as contrasted with a pointless meander), we need to know the final destination. To make sense of a play or a novel (of what used to be the ordinary kind), we need to see the last act or read the last chapter. And so on.

Now eschatology, at least the kind of eschatology that is relevant to the Christian Eucharist, invariably takes a narrative form. What it describes is an "end" in the sense of what comes last—the arrival of "the life of the world to come," perhaps. But what the description is about, what it expresses, is the "end" in the sense of the meaning of the whole to which it belongs. We may leave to one side the individualized eschatology for which the whole in question is the whole of a person's life, and the last things take place at death. Eschatology in scripture, and for the early church, concerns itself with a larger whole: the course of human affairs, the flux of events that make up the great drama in which each and every person takes a part. About that whole, the most basic assertion that eschatology makes is that it is a whole, because it has a point, a purpose, a direction, a meaning. It can be grasped as one, conceived as a single narrative, by grasping how the narrative ends.

The truth of such an assertion is not obvious. It is quite possible to be convinced that what happens in the human world is nothing but one damn thing after another, and that in the end everything amounts to sound and fury, signifying nothing—no plot, no meaning, no narrative; only a blizzard, as it were. Christian eschatology takes the opposite view. However haphazard and senseless the course of things may seem, they do have a direction, because they are moved not by human intentions and purposes alone but by divine intention and purpose. What is and has been going on is meant to go on; and what it is meant to go on *to* is "what no eye has seen, nor ear heard, nor the human heart conceived, what God has prepared for those who love him."[2] True, no such tendency is obvious. Here and now, the end is neither seen nor heard nor conceived. For exactly that reason, it has to be portrayed as an ending, as not yet, as last things, seen and heard as the final act of a drama. The form that eschatological discourse takes is prediction, if you like; but it takes this form in order to say something about the present.

What has any of this to do with the Eucharist? That depends on how the specifically Christian element in Christian eschatology — the association of the last things with the coming of Christ — is understood. That the New Testament makes the association is beyond cavil. Just what the association amounts to has been disputed ever since Weiss and Schweitzer called attention to it at the turn of the last century.[3] Dix takes a position on the whole issue that is worth noting and also, I think, worth developing.

The Shape of the Liturgy is not primarily a theological treatise. Dix himself thought of it as a study in "comparative religion," with the proviso that he was studying the practice of worship in a religion that was also his own.[4] The book is remembered, rightly, for its exposition of the "four-action shape" of what Dix always calls "the eucharist," by which he means that part of the eucharistic liturgy which for most of us today begins with the offertory. He never tires of insisting that the eucharistic liturgy is something

---

2. 1 Cor. 2:9; Paul is paraphrasing Isaiah.
3. Albert Schweitzer's *Quest of the Historical Jesus* (New York: Macmillan, 1910) put the eschatological interpretation of the Gospels squarely within the theological horizon, though Johannes Weiss had proposed it some years earlier. This focus on eschatological interpretation of the Gospels has continued; see N. T. Wright's overview in *Jesus and the Victory of God* (Minneapolis: Fortress, 1996), 3–27.
4. Dix, *Shape of the Liturgy,* xii–xiii.

done more than something said or heard or watched, and that to do it is to perform the same four actions that Jesus is recorded as performing at the Last Supper — taking, blessing, breaking, and giving. To these correspond the offertory, the *anaphora* or great thanksgiving, the fraction or breaking of the bread, and the communion. Together, these actions give the Eucharist (in Dix's sense) its "shape," a sequential, narrative shape, enacted "for the *anamnesis* of me."

What it means for a Christian assembly to enact this four-action shape follows from Dix's understanding of Christian eschatology in general and of Christ's coming in particular. For most Christians, perhaps, if they ever consider, there are two comings, two advents of Christ. One of these, the first advent, belongs to the past. It finished happening long ago. The other, the second advent, belongs to the future. It has not happened at all. Each of the two, then, as they are commonly thought of, is a single event, restricted to one point on a time line. For Dix this way of thinking is vastly misleading if not utterly mistaken. It amounts to saying that both of Christ's advents are wholly historical, wholly "in" time, and so not eschatological at all. We have seen that in eschatological discourse, last things disclose divine intention. For Dix the intention that is the center of Christian eschatology is shown in Christ's "coming in the clouds of heaven" — a symbolic phrase that the earliest Gospel ascribes to Christ himself, both at his trial and, just previously, in his speech to the disciples about the last things (Mark 14:62; 13:26). But we miss the point of the phrase if we construe it as an advent from heaven. The imagery of coming in clouds of heavenly glory has its source in the eschatological visions of the book of Daniel, where "one like a son of man" comes on the clouds to the "Ancient of Days." Christ's second coming in glory was still in the future when he spoke of it, but if it is his coming *to* God, his exaltation, his being "lifted up" in the Johannine phrase, then it is not in the future any longer, and it is not a separate event from his first coming. In other words, there are not two historical advents: one past, one future. Rather, Dix writes:

> There is but *one* "coming." ... And that is the "coming" of "One like unto the Son of Man" (who is "the people of the saints of the Most High," *i.e.*, Christ and the church) *to the Father*. This is the end and meaning of human history, the bringing of man, the creature of time, to the Ancient of Days, in eternity. The same eternal fact can touch the process of history at more than one point, and if there is an apparent difference in the effects of such contacts, that difference is entirely on the side of the temporal process, for eternity knows no "difference," and no "before" or "after."[5]

The "end and meaning of human history" have already been disclosed, within historical time, in the (one) advent of Christ. Instead of two "descents," a first coming and a second, Dix finds it more congruous with the earliest Christian eschatology to think of a single "ascent." Christ's coming embraces the Resurrection and the Ascension, which are not properly historical events at all, since they constitute an entry into nonsequential eternity. This entry, moreover, inasmuch as it includes the "people of the saints of the Most High," is what redemption consists in — not an apocalyptic disruption or cutting-off of the flow of horizontal history, but the entry of human living into the life of God.

From this the eschatological meaning of eucharistic worship follows. It is the meaning expressed in the "shape of the liturgy," in offering, consecration, oblation, and communion, the fourfold

---

5. Dix, *Shape of the Liturgy,* 262–63. The passage continues: "This view of eschatology as manifesting the purpose of history already within time does not deny a 'last judgement,' " and to that further point it will be necessary to return presently.

sequence of actions that shows what it was for Christ, and what it is for the church, to come to the Father or, in other words, to enter the reign, the purpose, the kingdom of God.[6] On this reading, redemption cannot be associated with Christ's passion and death to the exclusion of the rest of what we have come to call the paschal mystery. The passion is one episode, one moment in the redemptive eschatological drama — one that is entirely historical, one that lies entirely on the line of temporal sequence that runs between past and future, one that is finished — but not the only one. Take it as the only one, and you will have no choice but to interpret the Eucharist as the sacrament of redemption in one of two mutually exclusive ways: either it is an act that repeats, in the present, an absent event in the past; or it is an act that reminds you, now, of what happened then. The first is the medieval Catholic option; the second, the equally medieval (in this respect) Zwinglian option which (on Dix's notorious interpretation) was Cranmer's option also. *Tertium non datur*— there is no third alternative, although Calvinists and Lutherans have attempted to find a way out of the dilemma.

Dix avoids this dilemma entirely by going behind both of the historical understandings of the Eucharist, and the soteriologies they rest on, to the more eschatological conception that by the time of the Reformation had been all but forgotten. As a result, he is able to bring off the tour de force of writing a thick book on the Eucharist without mentioning the eucharistic "presence" of Christ even once.[7] Yet there is a sense in which that and nothing else is what the whole book is about — Christ's presence, his parousia, his advent, which is *one* in that he comes once to one God and yet *many* in that he comes with all his saints in all their

---

6. Dix, *Shape of the Liturgy*, 593, 76.
7. More exactly, he mentions it toward the end, in order to point out that he has had no need to mention it; see ibid., 725.

liturgies. For on this view the Eucharist is the eschatological event, the last things that manifest what human life is for by enacting its proper orientation to divine transcendence. The liturgy neither repeats nor recalls the past. It shapes the present.

Because he was concerned primarily with how liturgical practice has developed, rather than with eucharistic theology, Dix never brought his insights together in a unified argument. If they are to be taken seriously and followed through on, certain limitations of *The Shape of the Liturgy* have to be addressed, two in particular. Dix restricts himself unduly to what is after all only a part of the eucharistic liturgy as it is celebrated today, though undoubtedly the climactic part. And his discussion of eschatological meaning has an unduly narrow focus on one symbolic phrase, though that one is undoubtedly central.

1. There is more to the Eucharist than the four-action sequence. Dix was perfectly well aware that from very early times eucharistic liturgy began with a *synaxis* or "meeting" consisting of scripture readings, psalmody, sermon, and corporate prayer. But his inclination is to regard the *synaxis* and the liturgical action that follows it not only as separate liturgies that gradually fused — a historical point that scholars are still debating — but also as theologically independent even after their fusion. Thus the eschatological meaning of the rite belongs entirely to its latter half, irrespective of what we now call the liturgy of the word. I would suggest, on the contrary, that this meaning, which Dix rightly says is the meaning of Christ's advent or coming or parousia, belongs to the whole two-part rite; more especially, it is precisely because it follows the *synaxis* that "the eucharist" (in Dix's sense) is the eschatological event that it is.

2. There is more to Christian eschatology than Daniel's image of one like a son of man coming on the clouds of heaven to the Ancient of Days, though Dix is right to stress its centrality. As

Geoffrey Wainwright has shown in his classic study of eschatological symbolism in Christian liturgy,[8] the images used in early liturgical texts to connect the eucharistic rite with the last things are many and various. Categorizing them is hazardous, but for the most part they cluster in two groups, which in turn stand in a narrative order, as two scenes of one eschatological drama. The first scene is a trial, the second a banquet. The first group of symbols revolves around judgment, the second around celebratory eating and drinking. Because of the obvious affinity between this second group and communion, the fourth of Dix's four actions, the Eucharist has often been described as a foretaste of the eschatological supper of the Lamb, or in Wainwright's phrase as an antepast of heaven.[9] As he puts it, "in so far as the kingdom is conceived (and it is perhaps the dominant conception) as a feast for the citizens,"[10] eucharistic worship anticipates and enacts the eschatological reign of God that is the divine purpose for human living. Still, the kingdom of God, however conceived, is not finally established without the king's separation of the sheep from the goats. The last things begin with judgment; then, for those who have passed through this judgment, comes the banquet. Thus in the creeds, which adopt the imagery of Daniel, the Christ who comes in glory comes to judge.

Dix is not unaware that judgment precedes feasting in Christianity's narrative of last things, any more than he is unaware that a liturgy of the word normally precedes communion in the Christian Eucharist. But he does not build either of these facts into his conception of eucharistic eschatology, and much less does he see any parallel between them. That there is such a parallel, and that

---

8. Geoffrey Wainwright, *Eucharist and Eschatology*, 2nd ed. (London: Epworth Press, 1978; New York: Oxford University Press, 1981).
9. Ibid., chap. 2, 18–59.
10. Ibid., 58.

it is not merely formal — that, on the contrary, the eschatological meaning of the Eucharist turns on it — is the main point of this essay.

In the first place, then, the communion rite depends on the *synaxis* for its meaning. It is not performed for the *anamnesis* of just anyone, and the four-action shape is not intelligible apart from a context that makes this explicit. True, the prayers that make up the second action, the Great Thanksgiving, state by name who it was that took bread, blessed it, broke it, and gave it to his disciples. Still, if the Gospel episode of Peter's "confession" has anything to tell us, it is that knowing when and how to use the right name is one thing, and knowing what the name means is something else. The Gospels themselves were written, arguably, to identify the Jesus of such acclamations as "Jesus is Lord!" — to specify who he is and explain what his lordship involves. Similarly, the *synaxis* identifies the person whose redeeming act is articulated in the "shape of the liturgy." But in the second place, precisely because the opening liturgy of the word functions in relation to the whole rite by identifying Jesus Christ — specifying who is being remembered, before whose Father, in whose Spirit — it is at the same time an event in which those who take part in it are judged. "Doing" the *synaxis* is at once "rendering an agent" — Hans Frei's phrase — and rendering judgment. The agent is Christ the Word, mediated in words, made present in and as proclamation, and judgment consists in being presented with that Word and welcoming it — or not.

In this regard, eucharistic theology has something to learn from a seemingly unlikely teacher: Karl Barth, whose whole vast theological project is the working-out of one theme: the unity of the Word announced in John's prologue with the word of scripture and the word of preaching. Christian proclamation is an event of Christ's presence. To put this in terms of a more liturgical

Christianity than Barth's tends to be,[11] it need only be added that scripture and preaching alike have their proper setting in the church, that the church is most fully and finally itself when it is worshiping its Lord on the Lord's Day, and that the norm of Lord's Day worship in the church is the Eucharist. What defines it as worship of a specific Lord is the proclamation, the liturgy of the word, with which it begins.

By that I do not mean only that the eucharistic *synaxis* always includes a reading from the canonical Gospels, though it does. I mean that the whole liturgy of the word is "gospel," announcement, *kerygma*. Sunday by Sunday it sets forth now one, now another aspect of what Austin Farrer called the narrative icon of Christ. The particular gospel lesson is only one of the elements of narrative that intersect at any given Eucharist. The liturgical "rendering" of Christ's identity draws together several story lines. One of these is the annual sequence of liturgical seasons, which begins with the narrative pattern of expectation and manifestation, pivoting on Christ's nativity, and goes on to the greater pattern of humiliation and exaltation, pivoting on the paschal mystery of Christ's death and resurrection. Psalms and the lessons that precede the liturgical gospel weave into these patterns the narratives of Israel and the church. All this and a great deal more contribute to the weekly (re-)presentation of the identity of Christ — what it is to be human divinely, what it means to come to God.

Insofar as it mediates this meaning, the liturgy of the word is as much an "extension of the Incarnation," of Christ's first coming, as is anything else in the Eucharist, which is why it is a judgment. As Wainwright observes, a strong theme of New Testament eschatology is that the world has "already" been judged

---

11. See "Liturgy and Theology: Conversation with Barth," chap. 4 in Don E. Saliers, *Worship as Theology: Foretaste of Glory Divine* (Nashville: Abingdon, 1994), 69–81.

in its reception of the incarnate Word. At the coming of light, darkness must hide or attack, or else cease to be darkness. Either way, its being dark is made manifest and so condemned. But this verdict is not another event, consequent on Christ's having come. His coming, his parousia, his being present *is* judgment. Those people who encounter Jesus are judged in the very act of their response to the encounter.

It follows, if we agree with Dix that there is finally "but *one* 'coming,'" that the Eucharist, which is that coming manifested in time, demands of those who take part in it a response to the Christ who comes. It may be a response that constitutes condemnation. That would seem to be Paul's point in the difficult passage that speaks of the Eucharist both as the occasion of an offense on the part of the Corinthian church and as the vehicle of judgment on that offense (1 Cor. 11:27-34).[12] More generally, those who are "in" Christ, the baptized, whose privilege it is to worship eucharistically, cannot on that account be at ease in Zion. *Anamnesis* of Christ is, in Johann Baptist Metz's phrase, a dangerous memory, and the Eucharist that is celebrated to convey it has not conveyed it unless the celebration interrupts and redirects the celebrants' lives.[13] For what they celebrate is the coming in glory of a crucified Lord whose death was the divine condemnation of sin, and to accept his coming is to accept that judgment, by repenting.

For just that reason, however, the last word about the Eucharist as last things should be a word of hope. Judgment, Rowan Williams has written, "is not an activity in which Jesus engages: it is an event in which his 'word,' his image, his history, 'acts' in the world to convict and transform." The eschatological Eucharist,

---

12. See Wainwright, *Eucharist and Eschatology*, 81-83.
13. See Bruce T. Morrill, *Anamnesis as Dangerous Memory: Political and Liturgical Theology in Dialogue* (Collegeville, Minn.: Liturgical Press, 2000), 139-87.

I have suggested, is such an event. But the judgment effected by Christ's presence is a just judgment, Williams continues; "it is not an expression of human partiality, because Jesus' work is solely to embody and enact the Father's will...; and that will is for the acceptance of the whole world."[14]

Maranatha. Come, Lord Jesus.

---

14. Rowan Williams, *Resurrection: Interpreting the Easter Gospel* (London: Darton, Longman & Todd, 1982; New York: Pilgrim Press, 1984), 14. See also Wainwright, *Eucharist and Eschatology,* 80–93.

8

The Historic Ought-to-Be and the Spirit of Hope

ROBERT D. HUGHES III

THE PREVIOUS CENTURY'S recovery of eschatology as a focus of contemporary theological interest has been hampered by a failure to appreciate the role of the Holy Spirit in the movement of history toward its divinely appointed end. This lacuna resulted in gaps between history as written and history as lived, word and referent, and eschaton as both transcending history and yet immanent in it as its true end, as precisely historical. One critical result is the inability to distinguish hope from optimism in the face of the century's despair. This essay seeks to begin addressing this lack.

The twentieth-century's recovery of eschatology has depended upon new insights into both concepts and texts, insights deriving from the rise of historical consciousness and the resulting methods of research and writing in the two preceding centuries. In this sense, the recovery of eschatology derives from modern historical consciousness. There is an increasing recognition, however, that as a matter of history, historical consciousness, the "myth of history," is a direct legacy of the Bible and its vision of a present determined by a meaningful past (covenant) and a hopeful and concrete future (the commonwealth, reign, or kingdom of God). One of the most carefully documented and thoughtful demonstrations of this complex interdependence remains that by W. Taylor Stevenson, late professor of theology at Seabury-Western.[1]

In addition to the biblical foundation, Western historical thought has also been influenced greatly, if often unknowingly, by the twelfth-century work of Joachim of Fiore, who explained history in terms of a succession of ages governed by the persons of the Trinity. This kind of theological move continues to have resonances both in modern historical consciousness and in apocalyptic versions of Christianity, including the various dispensationalist theories of cultic American Protestantism.[2]

Thus, the relationship between Jewish/Christian eschatology and modern history, as lived and written (i.e., the meaningful course of human public events and the written interpretation of such) is extraordinarily complex. This complexity is often obscured by the growing secularism in the scholarly community that writes history from a desire to interpret it in terms of nontheological ends. It is also obscured by a tendency among many Christians to collapse the public, historical dimensions of eschatology back into a subjective appropriation of what had become a merely individualistic discussion of eschatology as death, resurrection or eternal life, heaven, and hell.

Certainly, the theologian who has done most to recover a robust and balanced eschatology in recent years is Jürgen Moltmann, beginning with *A Theology of Hope*. In a later work, *The Coming of God,* he considers the problem at issue here with great clarity as he describes the search for "a concept of the

---

1. W. Taylor Stevenson, *History as Myth: The Import for Contemporary Theology* (New York: Seabury, 1969); see also Van A. Harvey, *The Historian and the Believer* (New York: Macmillan, 1966).

2. Perhaps the clearest account is Yves Congar, *I Believe in the Holy Spirit*, trans. David Smith (New York: Crossroad, 1997), 1:133.

future which neither allows the history 'which continues to run its course' to swallow up eschatology, nor permits the eternity that is always present to put an end to every history. The eschaton is neither the future of time nor timeless eternity. It is God's coming and his arrival."[3]

This essay proposes to clarify the meaning of eschatology by giving an account of the relationship of the historic ought-to-be that underlies all history, written or lived, as the ideal which gives it meaning, to the need for a deeper understanding of the eschatological role of the Holy Spirit in the divine economy. A proper understanding of their relationship offers new possibilities for relieving the tension between history and its theological end.

One dimension of this relationship is the role of a historic ideal or ought-to-be in the writing of any history. This concept has been most fully developed by American Jewish philosopher Paul Weiss in *History: Written and Lived*.[4] Weiss follows his usual fruitful method by eschewing an abstract philosophy of history, and instead looks at what historians actually do in the practice of their discipline. This approach allows him to ask what must be true of history as lived if history as written is a discipline making legitimate truth claims. One such factor is the historic ideal, or ought-to-be, which is at once a critical principle allowing the historian to determine what of the past is relevant for the present, and an actual causative factor that allows the accumulated past to be present. It has real ethical content,[5] even though it is neither

---

3. Jürgen Moltmann, *The Coming of God: Christian Eschatology*, trans. Margaret Kohl (Minneapolis: Fortress, 1996), 22; *Theology of Hope: On the Ground and the Implications of a Christian Eschatology*, trans. James W. Leitch (New York and Evanston, Ill.: Harper & Row, 1967).
4. Paul Weiss, *History: Written and Lived* (Carbondale: Southern Illinois University Press, 1962). Weiss sketches the outlines of the historic ideal or ought-to-be and its relation to God in the Introduction, and then a full account in the final two chapters. The nature of this essay does not allow a close analysis, but the following points come from these passages.
5. Ibid., 18.

the absolute Good (which is larger and includes private as well as public life) nor simply the desired outcome of any age.[6]

For history as written to be true, Weiss believes, the past must also exist outside the present, and, he insists, it is God's role to be the one who remembers and preserves the past, making historical truth claims possible. God is also the one who always presents the historical present with the ought-to-be, providing history with a meaningful future grounded on the past, and guaranteeing that history as written (*Geschichte*) will bear some resemblance to the fullness of history as lived (*Historie*).[7] Indeed, without taking account of the historic ideal and God (whom Weiss always interprets in nonreligious, philosophical terms), the historian will not even be able to do the work of history properly, let alone know why what is written could be true.[8]

In this light, I suggest the Christian eschatological vision needs to be cast as a concrete historic ought-to-be in order to avoid mere apocalypticism; in turn, the historic ought-to-be as such is best expressed as a Christian eschatological vision if it is to be truly causal in history and not a mere ideal. That is, Weiss lacks an account of precisely how God presents the historical ought-to-be to history precisely as historical and within history. The Christian tradition can supply this need only if it reassumes the burden of the truly public and historical in its account of the last things. Critical to both points is a recovery of a consciousness of the eschatological mission of the Holy Spirit, the *missio Spiritus,* as the only means of bringing past and future together in a theologically and historically significant present.

The climate for attempting such an account is made difficult by the tension addressed by Moltmann above. Stevenson gives

---

6. Ibid., 16.
7. Ibid., 217–30.
8. Ibid., 230.

an acute analysis of this tension, which he calls the "great disjunction," from which he traces most of the classic bifurcations within modern Western thought now so heavily critiqued by postmodern thought.[9] That is, for Stevenson, the false disjunction between *Historie* and *Geschichte* is reflected in further bifurcations among past/present/future and word/referent/recipient. This is precisely the state of affairs that Weiss predicted when history is written in ignorance of the historic ought-to-be and of God. Stevenson responds to this need with a reading of history as myth centered on the "original relational event" of Jesus Christ.[10] This program goes a long way to giving one specific instantiation of what Weiss demands, and also, in the end at least, is clearly related to Moltmann's program.[11]

This disjunction, however, is only partly resolved by recognizing the grounding of the myth of history in the Christ event, which is Stevenson's strategy. This still leaves a gap between the Resurrection (or the Ascension, if you will) and the parousia (second coming of Christ) as the final herald of the commonwealth. That is, there is no real history of ultimate theological significance between Resurrection and parousia. Nothing of salvific significance happens in that gap except individual conversions, which are, by definition, private rather than public, and to that degree not historical — hence the ahistorical approach of many evangelicals to the present and the postbiblical past, and of nearly all interpretations of the parousia as the termination of history but not as its fulfillment (except in the classic liberal theologies, where the problem is the reverse). Note that in Moltmann's terms, this kind of eschatology is epiphanic rather than covenantal in form.

---

9. Stevenson, *History as Myth*, 80ff., for the false disjunction between *Historie* and *Geschichte* as found in the work of Bultmann; see 107ff., for the implications for hermeneutics.
10. Ibid., 124–46.
11. Ibid., 155.

All the other disjunctions come rushing into this gap. The church as the body of Christ becomes at best a mere metaphor, its mission only a gathering of individual souls from the burning. The sense of the actual historical church, warts and all, as an ongoing instrument of the world's salvation, is lost. The eucharistic *anamnesis* is reduced to a mere memorial or a participation in a future heavenly reality and stripped of its sacramental character of re-presentation, precisely as the epiclesis disappears from the Great Thanksgiving. There is no longer a real Spirit to inspire text and reader alike, or shape a community of faithful interpretation, leaving us with the recurring nightmares of nominalism from which we still suffer in philosophy and theology, as symbol is disjoined from referent and recipient. Ethics degenerates into quietism or a merely individualistic Puritanism as the social and prophetic implications of the gospel are rejected because the ought-to-be is no longer truly historical, or, if historical, no longer truly expressed as gospel.[12]

All of which is to say that these disjunctions result in part from the Western tendency to ignore the *missio Spiritus* in the present and its cosmic and eschatological dimensions in particular. We do this by (1) collapsing all elements of the *missio Spiritus*, everything properly appropriated in the economy to the Spirit (in particular everything in the third paragraph of the creeds) onto Christ, in which case we are left with the problem just identified — the gap between Resurrection and parousia; or (2) we identify Spirit with the human spirit or some such;[13] or (3) we

---

12. Among evangelical traditions the great exception, of course, is Wesleyanism. It is no accident that this movement is also the parent of Pentecostalism and the Anglo-Catholic revival.

13. Geoffrey W. H. Lampe, *God as Spirit* (Oxford: Clarendon Press, 1977). This is the equivalent in pneumatology of the problem Tanner identifies in christology as it becomes shaped by the subjectivist *"pro me* of modernism." Kathryn Tanner, "Jesus Christ," in *The Cambridge Companion to Christian Doctrine*, ed. Colin E. Gunton (Cambridge: Cambridge University Press, 1997), 252ff.

reduce the Spirit's role to mere "sustainer" and "sanctifier of the faithful" and interpret the *missio* only in the individualistic terms of heaven and hell, without reference to the cosmic and social dimensions. We lose our sense of the Spirit as she who guides history toward the consummation of the sacramental consecration of all material reality. That is, we render once again the ought-to-be either ahistorical or noneschatological, losing precisely its function as a real ideal.

Only a full recognition of the Spirit and its *missio* can resolve these problems. We must begin with a full recovery of the appropriate Trinitarian missions, in which we recognize that all the external acts of the blessed Trinity are undivided, in the sense that all such actions involve their mutual cooperation. As Robert Jenson has shown, that does not and should not mean that the contributions of each of the three to one mutual act be indistinguishable.[14] Indeed, much of Jenson's subsequent systematic work is structured by spelling out the Trinitarian rhythm of the works of God *ad extra*.[15] In two recent articles, I have attempted, in a manner different from Jenson's, but I believe compatible with, and certainly inspired by, his work, to show a Trinitarian rhythm in the Holy Spirit's mission; as the Spirit cooperates with the Father/Mother in the *missio dei*, then with the Word/Wisdom in the *missio Christi*, and finally as the first and second persons cooperate with the Spirit in her own proper *missio* of the sacramental consecration and hence fulfillment of the entire material creation, resonances of this triunity of action are aroused in all the Spirit indwells.[16]

---

14. Robert Jenson, *Systematic Theology I: The Triune God* (New York and Oxford: Oxford University Press, 1997), 110–14.
15. Robert Jenson, *Systematic Theology II: The Works of God* (New York and Oxford: Oxford University Press, 1999), *passim*; see, for example, 26ff. for the Trinitarian structure of the act of creation.
16. Robert D. Hughes III, "Starting Over: The Holy Spirit as Subject and Locus of Spiritual Theology," in Robert Boak Slocum, ed., *Engaging the Spirit: Essays on the Life*

A robust pneumatology, with a fully historical and eschatological scope, along the lines I suggest or otherwise, will have at least the following characteristics and consequences:[17]

1. The Spirit brings the Word to life in the process of hearing, reading, and interpretation (Calvin, Barth). It is not the text that brings the presence of a previously absent spirit to a reader, but rather an already present Spirit who presents the reader with the text (the Spirit gives the text as a present, brings it into the present, makes it a vehicle of presence and re-presentation).

2. The Spirit is also the sanctifier of human culture as a means of grace, and the resolver of the ambiguities of history, as the theology of Tillich has so powerfully shown.[18]

3. The Spirit fills the gap between Resurrection/Ascension and parousia by creating those structures of *koinonia* that bind the people of God into the church as body of Christ as a sacramental reality, not just a metaphor, but a sacrament of the commonwealth to come as well as of the Jesus who has inaugurated it. The church and its time and its actions become part of the account of salvation, not merely a vehicle of memorial and proclamation "in the meantime."

4. In short, only the Spirit bridges the gap between *Geschichte* and *Historie;* Word, referent, and hearer/reader; faith and knowledge; the "yield of the past" and "the meaning of the future"

---

and Theology of the Holy Spirit (New York: Church Publishing Incorporated, 2001), 85–102; and Robert D. Hughes III, "A Critical Note on Two Aspects of Self-Transcendence," *Sewanee Theological Review* 46 (2002-3): 112–32.

17. For pneumatology in general, in addition to the essays in *Engaging the Spirit,* see Veli-Matti Kärkkäinen, *Pneumatology* (Grand Rapids, Mich.: Baker Academic, 2002) and Alasdair I. C. Heron, *The Holy Spirit* (Philadelphia: Westminster Press, 1983); among significant recent theologies, the pneumatologies that come closest to what I envision are Congar's *I Believe in the Holy Spirit;* Paul Tillich, *Systematic Theology* (Chicago: University of Chicago Press, 1951–63), vol. 3; and Elizabeth A. Johnson, *She Who Is* (New York: Crossroad, 1992).

18. Tillich, *Systematic Theology,* III; Robert C. Kimball, ed. *Theology of Culture* (New York: Oxford University Press, 1959).

(Bultmann via Stevenson);[19] between the living and the dead, this life and eternal life. This is not to make the Spirit a "God of the Gaps," which may be filled by later scientific inquiry. These gaps are never actually there. They arise when we attempt the human historical or theological enterprise in denial of the Spirit as the "Go-Between God."[20]

5. The Spirit carries out her *missio* by indwelling the present moment, re-presenting the graceful past as precisely the ground by which the historic ought-to-be is presented to the present as both real ideal and real hope. As the Spirit of Covenant and Sabbath Holiness,[21] the Spirit presents this ought-to-be within history *in propria persona,* just as had the incarnate Word in Jesus. This is one of the ways in which the Spirit is *another* advocate, *another* Christ.[22] This is the Spirit as covenant partner executing what we may call the objective, historical dimension of the *missio* as hope.

6. The Spirit provides this hope not only to church and world on the objective side, but also to individuals and communities on the subjective side by the gift of the theological virtues, specifically the virtue of hope. This personal indwelling in the form of the three theological virtues of faith, hope, and love — notably, in this case, as hope (the virtue that resonates with the Spirit's own proper *missio*) — is the personal, subjective, and even epiphanic dimension of the eschatological *missio.*

It is important to note that the theological virtues are at once gifts of the Holy Spirit; but these gifts are not something separate from the personal indwelling of the Spirit as such. The Spirit is properly named in the tradition both "Gift" and "Love."[23] The

---

19. Stevenson, *History as Myth,* 80.
20. John V. Taylor, *The Go-Between God: The Holy Spirit and the Christian Mission* (Philadelphia: Fortress, 1973).
21. Abraham J. Heschel, *The Sabbath* (New York: Farrar, Straus and Young, 1951).
22. Raymond E. Brown, *The Gospel According to John XIII–XXI,* Anchor Bible 29A (Garden City, N.Y.: Doubleday, 1970), appendix on "The Paraclete," 1135-44.
23. Augustine, *De Trinitate,* XV: 28–29.

theological virtue of love is thus the impact on a believer of the personal indwelling of the Spirit, not something separately packaged and delivered. I suggest the same is true of faith and hope. These are not gifts separable from the person of the Holy Spirit, but who that Spirit *is* as gift in the entire divine economy in the rhythm of her Trinitarian mission. As this cosmic mission impacts individual believers through the personal indwelling of the Spirit in the present, the result is growth in these three virtues, the resonance in us of what the Spirit is by nature in her *missio*. The Spirit's giving is always self-donation and never less. This origin of the virtues in the Trinitarian rhythm of the Spirit's *missio,* as an outward expression of the inner substantial relations of the divine triadic life, is the source of both the distinctness and the unity of these virtues.

True hope must thus be grounded not merely in a utopian apocalyptic commitment to the future. It must remain grounded in faith in "the yield of the past," the entirety of past history read under the signs of covenant and cross, and read realistically in the fullness of its ambiguity as illuminated by those symbols.[24] True hope thus requires humility as its mother, in an ongoing practice of repentance in the face of the proclamation of the gospel which is the "yield of the past" as that proclamation ruthlessly exposes the failure of the human community at every moment fully to live up to the ought-to-be with which the Spirit presents it. Hope is thus never optimism.[25]

True hope must also be grounded in the praxis of love in the present, as the Spirit creates the church as beloved community through concrete sacramental structures of *koinonia*, binding faithful, loving, and hopeful individuals into the body of Christ.

---

24. Tillich on the ambiguities of life and history in *Systematic Theology,* III:138–277, 362–426.
25. Moltmann, lecture in Cambridge, Mass., 1967.

The Spirit then empowers that body for its mission of proclamation of the yielded past of the Gospel, calling all persons into membership in the people of God, in loving service to all (the classic dominion of charity in all traditional spiritual theologies, 1 Cor. 13). This love is also unsentimental, realistic, and unromantic. It stands under the signs of covenant and cross as well, ministering to the deep wounds caused by sin in past and present, including the church's own sins.

This manifestation of love terminates in a prophecy of liberating hope which holds before the world and all its people a true historic ought-to-be of justice and peace for all in the divine Commonwealth. This latter allows the believer to see the Spirit at work in the present manifestations of love in juncture with the yielded gospel past and the hopeful future. True eschatological hope is thus fully Trinitarian, grounded solidly and realistically in past and present as well as future, in the fullness of the Trinitarian economy.[26]

7. This is the only solution which holds together the notion that the present moment, the here and now, the *Dasein* of humanity, is of ultimate theological significance, as the Spirit builds the beloved community into the sacrament of the coming commonwealth, while maintaining its grounding in the Christ event (recalling the words and deeds of Jesus), and yet assuring that the end, when it comes — indeed, as it comes — will be an irruption of God's graciousness, and not the mechanistic working out of some optimistic trend inherent in human nature and the world. If we think otherwise, we have failed the test of Constantinople I; we have not confessed that the Spirit is both distinct from the Father and the Son, and is yet fully God. Without the Spirit and

---

26. The debt here to David Tracy's three modes of theology in *The Analogical Imagination* (New York: Crossroad, 1981) is, I trust, obvious. For a closer analysis see my "A Critical Note on Two Aspects of Self-Transcendence."

her *missio* in the present, the eschaton is either pure apocalyptic or mere religious metaphor for a historic ought-to-be, which is really to be explained better in worldly causal terms. Only in the Spirit, and *hence* in Christ, is the eschaton truly the historic ought-to-be; only in these terms can the historic ought-to-be be recognized as both truly historical (the apex of the myth of history and yet also truly active in the present) and justifiable in terms of goodness, truth, and beauty as precisely an "ought" and not merely a *terminus ad quem*.

In short, without the Spirit and her *missio*, we are literally hope-less, either living historically in a present with no true end, or significant past, or living ahistorically, merely anticipating an apocalyptic end which is no true hope for the world as world.

The eschatological prayer must therefore be twofold: not only *"Maranatha, Veni, Domine Jesu,"* but also *"Veni, Creator Spiritus."*

9

Where Lies the Path of Hope in Everyday Life?

THOMAS HUGHSON, S.J.

The American Dream

"WHERE LIES THE PATH OF HOPE?" is a generic human question prompted by myriad kinds of straitening circumstance. A principle here is that the question and whatever answers can be found also are contextual. Asking the question in cultural context becomes "Where lies the path of hope in everyday American life?" Then the query carries the force of a condition in which doubt has arisen about the American dream. Pursuing the American dream is the default option operative unless and until something intervenes, something possibly as gentle as a doubt. Does adherence to unimpeded freedom, upward mobility, home ownership, and a good earthly life gained by hard work leave anything out of our common humanity?[1]

Even under democratic self-governance as the presupposed condition for freedom, and even when freedom is exercised in legitimate, profit-making labors, our experienced humanity remains as a touchstone by which to take the measure of the whole

---

1. These are the four main elements of the American Dream in Jim Cullen, *Restless in the Promised Land: Catholics and the American Dream* (Franklin, Wis.: Sheed & Ward, 2001). Also see Jim Cullen, *The Art of Democracy: The Short History of an Idea* (New York: Oxford University Press, 2003).

reality. Is the American dream, in hope or achievement, adequate to our humanity? What kind of human being does it make us? If chasing the pot of gold at the end of the American rainbow introduces relentless stress into every important relationship, where does the path of hope lie in everyday American life? The question does not ignore or lack respect for the massed witness of millions of immigrants who have immigrated to America to seek that dream, whether recently as in the good-natured film, *My Big Fat Greek Wedding*, or longer ago as in *The Gangs of New York*. Rather it wonders about the American dream becoming a vise-like trap, defended with the legendary ferocity of idol-worshipers, when not sustained by and subordinate to something greater than itself.

The doubt may be nothing new. From July 4, 1845, to September 6, 1847, Henry David Thoreau lived at Walden Pond.[2] His option exemplified downward mobility, a simple earthly life, temporary residence, and concentration of freedom in a contemplative rather than acquisitive mode. He had observed the bustling way of life, prone to unremitting toil, characteristic of pre–Civil War Boston and vicinity. He opined that "[t]he mass of men lead lives of quiet desperation."[3] He wasn't looking at dispossessed Native Americans, at those in slavery (relatively few in Massachusetts but many further south), at new immigrants laboring to survive. His remark was directed at those dutifully devoted to earning a living in what Max Weber later would call the "iron cage of modernity." He paid particular attention to the quality of inward life in those voluntarily given over to such hard work while making no effort to consider the link between what they did and why they existed. Not raising one's eyes from whichever

---

2. Henry David Thoreau, *Walden* and *Civil Disobedience* in Paul Lauter, ed., *Henry David Thoreau: Walden and Civil Disobedience: Complete Texts with Introduction, Historical Contexts, Critical Essays* (Boston: Houghton Mifflin Company, 2000).
3. Ibid., 43.

kind of workbench that gave a livelihood was lacking in wisdom, and living in a manner of quiet — because voluntary — desperation. Walden Pond was an alternative path of hope that changed him. Was it a path of success? Afterward he wrote that he was a "sojourner in civilized life again."[4] Most would have imagined him a sojourner at Walden. Would his observation about busy Americans in 1854 pertain to people today?

Three critically acclaimed films lead one to think so. Each one can be understood to address and answer, in very different ways, the tacit, presupposed question, "Where lies the path of hope in everyday American life?" Academy Award–winning *American Beauty* portrays a hard-working California businessman whose infatuation with the beauty of a daughter's cheerleader friend undermines his economic zeal and alters his suburban family life. A counterconventional experience of beauty moves him into deeper and eventually tragic personal integrity. Hope in the film lies with beauty, art, and an emerging personal integrity, not with relentless selling, a home, financial freedom, and a good suburban life.

Far from Heaven shows socially unacceptable impulses bursting through the cultural constraints of a very 1950s Connecticut couple. Though their marriage turns into a tragedy, the husband and wife seem in some way gaining in personal integrity as they head their separated ways into an unforeseen future. The audience already knows, and the couple's bereft if stereotyped children will find out, it will be the 1960s and 1970s. Hope, cued in the final scene, springs from cathartic confrontations and does not consist in longing for return to a Technicolor but segregated, homophobic American dream of the 1950s.

Adaptation weaves variations on passionate devotion to something beyond oneself — the stuff of success and faith: a rare species

---

4. Ibid., 39.

of orchid, investigative journalism, screenwriting. Madcap capers with real-life consequences give Hollywood screenwriter Charlie Kaufman a basis for learning that love involves risk to the self. In unusual fashion he comes to integrate personal authenticity with artistic creativity. Hope emerges from that conjunction, not from success in the orchid theft, or from over-the-boundary investigation that obsesses on the orchid hunter. Charlie can write creatively again once he lets love replace narcissism. His artistic achievement goes beyond financial success (though rewarded too) and in that respect exceeds the American dream. The three films show that American popular culture contains elements close to religion.[5]

Suppose a second version of the question proceeded from an explicitly Christian frame of reference so that it ran, "Where lies the path of Christian hope in everyday American life?" What would the answer be? First, though, what does the question mean? It does not emerge from the struggle for physical subsistence or political franchise, as it might if raised by liberation theology in regions of India, Africa, or in a Quito slum. Coercion by an illegitimate government's security apparatus does not incite the question, as if asked by Archbishop Desmond Tutu under Afrikaner apartheid regimes before Nelson Mandela's presidency. The question might resonate more with the black struggle against de facto racism in the United States after the end of de jure racism. For others the question comes out of a "normal" pilgrim existence in prolonged negative conditions, whether in relationships, work, society, or even church, for one reason or another. It is primarily

---

5. On connections between religion and popular culture, see for example, Tom Beaudoin, *Virtual Faith: The Irreverent Spiritual Quest of Generation X* (San Francisco: Jossey-Bass, 1998); Marjorie Garber and Rebecca Walkowitz, eds., *One Nation under God? Religion and American Culture* (New York: Routledge, 1999); Eric Michael Mazur and Kate McCarthy, eds., *God Is in the Details: American Religion in Popular Culture* (New York: Routledge, 2001); and William Dean, *The American Spiritual Culture: And the Invention of Jazz, Football, and the Movies* (New York: Continuum, 2002).

a prepolitical question, located in cultural, social, and personal reality. It is the focused, better side of a question like, "What's the use?" or of a periodic assertion that "enough is enough." The mood is more that of *Waiting for Godot* or *Death of a Salesman* than of Martin Luther King Jr.'s "I Have a Dream" speech or James Cone's black liberation theology.

An explicitly Christian version of seeking the path of hope in everyday life means looking for a way to regain confidence in a good already chosen as something valuable, of God, and never renounced. It is wanting to persevere in a worthwhile cause in a way that resembles a new beginning more than soldiering without knowing how or why. Doubt about a goal's feasibility, not about its value, differs from a crisis in faith. Faith's conviction that God has revealed deeds, words, symbols, and truths in Christ, that they call for placing daily hope in his Lordship amid adversity, remains firm. What falls into obscurity is exactly what that placing of hope means in the specific cultural context and historical situation of postmodern America. When individual and ecclesial pilgrims get lost, they wonder if the map is mistaken or if landforms have shifted, if old markers have been effaced. Pilgrim's progress takes a moment to wonder.

Hope has to do with sustaining movement toward something good, God above all, in difficult circumstances. Seeking a path of hope is looking for ways to renew or revise an original decision. Kids ask, "What's the use?" of their resolve to do homework when results don't materialize. One spouse might wonder something similar about fidelity to a promised love when long-term depression afflicts the other. An executive committed to ethical integrity could doubt its importance if economic success consistently flows to those whose decisions ruthlessly exclude all values except individual self-interest. The ecumenical movement, inspired by the Holy Spirit, strong in purpose, yet trying to bear with advances that languish, can lead its supporters to wonder about realistic prospects for deeper Christian unity. Asking, "Where lies the path of hope?" occurs when, over time, negligible results seem to negate the wisdom of sustaining an original decision on behalf of authentic personal, familial, social, cultural, or ecclesial goods.

The question also points to an irremovably contextual aspect of Christian hope. Hope, along with the entirety of redemption, occurs in specific people in particular cultures. The New Testament contains a dramatic, otherworldly answer that arose in one context, the polytheistic Roman Empire.[6] The answer was not hope for an earthly pie in a heavenly sky but for divine rending of the skies and of all human horizons closed to God, yet armed with power and prestige enough to oppress tendencies toward the good. The apocalyptic panorama and heavenward expectation in the book of Revelation cannot be regarded as obsolete or inefficacious. This most otherworldly vein of Christianity, contrary to Marx's theologically illiterate dismissal of religious faith, has been anything but an opiate that anesthetized a sense of responsibility for historical change. To the contrary, the apocalyptic mode of New Testament hope set in motion energetic historical tasks that helped produce modernity, and not just capitalism.

So much so that Jürgen Moltmann has argued that in modernity, "The interpretative framework which mobilized Europe's seizures of power over the world and gave them their orientation was millenarist expectation...."[7] That goes far beyond

---

6. Pauline studies are revising the view that Romans 13:1ff. by itself represents Paul's attitude toward the Roman Empire. See Richard Horsley, ed., *Paul and Empire: Religion and Power in Roman Imperial Society* (Harrisburg, Pa.: Trinity International Press, 1997), and Walter Pilgrim, *Uneasy Neighbors: Church and State in the New Testament* (Minneapolis: Fortress, 1999).

7. He goes on to spell this out as: "the expectation that when Christ comes, the saints will reign with him for a thousand years, and will judge the nations, and that this empire

Max Weber's familiar argument that a specific sort of Calvinism shaped the development of modern, especially American, capitalism. It adds to the well-known fact that English colonists settled the Atlantic coast of North America under the impulse of a biblical vision formed by the book of Exodus. Moreover, and also effective in modernity, the book of Revelation presents the beginning of a way to overcome oppressive social, political, and economic forces by conceiving of them in the figure of a powerful yet, in principle, defeated Antichrist. This is probably the clearest New Testament concept of social sin requiring resistance by Christians.[8] Together with the story of the Exodus, it displays the often-ignored emancipatory potential of the Bible.

Because the record of modernity has been so ambiguous, there is also need for Christian critique of excessive, one-sided influence from the apocalyptic strain. Neither a millenarian nor a broader apocalyptic orientation represents a complete picture of Christian hope. Still a millenarian vision certainly reenergized American Protestantism in the Second Great Awakening, and this revival movement affected all Christian traditions in the United States. Because of this it has been an influence in American culture beyond its explicit adherents. Even so, I doubt that upon reflection it presents a path of hope in everyday life to those not already in a millenarian tradition.

---

of Christ's will be the last, golden age of humanity before the end of the world," in Jürgen Moltmann, *God for a Secular Society: The Public Relevance of Theology*, trans. Margaret Kohl (London: SCM Press, 1999), 9. Michael A. Scanlon, O.S.A., takes a similar position, pointing out the influence of Joachim of Fiore, in "Hope," an entry in Joseph A. Komonchak, Mary Collins, and Dermot A. Lane, eds., *The New Catholic Dictionary of Theology*, 3rd ed. (Wilmington, Del.: Michael Glazier, 1989), 492–98.

8. Edward Schillebeeckx explains the figure of the Antichrist in the book of Revelation as personified evil that tyrannizes over society, economy, and state. As oppressive social sin it is something Christians are obliged to resist. Though the book of Revelation does not advocate the use of force, it allows no room for complicity either. See his *Christ: The Experience of Jesus as Lord*, trans. John Bowden (New York: Seabury, 1980).

Personal Prayer: Path of Hope, Yet...

Besides millenarianism, Christian tradition harbors another kind of spiritual reflex that also seeks the path of Christian hope in everyday life in an alternative to any cultural status quo. This too involves profound renunciation of everyday life, because participation in almost any economy, culture, political system, and society is deemed a compromise with worldly ways. This second Christ-against-culture impulse turns away from life in time and history but establishes itself by preoccupation with future, eternal glory on the other side of death, not at the end of history. Yet it was St. Augustine who transposed an inner-historical conflict into sharp contrast between life in time and eternal life to come.[9] Hope concentrates on eternal life while turning away from the concrete particulars of the church's temporal, corrupt, cultural context. Augustine's path of hope was, "...the rational creature's long quest in time for...[the] true and stable 'homeland,' for the blessedness of finding...[the] true identity in 'adhering to God' and loving all other creatures in God."[10] The "Our Father" in Matthew and Luke, Augustine proposed at one point, invited believers onto this path of hope.

At one point Augustine explained Jesus' teaching on hope as concentrated into the petitions in the "Our Father," seven in Matthew's version, five in Luke's.[11] Moreover, praying the "Our Father" with belief brought a Christian like Laurentius, to whom

---

9. Scanlon points to limits in St. Augustine's valid but incomplete perspective on hope. In order to distinguish Christian hope from the earthly fate of the (collapsing) Christian Roman Empire, "...Augustine both individualized and dehistoricized its meaning.... Christian hope is the grace engendered expectation of life eternal in 'the age to come.' As long as the fundamentally hopeless reality of 'this age' lasts the Christian is a restless pilgrim." "Hope," 497.
10. Brian E. Daley, S.J., *The Hope of the Early Church: A Handbook of Patristic Eschatology* (New York: Cambridge, 1991), 149.
11. St. Augustine, *Enchiridion on Faith, Hope, and Love*, trans. J. B. Shaw, introduced by Thomas S. Hibbs, with analysis and historical afterword by Adolph von Harnack (Washington, D.C.: Regnery, 1961, 1996), CXIV–CXVI, 132–34. For a brief discussion,

Augustine addressed the *Enchiridion,* into hope that flowed from faith in the articles of the creed.[12] The first three petitions in the Lord's Prayer, "Hallowed be Thy name," "Thy kingdom come," "on earth as it is in heaven," expressed hope for eternal life in God's kingdom after death. The life of grace, of course, began in the present life. The next four, "give us this day our daily bread," "forgive us our trespasses," "lead us not into temptation," and "but deliver us from evil" all concerned "wants of this present life."[13] The latter four might be interpreted helpfully to Christian life as means to the eternal end sought by the first three.[14] Nonetheless, Augustine's text did not make that kind of link. Instead he contrasted a future of eternal peace hoped for in the first three petitions with present evils outlined in the last four.

This path of hope consists in appropriating the letter and spirit of the "Our Father." It involves daily expectation of God's help in fulfilling the difficult demands of life in the Spirit, a way of life that struggles to follow Christ's teachings, which avails itself of means to salvation accessible through the church in order to die a "happy death" and enter heaven. "Hope is personal hope for heaven after death."[15] This perspective has been prominent in much of Christian tradition. Accordingly, hope "is the theological virtue by which we desire the kingdom of heaven and eternal life as our happiness, placing our trust in Christ's promises and relying not on our own strength but on the help of the grace

---

see S. M. Ramirez, "Hope" in the *New Catholic Encyclopedia,* vol. 7, prepared by an editorial staff at the Catholic University of America (Washington, D.C.: Catholic University of America, 1967), 133.

12. Private or personal praying of the "Our Father" is indicated by the fact that Augustine in *Enchiridion* III, 3 declared that, "God is to be worshiped with faith, hope, and love," and did not situate either the creed expounded in chaps. I–CXIII, or his exposition of the "Our Father" in CXIV–CXVI in a liturgical act of public worship.

13. *Enchiridion,* CXV, 133.

14. Ramirez, "Hope," 133.

15. Ibid., 495.

of the Holy Spirit."[16] It opens us to a new future in which we "expect with confidence to attain eternal life," and whatever contributes to our arriving at that end.[17] It steadies, thought Thomas Aquinas, our reliance on God's promises precisely in those difficulties, trials, and tribulations that could lead to reliance on human resources alone or to fatalism.

Twentieth-century reception of hope as a theological virtue reconnected it to the outcome of history as a whole, not only one's own. Hope, in view of the New Testament's broader eschatology, has come to be understood as enabling those plunged into Christ's death and resurrection by baptism to "live with confidence in newness and fullness of life, and to await the coming of Christ in glory, and the completion of God's purpose for the world."[18] This hopeful vision allows the "Our Father" to project both individual and communal dimensions of God's kingdom. This hope expands its scope to take in not only the church but also all those who enter the kingdom in ways known only to God. The path of hope steers graced human agency beyond waiting for completion of God's purposes to patient, constructive action toward "a more just and peaceful world" that in every era asymptotically approaches but never absolutely becomes the kingdom of God.[19]

In addition, exclusive concentration upon human redemption can expand to include the cosmos. New Testament references to God's kingdom in passages such as Romans 8:18–25 (creation groans and labors for its fulfillment) and Revelation 21–22 (new creation and New Jerusalem) point in that direction. Hope then looks to God's promises and action not only for individual and

---

16. *Catechism of the Catholic Church* (Liguori, Mo.: Liguori Publications, 1994), n. 1817, at 447.
17. Ramirez, "Hope," 133.
18. The *Prayer Book Catechism*, 861, quoted in "Eschatology," in Don S. Armentrout and Robert Boak Slocum, eds., *An Episcopal Dictionary of the Church: A User-Friendly Reference for Episcopalians* (New York: Church Publishing Incorporated, 1999), 188.
19. Scanlon, "Hope," 497–98.

communal human salvation but also to redemption of the physical universe into which human beings are inextricably, it seems, woven. Thus, a path charted by analysis of hope as a theological virtue, whether in an Augustinian or modern framework, consists in carrying out everyday matters in the spirit of an "Our Father" prayed on behalf of all humanity, all creation. This can inspire a path of virtue, and a spirituality.

And yet by itself it fails to encompass Christianity's hope. It would sidestep communal, liturgical expressions of hope. The Christian East, the Anglican/Episcopal tradition, black churches, Roman Catholicism, and many Protestant churches all affirm that public worship is central to Christian existence. A path of hope that did not link the theological virtue of hope with liturgy would be a detour around an essential mediation of the *memoria Jesu*.[20] It would omit regular contact with the ground of Christian hope and would give a misleading impression of Christianity as a multitude of private ties with God.

Liturgy: Path of Hope, and Yet...

The annual liturgical cycle of Christian feasts and Sunday worship lays out a path of hope that again and again lifts the negations of everyday life into the *magna et mirabilia* (great and marvelous deeds of God).[21] Over the period of a year, going to church on

---

20. The entry on "Liturgy" in *An Episcopal Dictionary of the Church* states that, "The church's public worship of God is the work of the Christian people. The life of Christ active in the church by the Spirit is expressed through liturgy," 307. Appreciating the role of liturgy characterizes Stephen L. Carter's argument for the civic importance of religion understood in terms of a worshiping community, *The Culture of Disbelief: How American Law and Politics Trivialize Religious Devotion* (New York: Basic Books, 1993).

21. See the entry *"Magna et mirabilia"* in *An Episcopal Dictionary of the Church*, 316. *Magna et mirabilia* is phrasing from Canticle 19 in the Book of Common Prayer, based on Rev. 15:3–4, itself alluding to the Song of Moses after crossing the Red Sea, in Exod. 15:1–18.

Sunday brings congregants to the breadth of scripture, from Genesis to Revelation, while linking them sacramentally to the divine initiatives culminating in Christ's death and resurrection. Every year the liturgical season of Advent moves the church along a path of hope, taking participants through prophecies into the birth of Christ. Each Lent opens a journey of hope from Ash Wednesday repentance through Good Friday into the victory of Christ over sin and death that Easter Vigil and Easter Sunday celebrate. Sunday worship commemorates the day and reality of Jesus' resurrection. Fifty days after Easter the feast of Pentecost recalls and renews the descent of the Holy Spirit that completed Jesus' saving event.[22]

These liturgical celebrations continually renew Christian hope by keeping people in the presence of the divine realities that are the ground of their hope and that begin to make God's kingdom present on earth. Indeed, the "eucharist involves the believer in the central event of the world's history."[23] That God has been faithful over and again renews hope over and again that God will fulfill the marvelous promises revealed in Christ and recorded in the New Testament. A path of hope, then, heads to and from the church building. Indeed, personal appropriation of that path by consulting the designated scripture texts ahead of time, then afterward wondering how to let Word and Sacrament make a difference in everyday life, is a valuable spiritual practice. Reflection afterward can mean realizing that, for example, the "eucharistic celebration demands reconciliation and sharing among all those regarded as brothers and sisters in the one family of God and is

---

22. Besides its internal structures evolved from New Testament practice, Episcopal liturgy "is also shaped by the seasons, feasts and fasts of the calendar of the church year and the lectionaries for the Holy Eucharist and the Daily Office..." ("Liturgy" in *An Episcopal Dictionary of the Church*, 307).

23. *Baptism, Eucharist, and Ministry*, Faith and Order Paper No. 11 (Geneva: World Council of Churches, 1982), section 20, 14.

a constant challenge in the search for appropriate relationships in social, economic, and political life (Matt. 5:23f; 1 Cor. 10:16; 1 Cor. 11:20–22; Gal. 3:28)."[24] Moving from liturgy to the rest of life and back again is an ongoing journey of hope.[25]

Yet on any given Sunday the liturgy, like art, is brief, while everyday life is, usually, twenty-two or twenty-three hours longer. More to the point, to presume that everyday life is a malleable set of circumstances that Christian worshipers simply and directly shape according to liturgically renewed hope is to misconceive social existence in an individualist direction that ignores the ubiquitous presence of historically affected social structures, which is not to say that Christian worship makes no difference in how people conduct their lives in a hopeful direction. To the contrary, there is much social-scientific evidence that individual churchgoing produces positive kinds of conduct because "values matter."[26] Congregations and individuals do have potential to affect their environment in a hopeful direction.[27] This is the import of "the liturgy after the liturgy," an ecumenical description for prolonging attitudes like reverence into ethical decisions.

And yet the problem is that liturgies can just as easily acclimatize people to a dubious or objectionable status quo. Without doubt, in principle it is true that, "[a]ll kinds of injustice, racism,

---

24. Ibid.
25. The Vatican I *Constitution on the Sacred Liturgy* teaches that, "... liturgy is the summit toward which the activity of the Church is directed; it is also the font from which all her power flows," in Austin Flannery, O.P., general ed., *Vatican Council II: The Conciliar and Postconciliar Documents* (Northport, N.Y.: Costello Publishing Co., 1988), section 10, 6. Presumably, the centrality of liturgy is a principle that structures the lives of those who participate in liturgy, not only the activities of the church as a whole.
26. Isabel Sawhill, "Framing the Debate: Faith-Based Approaches to Preventing Teen Pregnancy," in E. J. Dionne Jr. and Ming Hsu Chen, eds., *Sacred Places, Civic Purposes* (Washington, D.C.: Brookings Institution Press, 2001), 21. See also Patrick F. Fagan, "Conservative Triumph: Successes of Worship and Family in Preventing Teen Pregnancy," and Eugene F. Rivers III, "Effectiveness over Ideology: Church-Based Partnerships in Crime Prevention," in *Sacred Places, Civic Purposes*, 39–49 and 94–95, respectively.
27. See, for example, Avis C. Vidal, "Many Are Called, but Few Are Chosen: Faith-Based Organizations and Community Development," in Dionne and Chen, *Sacred Places, Civic Purposes*, 127–39.

separation and lack of freedom are radically challenged when we share in the body and blood of Christ" in the Eucharist.[28] And yet in fact it is equally the case that this eucharistic challenge is not immediately clear to pastors and congregations. The reason is that the internal structures and content making up public worship — the set prayers, the scripture readings, the eucharistic canon, communion — do not define or determine any specific relationship between worship and its cultural context. Liturgical representation of the *magna et mirabilia* sets forth a broad framework for interpreting social reality, but this broad perspective lapses into a lofty, ineffective ideal unless study, thought, reflection, research, and preaching mediate its application to a specific context.

And that is part of the fact that everyday life in America is not simple, transparent, or malleable. Thinking so can misguide hope. For example, George Kelling describes how some congregations hoped to help the homeless but ended up impeding a more basic remedy.[29] In 1989 New York's subway system was a disaster. Ridership declined steadily despite massive amounts of money infused into rebuilding the infrastructure. The problem was squalid conditions, disorderly behavior, and fear of crime. Almost everyone attributed this to the presence of the homeless, thinking that "emergency care, jobs, apartments, and welfare"[30] would solve the problem of homelessness. So a number of suburban congregations with great goodwill and hope decided to provide food and clothing in subway stations on weekends.

But Kelling's analysis saw the problem stemming not from the presence of the homeless but from proliferating unlawful behavior, such as turnstile-jumping, "graffiti, predatory panhandling,

---

28. *Baptism, Eucharist, and Ministry*, section 19, 14.
29. George Kelling, "Defining the Terms of Collaboration: Faith-Based Organizations and Government in Crime Prevention," in Dionne and Chen, *Sacred Places, Civic Purposes*, 61–76.
30. Ibid., 64.

youths loitering around the toll booths obviously casing them *and* the passengers, public urination and defecation, open sexual activity and fare scams...."[31] The fact that the police were *"doing absolutely nothing*... said 'Enter the subway at your own risk.' "[32] He uncoupled subway disorder from the homeless, and tied it to criminal behavior that could be policed. This restored the subways, which had not been a safe haven for the homeless in the first place.

The churches had not grasped the extent to which a variety of public policies guaranteed a population of street people, and that feeding and clothing them in subway stations exacerbated rather than ameliorated the problem. The congregations hoped to feed the hungry and clothe the naked, but their path of hope to and from worship seems to have been too simply understood. They seem to have gone from liturgy to everyday life and back too hastily, too simply, as if everyday life were an obvious clay amenable to direct reshaping. The effect was to defer essential questions about who the homeless were, about public policy putting deinstitutionalized mentally ill people on the street, and about how to make subways safe. They did what they could, they took action, they refused indifference toward the distressed. But they did not get this particular problem right.[33]

The issue is not, did Christian worship affect the lives of these generous, concerned congregants in a positive, hopeful way, or not? It clearly did.[34] The issue is whether worship also sufficed

---

31. Ibid., 65.
32. Ibid.
33. Kelling remarks that *"[f]or a faith institution, with its special mandate and role in society — often that of moral arbiter — getting the problem right ought to be the sine qua non of any effort to decide how to position itself on any problem"* (emphasis in the original text), ibid., 73.
34. See, for instance, direct, positive correlation between frequency of church attendance and frequency of volunteer work in the civil community reported in the Princeton Center for Research in Religion publication, *Emerging Trends* 21, no. 9 (1999): 4, as

to provide insight into and knowledge about what acting hopefully in a particular area of everyday life meant. It didn't. And so moving to and from liturgy cannot be by itself the path of Christian hope in everyday life. This can be stated in terms of Christians sharing in the priestly, prophetic, and kingly elements in Christ's mission. The path of hope is not a share in the priestly activity of worship alone. That is, to grant a liturgical monopoly on expressing hope would be resignation to the secularization of everyday life. It would be to accept without further ado the predefined scope of "religion" as that outside of which and in contrast to which the rest of (secularized) life occurs. "Religion" in that case is where people go when they enter church for worship. The very religion/secular contrast throws liturgy into relief as if it alone were the sum and substance of the real Christian difference. But this would overlook the inseparable prophetic and kingly dimensions of everyday, baptized life.[35]

The difficulty is that a reverent liturgy by itself does not contain the gift of being able to define its own relation to a cultural context. Rather, the insight — or blindness — of laity, bishops, pastors, preachers, congregations, or other church associations decides how the Eucharist relates to its context.[36] How to live congregationally or individually in accord with the spirit of the liturgy is not self-evident. For example, sociologists James D. Davidson and Ralph E. Pyle found two typical responses in how congregations responded to the economic boom of 1965 to 1995,

---

well as the correlation between church attendance and voter participation noted by Kenneth D. Wald in *Religion and Politics in the United States*, 3rd ed. (Washington, D.C.: Congressional Quarterly Press, 1997), 317.

35. See Vatican II, *The Dogmatic Constitution on the Church*, section 10, and John Paul II, *The Vocation and Mission of the Lay Faithful in the Church and in the World* (Washington, D.C.: United States Catholic Conference, fourth printing, 1997), sec. 14.

36. See chap. 14 in Bernard J. F. Lonergan's *Method in Theology* (New York: Crossroad, 1972) for attention to context as essential to theological method.

which widened the gap between rich and poor in the United States.[37] A "good fortune theology" sponsored hymns and homilies in worship services that celebrated God's material blessings to congregants and others on whom the Creator had seen fit to bestow a sign of favor. Hymns and homilies from a "social justice theology" issued prophetic summonses to more equality among all in those blessings under the demands of divine judgment and the biblical warnings against the dangers of wealth. While most congregations, Catholic and Protestant, black and white, fell somewhere in the middle of a spectrum between those alternatives, more lay toward good fortune theology. Doctrinal traditions and liturgical worship by themselves did not converge upon a generic Christian relation to the American context, 1965–95, despite the fact that all commemorated the self-sacrificial event of Christ's Last Supper.

The factual condition is that everyday life takes place in a world of meanings, institutions, knowledge, language, customs, and structures of interaction, many of whose main features have been molded by a centuries-long process of secularization. While not intractable, they are not able to be instantly reset either. The Renaissance and Reformation set in motion a wholesale reshaping of Western culture that gradually differentiated the major areas of human activity from one another and from the church. Removing them from ecclesiastical identity and supervision typically was seen as emancipation. As a result, the nation-state, philosophy, the economy, the sciences, technology, entertainment, education, recreation, the arts, all types of scholarship have, each of them, a distinct, autonomous set of guiding principles that no

---

37. James D. Davidson and Ralph E. Pyle, "Public Religion and Economic Inequality," in William H. Swatos Jr. and James K. Wellman Jr., eds., *The Power of Religious Publics: Staking Claims in American Society* (Westport, Conn.: Praeger, 1999), 101–14.

longer operates with explicit reference to an overarching religious frame of reference or to a central public presence of faith.[38]

According to the logic of differentiated spheres, liturgy and Christian hope belong inside the sphere of "religion."[39] Everyday life in the modern world predefines Christianity, the gospel, liturgy, and Christian hope as content in the specialized sphere of "religion" that occupies a role alongside other spheres of specialized meaning and activity.[40] Sharp differentiation of religion as sacred from all the secular spheres has been the signature of modernity. It has been positive in many respects. Unequivocal separation of state or civil authorities and institutions from those of the church, for example, has benefited protection of the human right to religious liberty, for the most part.[41] But another effect is that everyday life in any compartment or sphere tends to follow its own, unswerving, secular logic that is largely unaffected by anything like an orientation toward or influence from weekly worship or the liturgical year.

---

38. On secularization see Jose Casanova, *Public Religions in the Modern World* (Chicago: University of Chicago Press, 1994).

39. Some have begun to examine the limits in so sharp and total a division of religious from secular reality and to deconstruct the reciprocal, interlocked categories of "religion" and "secular" to learn who benefits from their opposition. See Talal Asad, *Genealogies of Religion: Discipline and Reasons of Power in Christianity and Islam* (Baltimore: John Hopkins University Press, 1993), and others (Jonathan Z. Smith, David Chidester, Walter Capps, Ninian Smart, Edward Said, Timothy Fitzgerald, Steven Wasserstrom, et al.) discussed by Kathleen M. Sands in "Tracking Religion: Religion through the Lens of Critical and Cultural Studies," in *Bulletin of the Council of Societies for the Study of Religion* 31, no. 3 (September 2002): 68–74.

40. It is not surprising, then, that some Christians, shaped by secularization, feel that their fellow believers trespass onto foreign soil when they focus on "secular" matters outside the sphere of "religion" by raising moral and religious questions about economic, military, and political matters, for example.

41. But not always and not in every case. An example of less protection of religious liberty because of sacred/secular, church/state differentiation is the failure of U.S. law adequately to protect the rights of Native Americans who do not make a sharp division between sacred and secular. Sacred/secular division renders some sacred realities, such as Native Americans' relationship with the land, invisible to U.S. law and vulnerable to intrusion. See Kathleen M. Sands, "Sacred Land, Communal Sovereignty: The Limitations of 'Religion' as a Constitutional Construct," a paper presented November 24 at the 2002 meeting of the American Academy of Religion in a joint session of the Church-State Studies Group and the Native Traditions in the Americas Group.

Of course, modernity's differentiation of spheres and its division of sacred from secular have troubling limits too.[42] But they do not demand from Christian hope a response of concentration solely on liturgy. It is no derogation from the centrality of liturgy to press forward with the question about hope in everyday life. Where lies the path of hope before and after liturgy, or in what has been referred to in the ecumenical movement as the "liturgy after liturgy"? Before and after liturgy, people are already inserted into and to some extent defined by networks of meaning and myriad institutions not based on (in any clear way) or derived from (in any direct, obvious way) the sources of Christian hope celebrated in liturgy. This means that the path of hope in everyday life does not consist exclusively in getting an ever firmer grasp on the habit of going to church, and so of setting aside the mentality, tools of trade, cultural associations, and perhaps scientific inquiry in everyday life in order to take up the censer, hymnal, and prayer book. Such a path merely ratifies modernity's predefined divide between sacred and secular.

Incarnational Humanism as Path of Hope: Authenticity (and Creativity) in All Things

The liturgy, however, carries an orientation beyond itself and into everyday life. No doubt that, like the Augustinian reading of the "Our Father," the Eucharist too brings congregants into Christ's heavenward self-offering to the Father. This grounds and

---

42. For example, liberation theology has criticized Vatican II for an overly optimistic reading of modernity that ignored an underside of racism, conquest, exploitation of resources, and underdeveloped nations. Nineteenth- and twentieth-century popes, of course, had earlier indicted modernity on a score of charges. An ecological critique accuses modernity in theory and practice of reducing physical nature to an object of scientific knowledge and an instrument of human purposes. Another critique of modernity, from the perspective of "radical orthodoxy," rejects the secularization of knowledge, as in John Milbank's invaluable but overdrawn critique of modernity and the secularization of knowledge in *Theology and Social Theory: Beyond Secular Reason* (Oxford: Blackwell Press, 1994).

legitimates renunciation as a direction or path for hope. When an organizing principle, restless dissatisfaction with anything less than the divine, the *contemptus mundi* theme in various traditions of Christian spirituality, can become an "eschatological humanism."[43] The early desert monks, and what H. Richard Niebuhr called the "Christ against culture"[44] tendency in any tradition, have tended to adhere to hope in that manner. Nonetheless, Acts 1 on Ascension Day portrays an angel challenging the apostles staring after the ascended Jesus: "Men of Galilee, why do you stand looking into heaven?" Moreover, the structure of the Eucharist itself contains an expression of earthward hope before and after liturgical remembrance of Jesus' surrender to the Father's will at the Last Supper, Gethsemane, and Calvary.

The Gloria ("Gloria in excelsis"[45]) in eucharistic worship draws believers into affirmation of the kenotic, earthward movement of the Word made flesh. This was and is the original act of self-emptying, of kenosis. Jesus' passion and death humanly appropriates the preexistent Word's being sent by the Father into temporal creation and human existence in its uttermost extent. As the Letter to the Philippians hymns, "... Christ Jesus, who though he was in the form of God, did not count equality with God a thing to be grasped but emptied himself, taking the form of a servant...."[46] Nor did Jesus' life, death, and resurrection

---

43. John Courtney Murray contrasted eschatological with incarnational humanism in post–World War II American Catholic thought. Eschatological humanism saw the permanence of sin, the transcendence of God, the discontinuity of any human effort with the coming of God's kingdom. It moved from prophetic perception of incompatibilities between American reality and God's kingdom to renouncing the value of American political life and culture generally. Murray, in "Is It Basket Weaving? The Question of Christianity and Human Values," in *We Hold These Truths: Catholic Reflections on the American Proposition* (New York: Sheed and Ward, 1960), 175–96.

44. H. Richard Niebuhr, *Christ and Culture* (New York: HarperCollins Publishers, 1956, 1957).

45. See the entry, "Gloria in excelsis," in *An Episcopal Dictionary of the Church*, 218–19.

46. Phil. 2:5–7, in Herbert G. May and Bruce Metzger, eds., *The New Oxford Annotated Bible with Apocrypha* (New York: Oxford University Press, 1977), 1424. That

culminate in the heavenward Ascension. Rather the earthward mission of the Holy Spirit completed his work. Christ did not retire from his redemptive mission after the Ascension. He is Emmanuel present "where two or three are gathered in my name" as well as the Logos through whom all creation continues to come into being.

After the eucharistic prayer or Canon, believers partake of Christ who makes himself accessible, coming to them in the forms of bread and wine. His redemptive power and presence continue to act in the ministry of Word and Sacrament. Historically, redemptive purpose did not cease at the Ascension and Pentecost but was communicated to apostles, disciples, and the whole church. Public worship of God in the Eucharist contains and communicates both participation in Christ's self-surrender to the Father and in that redemptive mission.

A problem may attend liturgical renewal in this regard. Has the renewal, frequency, and centrality of eucharistic liturgy deflected theological attention away from the abiding efficacy and importance of momentous, once-and-for-all insertion into Christ's redemption and mission imparted by the liturgy of baptism (and confirmation)? Baptism and confirmation orient and empower an outward direction to mission, not only to Eucharist and the other sacraments. Mission is essential in considering baptism and confirmation. Baptism is par excellence the sacrament of faith received, and is inseparable from confirmation. Together they also express and communicate a share in Christ's active mission to redeem all creation, which continues the divine kenosis. In them the redemptive finality of the kenosis of the Incarnation surfaces in both receptive and creative or productive mission: the Word's taking up of a created human nature for our redemption, for

---

this passage means something identical with the Incarnation has been disputed, but not conclusively disproved. A Pauline equivalent to the Johannine affirmation is accepted here.

the sake of transforming, affirming, blessing, and calling us to share in Christ's mission to carry the good news that all creation, not only "religion" is summoned to glorify God. That redemptive finality of the kenosis in the Incarnation is the basis for an "incarnational humanism"[47] that is a path of hope in everyday life. For the kenotic Incarnation has not stopped and as the underlying divine act in cross and resurrection remains the eternal divine promise. Nor has the kenosis of the Holy Spirit poured out into hearts ceased. The unceasing Trinitarian kenosis makes Christian hope a realistic approach to the present and future.

Yet incarnational humanism is not fully identical with going to and coming from eucharistic worship. Incarnational humanism affirms divine transcendence of creation as a facet of divine immanence in creation. It conceives salvation along the lines of Aquinas, that God is the fulfillment not the destruction of the human. It encourages involvement, albeit discerning and critical, with everyday life in the differentiated spheres of modernity. It does not ignore or prescind from whatever evils distort individual and social existence in a given culture. But it looks beyond negative judgment and to redemption of whatever good there is, often accessible only to discerning eyes of faith.

This is a path of hope laid out by Vatican II documents on the church, on the laity, and on the church in the modern world. Pope John Paul II develops it in *The Vocation and Mission of the Lay Faithful in the Church and in the World*. There he prolongs Vatican II's emphasis on the "secular character" of the lay faithful.

---

47. Murray, in "Is It Basket Weaving?" argued that this was the path for American Catholics because "[t]rue religion and humaneness...are not rivals but sisters," 195. And yet in view of human sinfulness he advised that while "the Church stoutly defends reason and its powers of knowing and of harmonizing its knowledge with its Christian beliefs...," the church remains prudently "less certain of man [sic] himself in his total being and less confident of his power to harmonize his whole human effort with his Christian faith, in that ever precarious synthesis known as Christian humanism," 196.

It expresses the church's own "authentic secular[48] dimension, inherent to her inner nature and mission, which is deeply rooted in the mystery of the Word Incarnate."[49] He locates their vocation to holiness and evangelical mission squarely in "their *involvement in temporal affairs* and in *participation in earthly activities.*" While this includes participation in church life, liturgical worship at its center, the lay vocation and mission are not completely identical with or reducible to churchgoing. The path of hope opened by the sacraments of initiation is not fully identical with the road to and from church on Sunday. It is a path that leads into everyday life as a locus for cooperating with God, as a set of conditions for "finding God in all things" as the spiritual heritage from St. Ignatius Loyola puts it.

Secularization tends to conceal this path. It pre-positions the path of Christian hope in everyday life within the segregated sphere of "religion." Sunday worship, a eucharistic liturgy, or a meeting of the Society of Friends, or for Seventh Day Adventists worship on Saturday, is churchgoing par excellence and sociologically is an index of being "religious." Its impact will seem to be on other matters considered "religious," perhaps including family life. But everyday life involves participation in other spheres too. What does it mean for Christian hope to affect everyday life in its economic, political, scientific, technological, cultural dimensions? An initial meaning is that, on the basis of the sacraments of initiation, the path of Christian hope resists confinement to "religion." Taking account of a secularized state of affairs in everyday life does not demand that either hope or Christianity

---

48. Of course, while true in principle that the venerable term "secular" can render the age-old term "temporal" without denoting modernity's process of secularization, it is also true that in fact Vatican II and postconciliar Catholic teaching on the "secular" does connote the temporal order precisely in the actual conditions of modernity.

49. John Paul II quoting Pope Paul VI's "Talk to the Members of Secular Institutes (2 February, 1972)" in section 15, 35 of *The Vocation and Mission of the Lay Faithful.*

has to play exactly the kind of "religious" role that historical processes of secularization have predisposed people to think are most "religious."

Or, rather, churches do not have to foreclose an option for deprivatization through redefinition of their public role. The processes of secularization have not completely foreordained the complete end of any public role for religion. The international history of modernity has not chronicled nor has the gradual differentiation of spheres determined the decline of religion, though Western Europe seems to be an exception that many sociologists thought was the rule. In the West, Christianity does not have to seek to reinstitute a medieval Christendom in which it held the place of the central source of legitimacy, official common meaning, and institutional order that united and maintained society. Instead, in any given society it can adopt a prophetic role vis-à-vis every sphere and that society as a whole. Religion differentiated into a sphere nonetheless can challenge to oppressive effect pretensions to absoluteness mounted by each and all of the other major spheres.

This path of hope in everyday life accepts the excess of Christianity and its hope over the compartment designated "religion," looking meanwhile into the meanings, truths, values, and institutions of its cultural context. Liturgies that link Word and Sacrament with the possibility of prophetic and "kingly" witness on a more just future for society, for example, point people along a path of hope that releases the power and vision of Christian hope to serve the common good and divine sovereignty, without identifying any given outcome with the fullness of God's kingdom.

The path of hope in everyday American life is not prayer alone, nor liturgy alone, nor both together apart from an understanding of cultural context. Prayer, liturgy, and knowledge of context are matters of intentional consciousness.⁵⁰ As intentional, acts of intentional consciousness make their objects present to the subject who has them. As conscious, they make the subject self-present. Intentional consciousness occurs on four levels beyond dreaming: (1) sensing, perceiving, feeling, imagining, speaking, moving; (2) inquiry, coming to understand, expression of understanding, working out implications of an understanding; (3) reflection on ideas, presenting evidence, passing judgment on the truth or falsity, certainty or probability of statements or positions; (4) deliberation on goals and courses of action, evaluating them, deciding on and executing them. Persons engage in self-transcendence when activating these operations. They have a pattern of movement that is "ever striving for a fuller and richer apprehension of the yet unknown or completely known totality, whole, universe."⁵¹ In effect, both Anglican and Catholic communions have recognized intentional consciousness as a traditional path of hope in affirmations of the real but limited capability of reason.⁵²

The intentional consciousness of each person and each Christian is a path of hope in everyday life. The spontaneous dynamic of our consciousness of anything moves from experience to a search for understanding, to a testing of ideas and understandings arising in experience in search of a judgment of truth or value, to a responsible decision based on the foregoing acts. These ordinary acts are distinguishable, but also are co-immanent in one another and cycle through each other. Fidelity to the exigencies of consciousness is authenticity. Authenticity is self-transcendence through acts of intentional consciousness, that go

---

50. This is to invoke the analysis of consciousness in *Method in Theology,* chap. 1.
51. Ibid., 13.
52. Anglican tradition, of course, has held onto three sources of authority: scripture, tradition, and reason. In *Fides et ratio* Pope John Paul II reaffirmed the importance of reason for a life of Christian faith, in *Origins* 28, no. 19 (October 22, 1998): 319–47.

beyond knowing to loving, deciding, and doing. Authenticity is the generically human invitation issued by human existence itself, not a specifically Christian summons based in the gospel.

Yet it inheres in and places its claim on Christian existence, as it placed and places its claim on the people of God's first covenant. The importance of truth-telling to the existence of Israelite society can be inferred from the Decalogue, which pronounces that, "You shall not bear false witness against your neighbor." This imitated YHWH's fidelity. Jesus was more than authentic but was no less than authentic. Christian existence can be understood as a vocation to authenticity empowered by divine grace. Authenticity always involves some degree of withdrawal from inauthenticity. Inauthenticity consists in being inattentive, being mistaken in understanding, making erroneous judgments, forming irresponsible decisions, refusing to love. Movement into greater authenticity occurs in intellectual, moral, and religious conversion that reorients and reforms persons and communities. Community is an achievement of common meaning, based on common experience, some shared ideas about it, with at least a few judgments of truth agreed upon, and a capacity for unified decision-making. The American dream is a matter of common meaning. Testing its adequacy belongs to the self-transcendence that is authenticity.

As the source for personal and social progress, authenticity is a principle and path of hope. It counteracts personal and social decline. Authenticity is actuation of the human capacity for self-transcendence in attention to experience, raising questions on that basis, ascertaining the validity of answers, arriving at judgments of value and decision from those answers. Love for God given in the Holy Spirit affects and renews authenticity. Authenticity is movement whose every step, as it were, fulfills human existence and brings a person or group closer to its last end. Authenticity is advance into and through acts whose full and transcendent object is uncreated, absolute truth, goodness, and beauty. Since this advance results from the difficult experience and dynamic of self-correction and conversion, it partakes of the character of hope that perseveres in spite of difficulties. In this way, human consciousness itself witnesses to hope, insofar as it invites each person to pay attention to experience, to seek understanding of experience, to judge the validity of truths and the genuineness of values, to self-giving in love.[53]

The American dream, testimony to the power of imagination, is the built-in, default path of hope in everyday American life. Any person's or artist's movement into deeper authenticity follows the spontaneity of intentional consciousness — probing, testing, and exploring the dream's adequacy to our common humanity. Does it represent some universal meanings, truths, and values, or does it generate a narrow nationalism? Finding a shortfall in some respects ends casual optimism, not hope, and by no means cuts away the possibility of redeeming the dream. This can happen when real or imaginative recognition of the dream's inadequacy opens space for realities not part of the dream — beauty and art, prayer and worship, a power of imagination that leads not to products but to human changes. In none of the three films, *American Beauty*, *Far from Heaven*, and *Adaptations*, does a flawed main character succumb to what Thoreau called quiet desperation. Each instead struggles away from that, in a flawed way, toward authenticity. Each is a pilgrim's progress out of inauthenticity. Despite admitted ethical problems about each struggle, the

---

53. Ernst Bloch, in his *The Principle of Hope*, originally *Das Prinzip Hoffnung* (Frankfurt am Main: Suhrkamp, 1959), trans. Neville Plaice, Stephen Plaice, and Paul Knight (Cambridge, Mass.: MIT Press, 1986), treats consciousness as anticipatory of the future on the basis of the "not yet," unfinished, incomplete nature of reality that we are conscious of. However, consistent with an atheist premise, Bloch does not account for transcendence in any given present except by reference to the future.

plots in the films are journeys of hope in everyday American life. When Thoreau staked out a mid-nineteenth-century experiment at Walden Pond, he too committed himself to search for an authentic life with personal and public dimensions. This path of hope in everyday life changed him for the remainder of his days because it was a movement out of specific kinds of widespread inauthenticity he had detected in pre–Civil War New England — forgetfulness of God as end of human existence, work without contemplation, relentless acquisition of goods while ignoring the moral demands of American citizenship.

The path of authenticity and creative imagination lies open to everyone. Christian hope does not substitute for it. That would be a variant on fideism in the matter of Christian approaches to the future. Rather, hope exercised in personal prayer and nourished by participation in liturgical worship provokes intentional consciousness into movement to deeper authenticity and withdrawal from inauthenticity. And that is the path of Christian hope in everyday American life. It is indissociable from revising inauthentic elements in the American dream. Changing a dream takes creative imagination. For example, to whatever extent this dream thrives on an individualist premise that social reality derives from rather than belongs essentially to our humanity and intentional consciousness, to such an extent the path of hope also is movement into affirmation of relationships as in some way constitutive of human and Christian existence rather than entirely consequential. How can we imagine our life together?

Conclusion

Where lies the path of Christian hope in everyday American life? First, renunciation and prayer are essential to a path of hope, and not simply because of an apocalyptic sense of pervasive sin but because God alone is God. Second, liturgy remains for both church and individual a privileged map, path, and journey of hope. However, each by itself is incomplete. Third, the least conspicuous but most influential side of the path probably is that of authenticity. Prayer, liturgy, and authenticity/creativity are irreducible. They all are exercises of hope that belong to Christian life. Authenticity sometimes may not be clearly evident among Christians, while conspicuously present apart from hope that is formally Christian. Authenticity is the path of self-transcendence through attention to experience, probing inquiry, careful judgments, and responsible decisions. It can result in creativity, using the power of imagination, which in its most concentrated form is art. The path of authenticity/creativity heeds what might be conceived as a promissory character inherent in human existence spontaneously presenting itself in the structured dynamic of intentional consciousness. God, of course, is the origin and end of prayer, liturgy, and authenticity/creativity alike.

Finally, it is worth commenting on the co-presence of prayer, liturgy, and authenticity/creativity in everyday Christian life in America. When Christians keep discipleship open to commitment to a just social future they exemplify authenticity insofar as they proceed from attention to social existence, to the situation of many kinds of people, from analysis of these facts and careful scrutiny of theories about the facts, from affirmation of the truth of human dignity as a touchstone for evaluating societal conditions and for responsible decisions about them. Praying the "Our Father" is hoping for God's kingdom to come on earth as it is in heaven, a hope that invites the ones praying to work for just social structures. Liturgical worship makes congregants bread for the world in the sense of seeking to have decent living conditions for all. The association of faith and justice can be considered the convergence of prayer, liturgy, and authenticity, the royal path of hope in everyday life in America.

In my judgment it would be even more hopeful if Christian churches exercised prayer and creativity enough to evolve a celebration of God as Creator, and of creation as dependent on the One it stems from. This could be a distinct liturgical feast for the Creator/creature relationship, emphasizing humanity inseparable from the whole physical cosmos.[54] At present, there seems to be nothing in Christian liturgy that ritually remembers the Genesis depiction of divine creation and the created but still incompletely known cosmos as already a *magnum et mirabilium*. Creation readings figure prominently in the Easter Vigil, but seem quickly left behind. Nor does the cosmic Christ of Colossians and Ephesians seem much in evidence liturgically.

---

54. Mircea Eliade analyzed many ritual reenactments of creation, which served to orient a people by relating them in the most basic way to their world, in Willard R. Trask, trans., *The Sacred and the Profane: The Nature of Religion* (New York: Harper & Brothers, 1961).

10

What Shall We Do While Waiting for the End?

ALAN JONES

What shall we do
while waiting for the end?

Hanging about for apocalypse
can be a pain.
There are only so many trips to the mall,
so many reruns, so many deals,
so many things to buy.

Sometimes, in my stupor,
I hear a voice telling me that my waiting
is not just hanging around
until the end.

The voice tells me to look
for something I've mislaid.
Expectant, radiant even —
a hint and promise, an annunciation
I'd forgotten.

Beware of God

ON A RECENT VACATION, I saw a T-shirt on a teenager with the slogan "Beware of God." Given the violent tendencies of fundamentalist religion, the warning is apt. It seems that, for many, hope involves the fiery destruction of millions of infidels. Religions easily turn violent and, in many cases, for the sake of intense love. The trouble is that the love is not universal. The love for which we turn violent is only available to true believers and the chosen people. Killing, then, becomes a duty. Pope Urban II launched the first crusade with the words, "Let the army of the Lord, when it rushes upon his enemies, shout but that one cry, 'Dieu le veult! Dieu le veult!' " This spirit is still alive — in the Christian apocalyptic Zionism of many American evangelicals who seem to want to engineer an Armageddon (and this attitude influences American foreign policy) and in the common beliefs of millions of Christians.

Beware of God. And with good reason. *Sacrifice lies at the heart of Christian hope*. René Girard writes of a sacrificial crisis in our culture, which, I believe, is related to hope. This crisis is "the collapse of the basic structures of communal life and the simultaneous disintegration of moral and psychological coherence."[1]

Hope is a word that sounds benign but isn't necessarily so. It is part of the vocabulary of apocalypse, which often means that a lot of people have to be dispossessed or even killed for the particular group to have its hopes fulfilled. That's why I've always had a revulsion to apocalyptic speculation. I can see its uses as a form of madness necessary when the world is mad. I can also understand

---

1. See Gil Bailie, *Violence Unveiled: Humanity at the Crossroads* (New York: Crossroad, 1995), 56, referring to René Girard's *Violence and the Sacred*, trans. Patrick Gregory (Baltimore: Johns Hopkins University Press, 1977), and Robert Hamerton Kelly (a Girard interpreter) echoing Barth's "gospel" versus "religion" notion, which is all right as long as we don't identify our own well-entrenched position as "gospel."

it psychologically. "These times are so awful that God will wipe away the injustices as if he were wiping clean a dirty dish." Then there is the phenomenon of false hope — a determined, upbeat cheerfulness that is depressing when the evidence on the ground is contrary to the official optimism. There are other problems with the hoping heart in that Christians have tended to hope in a future in which they are on top and others lose out. Church needs to watch its claims. It claims to have too many answers, and not enough time is given to guarding the questions.

Jesus, Our Only Hope?

When it comes to hope, Christians are divided. At the heart of the tragic and comic mutual incomprehension among Christians is the assertion that the only hope for us all is in Jesus. It is my hope too, but the way this hope is often affirmed is alarming and destructive. Nancy Guthrie is an evangelical Christian whose book *Holding onto Hope*[2] is a moving story of the struggle to find meaning in suffering in the face of the death of her babies. I was struck by the headline in the newspaper: "Book's Christian message a hurdle for non-believers." The text reads, "The hurdle is this: no heaven without Jesus. Anyone who doesn't stand on a relationship with God through his son — regardless of their religious or spiritual label — is shut out." This isn't just a hurdle for nonbelievers but for believers as well — at least for this one. And here's the frustration: In this obviously moving and caring book, we have a poor and damaging theology written by a caring and decent person. This incident is emblematic of the crisis at the heart of the understanding of the Christian hope. The irony is that, in a sense, Nancy Guthrie is right. There is no hope without

---

2. Nancy Guthrie, *Holding onto Hope* (Wheaton, Ill.: Tyndale Press, 2002). See the report in *USA Today*, July 6, 2002.

the Spirit, which Jesus embodied. "No heaven without Jesus," but maybe Jesus is more generous than his followers? We will be judged by who Jesus was and is. The Christian claim is that he is the prism through which all things are seen as they really are. This is our hope. WWJD. What Would Jesus Do? What Would Justice Demand?

Actions are more important than words, but words matter. In God, word and action are identical. It is not so with us. Why do so many Christians think that verbal assent is the primary criterion for salvation? I wonder if Nancy Guthrie and her fellow evangelicals can see the spirit of Jesus in the actions of nonbelievers? Where is the spirit of Jesus in a crazed and fanatical Christian? Surely, even in the best evangelical theology, judgment is eschatological. Only at the very end, will the outcome of a life be known? Think of all those who have rejected Christ because of us Christians. Think of all the ordinary lives blighted by religion.

Faith in Christ promises transformation, but this transformation is not exclusively for Christians, which strikes fear into many Christians and makes them angry. Anyone can be drawn to the attractive power of Jesus, and there are many paths by which he may be followed. Jesus does not belong to Christians. He is the property of the world. In Walter Wink's wonderful phrase, Jesus Christ is "God's rash gamble that humanity might become more humane." Wink also adds Rake's comment: "The future enters into us in this way in order to transform itself in us long before it happens."[3] Our hope lies in anticipating God's future by sharing in the life of Jesus now through the power of the Holy Spirit.

The church always needs to hear its own message before it proclaims it to the world. One of the things the church finds hard to face is the elusiveness of Christ — always ahead of us. And

---

3. Walter Wink, *The Human Being* (Minneapolis: Fortress, 2002), 250.

the church has never been comfortable with this, with a Christ it cannot control, a revelation it cannot regulate. One paradoxical ingredient, therefore, of Christian hope is that it looks forward to the demise of certain forms of tribal Christianity. We hope for the liberation of God.

Recovering the Art of Doing Theology

It seems to me that we (that is, the thoughtful believers) are going through a humbling, even a humiliating period of reassessment. At last, we are having to face the fact that dogma isn't "eternal" but, like everything else, has a history. The constant evolving image of God in our consciousness over the centuries is bound to have an effect on they way we articulate our hopes. Those who rightly affirm that Jesus is the same today, yesterday, and forever tend to forget that we aren't. Human consciousness changes. Moreover, it is impossible to get into the minds of those who have gone before us (even if we need to try). That's why history keeps on being rewritten. Who is this Jesus who is the same today, yesterday, and forever? Who is he for us now?

We have forgotten some very simple rules for talking about God. The irony is that it is often the rigid conservatives who know little of the tradition and have forgotten the rules for doing theology. Fundamental principles of theological discourse tell us that God is a mystery beyond all our imaginings, and, therefore, no expression of God can be taken literally. That's why we need thousands of names. And still, thank God, God remains elusive. The Augustinian principle is, "If you have understood, what you have understood is not God." The late Jesuit theologian Henri de Lubac suggested that people who seek to know God are rather like "swimmers who can only keep afloat by moving, by cleaving a new wave at each stroke. They are forever brushing aside the representations that are continually reforming, knowing full well that these support them, but that if they were to rest for a single moment they would sink."⁴ We are being challenged, once again, to entertain the belief that God really is. The fact that we are contingent and mortal, that we have no choice but to live in this particular time and not in another, should come as no surprise.

The older the world gets and the more information we have about history, the harder it is to hope. The future isn't what it used to be. The slaughterhouse of history doesn't make it easy to believe that "things will turn out well in the end." They often don't turn out well, and to affirm that history is going someplace is hard to maintain. History has no compassion. "It is now getting harder to veil the apocalyptic. Unveiled violence is apocalyptic violence precisely because, once shorn of its religious and historical justifications, it cannot sufficiently distinguish itself from the counterviolence it opposes."⁵ The church, in being overanxious not to be too Hellenistic, has fallen too much on the Hebrew side in affirming that history and history alone is the theater of God's action. If there's a God, surely the divine action might transcend time and space? Hope can degenerate easily into "history-is-on-our-sidism." But we have to face the fact that on a very practical level Christianity doesn't work. It doesn't pay off historically. There isn't much difference historically between believers and unbelievers. That's why the questing and questioning side of Christianity must be kept alive. Part of our task is to keep big questions open and alive (something fundamentalist religion can neither understand nor tolerate). Gil Bailie, referring to Heidegger, reminds us that " ... the business of philosophy is not so

---

4. Paraphrased by Elizabeth Johnson, C.S.J., and quoted in Martin Marty's *Context*, March 15, 2002.
5. Bailie, *Violence Unveiled*, 16.

much to uncover truth but rather to 'endure' with heroic determination the 'absolute questioning' that was philosophy's special calling."[6] This should also be our business.

Just think of what happened in the last century in those countries touched by the gospel: the slaughter of millions. I take Bailie's point (but little comfort) that those cultures touched by the Bible still do abominable things but with a guilty conscience. "However savagely we behave, and however wickedly and selectively we wield this moral gavel, protecting or rescuing innocent victims has become the cultural imperative everywhere the biblical influence has been felt."[7] Perhaps, but "eschatological verification" isn't much to go on. But it's sufficient.

Hope in a Desperate World

The experience of the radical powerlessness of human nature reveals the need for a continuous exodus from ourselves. We need to recover our capacity to be surprised. We've lost the sense of the revolutionary and shocking aspect of the Christian revelation. Our culture tends to think of life as a debate, an argument. The gospel is a wake-up call, and the church is always in need of the salvation it proclaims. The story still intrigues us and nags at us. Will it be different this time? Is the new really possible? Will there ever be another revolution? A real revolution? Can there be?

According to the Talmud, Adam and Eve spent only twelve hours in the Garden of Eden, hardly time to unpack. This is a reminder that human beings have always been on the move. Permanence is an illusion. "Here we have no abiding city" (Phil. 3:20). So where are we going? Are we not searching for a place that will take us in and give us shelter? If the best we can expect

---

6. Ibid., 248
7. Ibid., 20.

is only twelve hours in Paradise, we'd better look for permanent shelter elsewhere — either after death, or in some divine intervention.[8] This doesn't stop our longing for Paradise in one form or another (although we shouldn't underestimate our efforts to delay our arrival). Our basic drive seems to be to stay alive here on earth. "Better to be a live dog than a dead lion." This basic instinct to stay alive should not be despised. It is better to be looking at a Tuscan sunset than to be dead; to hug a child, to weep with the sorrowful, to visit the sick than to be dead. But this longing to stay alive and to be safe isn't exactly Christian hope. What makes Christian hope Christian? And how is this hope connected to and not disdainful of ordinary human hopes? Before we go any further, we should take a look at what makes us dread the future. What renders life desperate — without hope — for millions of people? We know the answers: poverty, injustice, indifference, frustration and violence, technology, and depression. Let's take a look at the last two.

The Future Doesn't Need Us

Technology is changing the way we understand ourselves. The irony of the miracle of the interconnectedness of the Internet is that more people seem to be cut off from each other. More and more of us feel unprotected perhaps because of the new interconnectedness. But it's an interconnectedness without either intimacy or compassion. That's why the subject of hope is particularly poignant at this time. I don't want to turn September 11, 2001, into a cliché, but if we place that terrorist act in the context of other world events (the Middle East and the darker effects

---

8. See *Newsweek*, August 12, 2002, "Visions of Heaven: How Views of Paradise Inspire — and Inflame — Christians, Muslims and Jews."

of globalization will do) we are going through a period of history which *feels* deeply apocalyptic even if our time is no more apocalyptic than any other. It is estimated that only 30 percent of the world's population have developed beyond the narrowly tribal while virtually 100 percent of those caught in the tribal have destructive technologies at hand as well as cell phones. The Old World (and the Old Church) is dying; you can feel it. We are caught between loyalty to the old and fear of the new. The pain is intense when a great ideal, which has lost its power, ceases to inspire and give hope. It feels like a terrible loss, the loss of humanity itself. Bill Joy, cofounder of Sun Microsystems, wrote an article in *Wired* magazine that was something of a sensation: "Why the Future Doesn't Need Us." He estimated that within fifty years, technological advances in genetics, robotics, and nanotechnology might mean the end of the human species. Human consciousness could be downloaded into machines. The feasibility of this is not the point. Its power lies in its effect on the human imagination. Hope in our time is a battle about the imagination. What images will form the future?

The Christian hope holds out the promise of a healed imagination — the vision of a world in which there don't have to be winners and losers. The world defines itself over and over again in terms of victory or defeat. Christians define the world as communion. This cannot be proved. It sounds silly and naive. Moreover, there are intractable issues such as theodicy (God has a lot to answer for), judgment, and time, which attach themselves to our hopes and longings. When we add to this the consequences of our living at a time when the notion of the sacred is being eroded, the crisis deepens. René Girard writes, "Apocalyptic prophecy means no more and no less a rational anticipation of what men are likely to do to each other and to their environment, if they go on disregarding the [gospel's] warning against it in a desacralized and sacrificially unprotected world."[9]

The Epidemic of Depression

Seen steadily and whole, life is hard to bear. No wonder millions turn to religion for relief. Religion is the opiate of the people. But nihilism is no less an opiate. The poet Czeslaw Milosz writes of the discreet charm of nihilism:

> Religion, opium of the people. To those suffering pain, humiliation, illness and serfdom, it promised the reward of an afterlife. And *now* we are witnessing a transformation. A true opium for the people is a belief in nothingness after death — the huge solace of thinking that for our betrayals, greed, cowardice, murders we are not going to be judged.[10]

When it comes to Christian hope, judgment is part of the deal. To think otherwise is to betray an emotional and spiritual childishness. Daniel Goleman not long ago pointed out our lack of emotional intelligence, which leads to hopelessness. "International data shows what seems to be a modern epidemic of depression.... Each successive generation worldwide since the opening of the century has lived with a higher risk than their parents of suffering from a major depression — not just sadness but a paralyzing listlessness, dejection, and self-pity, and an overwhelming hopelessness — over the course of life."[11] Time is simply one damned thing after another. And depression starts earlier and earlier, infecting childhood. The mystics have always known the flimsiness of our world, and when we pay attention (when we

---

9. Bailie, *Violence Unveiled*, 16.
10. See the *New York Review of Books*, November 19, 1998, 17.
11. Daniel Goleman, *Emotional Intelligence* (New York: Bantam, 1995), 240.

pray) the trap door opening to the bottomless pit below becomes apparent. That's why we resist spiritual growth. Western culture has produced people who are continually taken by surprise that life is hard, and it seems that for many, life feels both desperately urgent and utterly pointless at the same time. There is no avoiding the abyss (*el abismo de la fe,* as St. John of the Cross understood it). In this context of desperation, talk about hope comes as a challenge rather than a comfort. To be open to life is to be open to a series of demands. And it might hurt! Depression, which is a kind of violence turned inward on oneself, can easily become violence against others, and how freeing that violence is when it is done in the name of a cause or a god.

The Jewish/Christian Perspective — Is It Realism or Depression?

Violence at the heart of religious hope must be acknowledged. In Anne Mary Doria Russell's *The Sparrow* a character (also called Anne) muses on the mystery of faith:

> God was at Sinai and within weeks, people were dancing in front of a golden calf. God walked in Jerusalem and days later, folks nailed Him up and then went back to work. Faced with the Divine, people took refuge in the banal, as though answering a cosmic multiple choice question: If you saw a burning bush, would you (a) call 911, (b) get the hot dogs, or (c) recognize God? A vanishing small number of people would recognize God, Anne had decided years before, and most of them had simply missed a dose of Thorazine.[12]

---

12. Anne Mary Doria Russell, *The Sparrow* (New York: Fawcett Columbine/Ballantine 1996), 100.

Russell herself is a convert to Judaism after having been raised as a Catholic. Judaism is at home with the ironic. "When you convert to Judaism in a post-Holocaust world, you know two things for sure: one is that being Jewish can get you killed; the other that God won't rescue you." The moral of *The Sparrow?* "Even if you do the best you can, you still get screwed." She goes on: "But if you read the Torah, you realize that God has a lot to answer for. God is a complex personality. I wanted to explore that complexity and that moral ambiguity. God gives us rules but those are rules for us, not for God." This is hard stuff but needs to be said if our hoping is to be realistic.

Looking for a Good Story — The Recovery of Christianity as an Art

Hope has something to do with how we move through time and how we are judged and shaped by the decisions we make. Time is a part of creation (the world was made *cum tempore* not *in tempore*). Time is a peculiar creature, and our relationship to it can make us mad. Time will not stop, and there's an incurable sadness about it because the past cannot be undone. Time goes on and on but doesn't go anywhere, does it? The Christian affirmation of "the God of History" sounds pretty hollow in the light of history's long, bloody mess. And how deadly boring it all is. How easy to kill time with depression or violence. No wonder we fear it. Look what it does to us. It brings us to a dead end, and when people are cornered they turn nasty. The god Chronos feeds on its own children — moment by moment eaten up by time and we along with it. Never a final solution — the future is always coming at us, and we never catch up with it. So many of us live life as if we were on the run, knowing that life will catch up with us in the end and do us in.

We have various coping mechanisms to try to dodge time's decay. Power, money, some form of subservience or slavery in religion and politics — any number of strategies might buy us both time and safety. But in the end we run out of time, and there is no safe place. We lose our moorings. It's as if we have lost touch with our own resources. We have mislaid our hearts. We put a ceiling on our own growth. We underestimate ourselves and hide from the risk that growth involves. These are the fierce issues of theodicy. God has a lot to answer for — the slaughter, the holocausts, the senseless waste of human life, the relentlessness of time. We preach that God does answer for these, sort of, but only sort of. For others, hope may be easier that this. Not for me. The Christian Story as it has been told to many of us won't do anymore. We need new stories and a better way of telling them. We also need grace to live with the loose ends and with the mystery and muddle at the heart of life.

The playwright Tom Stoppard tells us "grown-up art is an art that withholds information."[13] Art's suggestive power points to a story beyond itself. The point of the story is to inspire and baffle at the same time. Good stories comfort and unsettle us simultaneously. Perhaps if Christianity were seen as an art — a way of imagination, instead of a set of beliefs — it might regain its power to undermine our resistance to and fear of the new? A work of art is something that brings a new thing into the world and enlarges and deepens our frame of reference. For example, Sartre's *No Exit* — the story of three people stuck with each other — changes and focuses our view of hell. Or in Beckett's *Waiting for Godot* something vague is made tangible in that absurd and awful picture of the awesome fragility of our lives. Suddenly our world changes or even collapses. We experience a little apocalypse. "The

---

13. See the *New York Review of Books*, September 23, 1999, 10.

horror when we realize that we have been turned into someone we hadn't planned — a picture of ourselves endlessly grinning — not as Pagliacci once grinned, to conceal a broken heart, but grinning because no-one has told us our heart stopped beating long ago."[14] A healthy horror might do us good. Is life like the description of the opera *Pelleas and Melisande?* Nothing happens. Nothing happens. Nothing happens. Everyone dies.

Christian hope always disturbs and sometimes destroys the world we have invented. It takes the tragic seriously and has no utopian pretensions. Judgment is necessary because we love to create stories about ourselves, stories that blame every kind of pain and problem on something or someone outside ourselves. This is how we fabricate our hopes. We use the power of the imagination to order the world in a way that makes us feel safe and comfortable. Its effect is to close down the world — rendering it hopeless because the new is not allowed in.

The Shape of Christian Hope

Perhaps the most important admonition for us is "No one knows the hour"? We are reminded that everything comes to an end, and the sense of coming to an end is built into all human and earthly reality. What is the revelation of Jesus Christ? We believe history is going someplace. It has a point. The world as a whole lives in a history which, whether we know or realize it or not, moves toward God's definitive victory in history as judgment and eternal salvation — the divine work in us and in the world of faith, hope, and love. In that sense we believe that the future has been disclosed to us. We know what we're supposed to be up to. We're not trash, and we weren't made for nothing. This is the ultimate

---

14. Peter Brook, *The Shifting Point* (New York: Harper & Row, 1987), 32.

diagnosis of our condition. We were made by Love for Love. We will be judged and acquitted by the life of Christ, who has entered into our life with sympathetic understanding of its fragility and unsolved enigmas. In the flesh. He lived it. This is what we mean when we proclaim that Jesus is Lord. This is theology, but how far is it experience? I think it is both theology and experience. Because of the revelation, God gazes at us from every human face, because all are brothers and sisters of the divine. We shall be judged to the degree we responded to or rejected the call to human solidarity. Christ says and will say: What you did — or did not do — to the least of my sisters and brothers you did to me. This is the judgment that we rightly dread. The uncompromising demand of the gospel is that God has created us neighbors in one community.

What else do we learn? We learn how futile it is to wallow in regret for that which cannot be changed and how atonement can be made for even the most terrible of errors.

Christians are unable to think about hope without reference to the birth of the incarnate Word (the image of Mary and her Son), the violence of the cross (the work of redemption), and the revelation of community and communion (the holy and undivided Trinity). These three give shape to Christian hope and make it specifically Christian. In the end, the test of the spiritual life is that we respond in love for its own sake, not for the sake of winning heaven or escaping hell.

Christian hope affirms that time is going someplace, moving with, in, and to the glory of God. With the coming of Christ, the way we experience and endure time is changed. The advent of Christ is the hinge of time. Everything changed because of his coming. The message is, "You are not alone!" We cannot change the past, but because of the Incarnation we have the means of reinterpreting and reintegrating the past and seeing God's future as the gathering place for all people. We see and experience time through the prism of God's love for us, and the organ of perception is the open and grateful heart.

If the church has anything to offer the suffering world, it is the message of hope, which does not dodge the issues of judgment and tragedy but is clearly and unequivocally generous and universal. Many Christians seem to be overly concerned that too many people are being saved. And we have to do some serious theological work with other religious traditions and repudiate the cruel nonsense that verbal acceptance of Jesus Christ is the only means of salvation. We shall simply have to accept the fact that the Christian world is divided as to the very nature of the gospel. Unless our hoping includes hoping for the whole human family, it is defective and dangerous.

Last summer, we were wandering around Ravenna and visited the Baptistry Neoneano. In the dome was the depiction of John the Baptist and Jesus. I was struck by Christianity's struggling to express something immensely exciting about human destiny and creation. A profound hope lies at its heart — a hope that all shall be well and all manner of thing shall be well. Christianity, as practiced, messes up horribly, but it still points to a great hope (and in Ravenna the believer is kept humble because not far away is another baptistry — an Arian one!). The messiness of it all is part of the mystery. Hope with flesh and bones. Will, the "adult" hero in Nick Hornby's novel *About a Boy* (which was made into an excellent movie), finally grows up when he realizes that he's all mixed up in this confusing connectedness that is human life. "Will couldn't recall ever having been caught up in this sort of messy, sprawling, chaotic web before; it was almost as if he had been given a glimpse of what it was like to be human. It wasn't too bad, really; he wouldn't even mind being human on a full-time basis."¹⁵ That's what being a Christian means — being a human being on a full-time basis.

The advent Jesus as both Baby and Judge offers access to God for all — including and especially those who have no claim of moral or spiritual privilege, the unqualified. The God of Jesus is the God who sends rain on the just and the unjust, who loves everybody — even the desperately wicked. Our hope is that God is building a peculiar community of "unqualified" people. John Dominic Crossan calls this the "unbrokered society" — the promise of a society that does not rely for its workings upon some privileged class's control of the means of access to power and acceptability. The welcome of God is like an invitation to a meal with no social rationale, no ritual for ranking guests and marking their various levels of wealth or importance. "Jesus makes no appropriate distinctions and discriminations. He has no honor. He has no shame." In our terms, he is shameless. And his "future" keeps impinging on our "present."

And the tragic is real because Jesus' mission is, in one sense, a failure. Yet it turns out to be our failure to discern the true nature of power and authority, the true nature of hope. Jesus proclaims God's indestructible regard for all, regardless of merit and achievement, and for this he is executed. Yet, what happens? He won't lie down! The action of Jesus reveals a living presence that endures rejection and even death.

What about us? We are to act in such a way that the nature of this radically loving, shameless, hospitable and just God becomes visible. (This is ludicrous. Look at us!) We often talk about "the sacramental principle," which is the inherent capacity of the material world to bear divine meanings. But we also know that these meanings emerge from a process of estrangement, surrender, and

---

15. Nick Hornby, *About a Boy* (New York: Riverhead/Penguin Putnam, 1998), 292.

re-creation — not a bland appeal to natural sacredness. It is a lie that God's in his heaven and all's right with the world.

Judgment hangs over us.

> Despite the troubles, our vast society hums with reassuring steadiness. The morning paper is delivered on time. One's favorite program is predictably there. The chain stores are stocked and the highways crowded. It is hard to imagine that under that great throbbing busyness, the clock of doom might be ticking — as it has ticked for every other great civilization in history. There are more dead civilizations than live ones.[16]

Most civilizations die from within. They die from the loss of shared purposes.

Sacrifice Is Built into Christian Hope

We question not to confuse but to guard the mystery. What kind of world is emerging, and how can we make it more human and less cruel? The story we tell ourselves is too narrow and has to begin over and over again, bringing distress with it. It is the only way to acquire the wisdom we need. Suddenly the gospel is not a list of facts to believe but an adventure in which we are participants. Octavio Paz tells us that "the examination of conscience, and the remorse that accompanies it, which is a legacy of Christianity, has been, and is, the single and most powerful remedy against the ills of our civilization."[17] And Richard Tarnas calls for a moment of remorse if true transformation is to take place.

---

16. John Gardner, *National Renewal,* joint publication of Independent Sector and National Civic League, September 1995.
17. "Poetry and the Free Market," review in the *New York Times Book Review,* December 8, 1991.

We will experience grief. He writes, "It will be a grief of the masculine for the feminine; of men for women; of adults for what has happened to children; of the West for what has happened to every other part of the world; of Judaeo-Christianity for pagans and indigenous peoples; of Christians for Jews; of whites for people of color; of the wealthy for the poor; of human beings for animals and all other forms of life. It will take a fundamental metanoia, a self-overcoming, a radical sacrifice, to make this transition."[18] Tarnas changes H. G. Wells's dictum that we are engaged in the race between education and catastrophe to the race between initiation and catastrophe.

> I believe our task is to develop a moral and aesthetic imagination deep enough and wide enough to encompass the contradictions of our time and history, the tremendous loss and tragedy as well as greatness and nobility, an imagination capable of recognizing that where there is light there is shadow, that out of hubris and fall can come moral regeneration, out of suffering and death, resurrection and rebirth.[19]

The Subversive Christian Heart

An autistic child was asked what parents are for. "They hope for you." Perhaps we can hope for each other. You can do for me what I cannot do for myself. Cynicism has no place in the Christian character as skepticism does, as does irony.

It's time for the West and American Christianity in particular to take the tragic seriously. Robert George, political scientist at

---

18. Richard Tarnas, "Is the Modern Psyche Undergoing a Rite of Passage?" in Tom Singer, ed., *The Vision Thing: Myth, Politics, and Psyche in the World* (New York and London: Routledge, 2000), 265.
19. Ibid., 266–67.

Princeton, writes, "We would do our best if we could make sure our students had a dose of the Augustinian sense that there is a tragic dimension to life, that there is a sense in which we live in a vale of tears. We could make them aware of the reality of sin, by which I mean chosen evil, which cannot be cured by therapy or by science. We don't do enough to call into question the therapeutic model of evil." The conquest of the self is part of what it means to lead a fully human life. To be conscious is to be sad. To be Christian is to affirm a deep joy behind the sadness and the tragic.

Michael Sells, the translator and editor of *Approaching the Qur'ān: the Early Revelations,* writes:

> Qur'anic reciters and commentators characterize the tone of the Qur'anic recitation as one of sadness (huzn). This is not a world-rejecting sadness. Indeed the sadness is at its most telling in those passages in which the world's mystery and splendor are evoked. Yet there is a sense that somehow the splendor and mystery are too great for the human to encompass — or that the human heart has somehow forgotten it actually has the capacity to encompass the splendor and the mystery. At this moment of reminder, the text expresses not fear but the sadness, which comes with a personal realization of a loss that is part of the human condition. The day of reckoning contains the possibility that this loss will be overcome with final reconciliation and sense of belonging, or that it will be revealed as permanent — and it brings into the present the reality of that moment of finality.[20]

My friend Al Shands puts it well in describing how a friend of his received the news of a death-dealing cancer. For Al's friend, this is all there is. There is no life after death.

---

20. Michael Sells, trans. and ed., *Approaching the Qur'ān: The Early Revelations* (Ashland, Ore.: White Cloud Press, 1999), 28.

When it's over it's over. What you see is what you get, ... I was beginning to experience a dark gap widening between us, separating and threatening. Though I was uncomfortable, I also felt he was onto something important.... The End is not something which is readily accepted in our society. We are loath to accept the tragedy of the End. We want to avoid the truth that life is in part inherently tragic. We see life as some kind of endless fulfilling continuum. But of course that is not the whole story. The truth is that the deepest experiences of the spirit also involve utter darkness and emptiness. It is when we are in the power of death that the mystery of our lives also opens up to us in the deepest ways.... We cannot avoid it. We do not want to avoid it because it takes us beyond the shallows of pessimism or despair to the Edge where we gaze trembling into the very mystery of God.[21]

Our hoping, longing heart in the light of the End is a function of our identity. To be a person of hope is to be one who cooperatively enacts The End of the World. And what is the End of the World? It is to have arrived at the place of freedom, in faith, hope, and love.

---

21. From a newsletter of St. Clement's Church, Louisville, Ky., November 3, 2002. Al Shands is the priest who convenes this house church.

11

"In Times Like These We Need an Anchor"
The Quest of a Storm-Tossed Church for a Sure and Certain Hope

HAROLD T. LEWIS

"Sure and Certain Hope"?

WHEN I WAS SIXTEEN, my grandmother died. Not content to sit among the mourning family members, I asked the rector if I could be the crucifer. At the end of the requiem Mass, I preceded the casket to the waiting hearse, and after the body was placed inside, I laid the ornate brass and oak processional cross next to it. At the cemetery, I retrieved the cross and led my grandmother's body to its final resting place, and listened as the priest pronounced the words of committal. I don't think I knew the meaning of "oxymoron" then, but if I had, I would have used that word to describe what was said as a clump of earth, in the form of a cross, was traced on Grandmother's casket: "Unto Almighty God we commend the soul of our sister departed, and we commit her body to the ground, earth to earth, ashes to ashes, dust to dust, *in sure and certain hope* of the Resurrection unto eternal life through our Lord Jesus Christ...."

To my young mind, something didn't click. To me, hope, by definition, was anything but sure and certain. Hope was an expression of something we would *like* to happen. We express a hope that it won't rain, so that we can go on a picnic; we hope that the girl in our class will go with us to the prom; we hope that Mother has made bread pudding for dessert. But there is nothing either sure or certain about those hopes. It might rain torrents. Our would-be date may already be spoken for. And Mother might serve us canned peaches because she didn't have time to make dessert.

But to the Christian, "sure and certain hope" is not an oxymoron at all. It is a statement of faith, based not on our feeble wishes and desires, but on God's own pledge and assurance. As Father Baring-Gould's rousing hymn puts it, "We have Christ's own promise, and that cannot fail."[1] That promise is no more powerfully manifest than in the Resurrection, through which we are "begotten again unto a living hope" (1 Pet. 1:3).

Hope in the New Testament

Hope (*elpis*) as a theological concept, while not absent from the Gospels, figures prominently in the Pauline epistles. The odds-on favorite among lessons read at weddings is the thirteenth chapter of Paul's first letter to the Corinthians, which ends with the words, "And now abide faith, hope, love these three; but the greatest of these is love." These three so-called "theological virtues" are, to the blessed apostle, the foundations of the Christian life, and they are mentioned as a group elsewhere in his letters to the churches he visited.[2] But it is clear that it is his theology of hope that most informs his writings and his preaching. Because of hope, Paul, who describes himself as "the least of the apostles," feels

---

1. Sabine Baring-Gould, "Onward, Christian soldiers," *The Hymnal 1982* (New York: Church Hymnal Corporation, 1982), 562.
2. See, e.g., 1 Thess. 1:3; Gal. 5:5–6; and Col. 1:4–5.

emboldened to preach the gospel in the first place: "Not boasting of things beyond measure... but having hope, that as your faith is increased, we shall be greatly enlarged by you in our sphere to preach the gospel in the regions beyond you" (2 Cor. 10:15–16). Such hope is present, too, according to Paul, as all Christians exercise their ministry: "There is one body and one Spirit, just as you were called in one hope of your calling" (Eph. 4:4). In his letter to the Galatians, Paul explains that hope is the reward for those who forsake bondage to the law, and whose lives become governed by God's grace:

> You have become estranged from Christ, you who attempt to be justified by law; you have fallen from grace. For we through the Spirit eagerly wait for the hope of righteousness by faith. (Gal. 5:4–5)

While hope, to Paul, is inextricably bound to the conduct of the Christian life on earth, his theology of hope is not devoid of an eschatological dimension. "For what is our hope, or joy, or crown of rejoicing?" he asks the Thessalonians. "Is it not even you in the presence of our Lord Jesus Christ at his coming?" (1 Thess. 2:19). To the Colossians, he speaks of "the hope which is laid up for you in heaven, of which you heard before in the word of truth of the Gospel" (Col. 1:5).

But Paul's theology of hope is nowhere more fully expounded than in the Epistle to the Romans, sometimes called "The Epistle of Hope."[3] Perhaps his most graphic example of hope is his recounting of the story of Abraham, whom he holds up as an example to Christians. There was no reason, given the facts, why the aged Abraham, whose wife was barren, could reasonably have expected to become the "father of many nations." But, Paul tells

---

3. See, e.g., John Paul Heil, *Romans: Paul's Letter of Hope* (Rome: Biblical Institute Press, 1987).

us, Abraham, "who against hope believed in hope," had faith in God nevertheless (4:18). Similarly, Paul maintains that adversity, far from depriving the Christian of hope, is actually a source of hope:

> We rejoice in our sufferings, knowing that suffering produces endurance, and endurance produces character, and character produces hope, and hope does not disappoint us, because God's love has been poured into our hearts through the Holy Spirit. (5:3–5)

In his valedictory remarks to the Romans, liberally peppered with advice on how to lead the Christian life, Paul again links hope to adversity, and makes it clear that it is on account of Christian hope that we are given the grace to be "kindly affectioned one to another": "Rejoice in your hope, be patient in tribulation, be constant in prayer, contribute to the needs of the saints, practice hospitality" (12:12–13).

The climax of Paul's treatise on hope comes in the penultimate chapter of the epistle, in which he prays that "the God of hope" will fill the Romans "with all joy and peace in believing, so that by the power of the Holy Spirit" they may abound in hope (15:13). Here Paul iterates his belief that we must be liberated from the gloom that dominates our thought processes when we regard things, as he says elsewhere, from "a human point of view" (2 Cor. 5:16). We have hope precisely because we can see, in Christ, and in particular in his resurrection, evidence of what God can do for his people.

Hope in the Hymnal

The church's hymnody reflects our biblical understanding of hope. In *The Hymnal 1982*, the theology of hope is a major theme in the majority of its seven hundred hymns, and the word "hope" appears in no fewer than seventy of them. In each of these, hope represents for Christians not only the very purpose of their existence, but the means by which they have that existence. Although never fully realized on earth, the earthly life contains glimpses of that eschatological hope which is a certainty in the life to come. Hope permeates our understanding of every season. In Advent, we sing "Our hope and expectation, O Jesus, now appear."[4] As we celebrate Jesus' nativity, we express the desire to share in the beatific vision of the angels:

Then may we hope, the angelic thrones among
To sing, redeemed, a glad, triumphal song.[5]

And even as we engage in introspective self-examination in Lent, hope is on our lips:

And thus my hope is in the Lord, and not in my own merit;
I rest upon his faithful word to them of contrite spirit.[6]

At the season of Easter, it becomes clear that our hope lies principally in the promise of the Resurrection:

My flesh in hope shall rest, and for a season slumber,
Till trump from east to west shall wake the dead in number.[7]

To one hymnwriter, hope in God is the only constant, a compass able to lead and guide us through the vicissitudes of life. Hope, moreover, endures, when all else in which we place our confidence disintegrates before us.

---

4. Laurentius Laurenti, trans. Sarah B. Findlater, "Rejoice, rejoice, believers," *The Hymnal 1982*, 68.
5. John Byrom, "Christians, awake, salute the happy morn," *The Hymnal 1982*, 106.
6. Martin Luther, "From deepest woe I cry to thee," *The Hymnal 1982*, 151.
7. George R. Woodward, "This joyful Eastertide," *The Hymnal 1982*, 192.

All my hope in God is founded, he doth still my trust renew,
Me through change and chance he guideth, only good and only true....

Mortal pride and earthy glory, sword and crown betray our trust;
Though with care and toil we build them, tower and temple turn to dust.[8]

For six decades before its inclusion in *The Hymnal 1982*, James Weldon Johnson's paean of hope, known in African American circles as "The Negro National Anthem," was sung lustily by the descendants of slaves who cherished a hope that they would be granted the inalienable and God-given rights granted to other Americans. Believing with Paul that "suffering produces endurance, endurance produces character, and character produces hope," Johnson could write:

Sing a song full of the faith that the dark past has taught us;
Sing a song full of the hope that the present has brought us;
Facing the rising sun of our new day begun,
Let us march on, till victory is won.[9]

Hope, in Samuel John Stone's famous hymn, is the very raison d'être of the church expectant:

One holy Name she blesses, partakes one holy food,
And to one hope she presses, with every grace endued.[10]

---

8. Robert Seymour Bridges, "All my hope on God is founded," *The Hymnal 1982*, 665.
9. James Weldon Johnson, "Lift every voice and sing," *The Hymnal 1982*, 599; also in Horace Clarence Boyer, ed., *Lift Every Voice and Sing II: An African American Hymnal* (New York: Church Hymnal Corporation, 1993).
10. Samuel John Stone, "The Church's one foundation," *The Hymnal 1982*, 525.

Hopelessness in the Church

The Oxford Dictionary of the Christian Church (ODCC), that great repository of ecclesiastical facts, some useful, some arcane, but all imbued with a distinctive Anglican flavor, defines "hope" as "the desire and search for a future good, difficult but not impossible of attainment." The definition makes it clear that Christian hope is in a class by itself: "Its primary end, its motive, and its author is God Himself, and like faith it may continue even when charity has been lost by mortal sin." Since hope is "confidence in God's goodness tempered by fear of His justice," the definition continues, it "is opposed to both despair and presumption."[11]

Professor Cross and his fellow editors of the *Dictionary* could probably not have foreseen the "unhappy divisions" in which the Anglican Communion finds itself today, and yet they seem to have aptly described our current climate. In the debate over human sexuality, Anglicans on all sides of the issue have too often lost not only charity but civility.[12] Moreover, while many give lip service to "the desire and search for a future good," there is in many places a sense of despair, as prophets of doom predict, for example, that the election and consecration of a gay man to the episcopate will be a "mortal wound" to the church. And there is no want of presumption in the words of those who claim to know not only the mind of Christ, but the exact date when that mind was revealed to the people of God. What I am suggesting is

---

11. F. L. Cross and E. A. Livingstone, eds., *The Oxford Dictionary of the Christian Church* (ODCC), 3rd ed. (Oxford: Oxford University Press, 1997), 790.

12. As I point out elsewhere, human sexuality is not the first issue over which Anglicans have found themselves seriously divided, and nor is it the only issue facing the church today. Unlike other historic controversies, however, sexuality engages us at the most fundamental level of our being and raises disturbing questions both about our personal identities and about the nature of settled truth. For many believers today, the church's position on homosexuality has become a litmus test for all sorts of issues relative to the place of Christianity in the modern world. See Harold T. Lewis, *Christian Social Witness* (Cambridge, Mass.: Cowley, 2001), 136f.

that many who purport to be steeped in the catholic faith seem perilously close to preaching a sectarian gospel, espousing a theology not unlike that of the fourth-century Donatists.[13] Moreover, as dioceses pass resolutions declaring who is orthodox and who is not, and as synods seem to grieve the Holy Spirit by defining the limits of the truth into which that Spirit is to lead us, we seem to be eschewing the idea of a sure and certain hope, and in so doing, we run the risk of becoming, literally, a hopeless church.

Perhaps we can take some small comfort in the knowledge that such expressions of hopelessness are nothing new. The church, as an institution, is conservative by nature — not in the narrow, political sense of the term, but in the sense that the preservation of the status quo is its default position. Change in any form is unsettling, a potential threat to the institution, causing that institution to rush instinctively to defend itself against the attack. In a statement issued in response to the election to the bishopric of New Hampshire of an openly gay priest, the bishop of Oklahoma wrote:

> The Church has spent a great deal of time studying and debating the place of homosexual men and women in its life. It is a subject that elicits great passion and it has the potential to split apart the Body of Christ. So did the inclusion of Gentiles in the first century! So did the breaking down of slavery in the nineteenth century! So did Civil Rights! So did the ordination of women!

---

13. The Donatists were a schismatic group in the African church who became divided from the Catholic Church because they maintained that the holiness of the church and the efficacy of the sacraments depended not only upon the worthiness of the officiating minister, but on the worthiness of the bishops who consecrated that minister. The matter was settled a millennium later by the Council of Trent, which declared that a sacrament confers grace *ex opere operato*, "irrespective of the qualities or merits of the persons administering or receiving it." See "ex opere operato," *ODCC*, 588.

Bishop Moody expresses a "sure and certain hope" when he adds: "I follow Christ as my Lord and Savior and Christ keeps breaking down barriers that religious people once thought were sacred. I think that our Lord is doing the same thing today with our attitudes toward homosexual men and women."[14]

"We Need an Anchor"

Because of the great importance of navigation in the ancient world, the anchor was regarded as a symbol of safety. It is not surprising, then, that Christians, whose church was not infrequently likened to a ship,[15] adopted the anchor as a symbol of hope. Just as the anchor is used to hold the boat secure, the anchor of Christ's unbounded love for the people of God will serve to hold his church secure. It will keep the Ark of Salvation from going adrift, or worse, from wreckage against uncharted reefs. Indeed, this symbolism was not lost on the writer of the Epistle to the Hebrews, who described hope as "as anchor of the soul sure and firm" (Heb. 6:19). Ambrose, the fourth-century bishop, writing about the epistle, built on this theme, and likened faith, strengthened by hope, to an anchor thrown from a ship which prevents it from being borne about.[16] In a modern evangelical hymn, we sing the words:

> *In times like these, you need an anchor;*
> *Be very sure, be very sure*

---

14. The Rt. Rev. Robert M. Moody, June 11, 2003 (Anglican Communion News Service, 3468).

15. The church has often been called the "Ark of Salvation," an image inspired by Noah's vessel for those who were saved from the Flood (cf. Heb. 11:7). This has further been enforced by Gospel stories in which Jesus taught his disciples in a boat (e.g., Mark 4:35–41). The word "nave" is derived from the Latin, *navis*, "ship." Architects of Gothic churches have often fashioned the ceiling of the nave to resemble a hull of a ship. During World War II, the World Council of Churches adopted as its logo a storm-tossed ship with a cross as its mast.

16. Ambrose, *Ep. Ad. Heb.*, cited in *The Catholic Encyclopedia* (New York: The Encyclopedia Press, 1913), 462.

> *Your anchor holds and grips the Solid Rock*
> *This Rock is Jesus, yes He's the One;*
> *This Rock is Jesus, the only One*
> *Be very sure, be very sure*
> *Your anchor holds and grips the Solid Rock!*[17]

In times like these, we must not fall into the trap of which St. Paul warns us, of sorrowing "as others who have no hope" (1 Thess. 4:13). In times like these, we must realize that our hope is and lies in Jesus Christ. In current debates, appeal has been made to the testimony of the councils, and to the teaching of scripture, and to a rather imprecise criterion predicated on what the church has always believed.[18] But councils have not been infallible; scripture has been subject to various interpretations and has been used, among other things, to justify slavery and the subjugation of women. And clearly, no teaching of the church has enjoyed universal acceptance.

Can we not learn as a church to appeal to the witness of Jesus Christ himself? Can we not appeal to the Person of Jesus Christ who is our hope? The Epistle to the Ephesians, according to John Macquarrie, describes "a new community, a new humanity" born of hope, in which there is "the breaking down of divisions and the overcoming of alienations." He adds:

> In this new community, the horizons of the hope that had been born in the experience of Israel were vastly expanded. But equally the hope was deepened and acquired new content. This transformation of hope had come about through

---

17. Ruth Caye Jones, "In times like these," *Lift Every Voice and Sing II*, 71.
18. This is reminiscent of an ancient test of Catholicity known as the Vincentian Canon, *quod ubique, quod semper, quod ab omnibus creditum est* ("what has been believed everywhere, always, and by all")

Jesus Christ — indeed, he was himself the hope of the new race.[19]

The twenty-first-century church will be imbued with hope when she owns that "God is working his purpose out as year succeeds to year."[20] The twenty-first-century church will be most faithful to the one hope of her calling when she recognizes that "tradition is not some solid rock from the dead past, [but] is understanding the complexity of the past so as to secure the future."[21] The twenty-first century church will best "lay hold of the hope set before us" (Heb. 7:18) when she takes at his word the promise of her Lord who promised to send the Holy Spirit to lead us into all truth.

---

19. John Macquarrie, *The Christian Hope* (New York: Seabury, 1978), 57.
20. Arthur Campbell Ainger, "God is working his purpose out," *The Hymnal 1982*, 534.
21. John S. Pobee, "An African Anglican's View of Salvation," Andrew Wingate et al., ed., *Anglicanism: A Global Communion* (London: Mowbray, 1998), 81-82.

12

Sorting Out Some Synoptic Scenes
The Destruction of Jerusalem and the Second Coming of Jesus

JEFFREY ALLEN MACKEY

TRADITIONAL ORTHODOX THEOLOGY claims for Jesus the Christ the position of the second person of the Holy Trinity. The second person of the Holy Trinity leaves the glory that was rightfully his for eternity past, humbles himself to a Bethlehem birth, and in the process "empties" himself of certain prerogatives of deity. Much of this is summarized in an early worship hymn recorded for us in Paul's letter to the Philippians, chapter 2:

> Have this attitude in yourselves which was also in Christ Jesus, who, although He existed in the form of God, did not regard equality with God a thing to be grasped, but emptied [ἐκένωσεν] Himself, taking the form of a bond-servant, and being made in the likeness of men. And being found in appearance as a man, He humbled [ἐταπείνωσεν] Himself by becoming obedient to the point of death, even death on a cross. (vv. 4–8)

The two Greek words I have placed in brackets here are from the same root that we translate "kenosis," which means "emptying."

So that Christ Jesus, in the incarnational act, empties himself of certain attributes of deity, or certainly limits himself in this area.

The early church would have understood this as an explanation for numerous facts. Early in the Gospel of Luke (2:40) the writer records what Jesus does after his return home following the encounter with Simeon and Anna in the temple, "And the Child continued to grow and become strong, increasing in wisdom, and the grace of God was upon Him." Certainly the second person of the Holy Trinity would not need to grow in wisdom, unless the attribute of wisdom had been limited or laid aside in the act of incarnation. At twelve years of age, again Jesus is taken to the temple, where he lingers behind when the caravan leaves for Nazareth. Joseph and Mary return to find him questioning and listening to the teachers. After the family returns home, Luke comments (4:52), "And Jesus kept increasing in wisdom and stature, and in favor with God and men." The lesson is essential as we move ahead to other areas of life where Jesus manifests a lack of limitless knowledge. Here in his incarnate state, the God-man, Christ Jesus, is self-limited.

This becomes particularly important as we encounter Jesus' teaching on the destruction of Jerusalem (which occurs in A.D. 70, thirty-some years after his death, burial, resurrection, and ascension to the Father's right hand), and the end of the age and his Second Advent or return. "About this, Jesus both says much, and admits his lack of knowledge of the day and the hour" (Matt. 24:36; Mark 13:32). This leads us to the scriptures in question as we seek to separate the known from the unknown in Jesus' mind and to try to comprehend what he intends by teaching something of each.

The Gospels that are the focus of our investigation are called the "synoptic Gospels," referring to Matthew, Mark, and Luke. These three Gospels are given the title "synoptic" because they seem to "come together." There is a very real sense in which they can be paralleled so that their common themes and contents can be seen alongside each other.[1] Often scholars teach that Mark is the primary Gospel writer with Peter as his source, with Luke and Matthew following subsequently. The order of events in these three Gospels follows very closely, and they have been published in what are called parallels or synoptics of the Gospels. The present author has chosen these three Gospels to be the focus of our search for what Jesus actually means in his teachings on the end of the age and the destruction of Jerusalem. They seem to deal with the issues historically, where the writer of the Gospel of John couches all of the similar teaching within the realms of theology and is therefore outside of the venue of this inquiry.

With these foundations, the self-limiting of the incarnate Christ, and the parallel records of the synoptic Gospels, we proceed. Often these issues have not been considered when church teaching on the Second Advent of Jesus is proclaimed. Coupled with these foundational concepts is the fact that in the discourses recorded in the synoptic Gospels, Jesus is answering two precise questions. They are delineated best by the record of Mark 13:4, "Tell us, when will these things be [the things he has been teaching about the destruction of the temple] and what will be the sign when all these things are going to be fulfilled?" This is also recorded in Matthew 24:3 and Luke 21:7. That the question is twofold is of utmost importance in our study, for this bifurcation of the questions will give us clarity of the twofold answers that follow. (The synoptic parallel scriptures we will be working our way through include Matt. 23:37–25:46; Mark 12:41–13:37; and Luke 12:26–21:36 [with several editorial omissions]). Commenting on Matthew 24

---

1. Several good versions of the Gospels arranged synoptically are in print. For this study I employed Burton H. Throckmorton Jr., *Gospel Parallels: A Comparison of the Synoptic Gospels* (Nashville: Thomas Nelson, 1992). It uses the New Revised Standard Version of the Bible.

(and therefore secondarily on the Mark and Luke parallels), W. F. Albright and C. S. Mann in their commentary on Matthew in the Anchor Bible series see

> Three distinct matters [that] are dealt with in these chapters xxiv–xxv: (a) The destruction of Jerusalem in the near future, seen by Jesus as judgment on the rejection of his vocation and ministry by official Judaism; (b) The persecution of the infant community by authorities and groups inside and outside Judaism; and (c) The continuing life of the Messianic Community, looking to "the End," whether the end of the present age or the end of the natural order. (285–86)

I feel they are limiting Jesus to his own followers rather than all believers within Judaism, but the fact of bifurcation in the emphasis is important to note. We should welcome such scholarly support.

> The synoptic Gospels unanimously proclaim the typical Jewish religious thought that there was, for first century believers, both the "this age," and "the age to come" (Matt. 12:32; Mark 10:30; Luke 18:30; 16:8; 20:34). Jesus, himself, foresaw the day when heaven and earth would pass away and the books of history would be closed with a consummate judgment following the general resurrection and the corresponding celebration of the blessed around the table of the Lord.[2]

This is essentially the explanation of the general conviction surrounding the second question asked of Jesus, and reflects the overall feeling of his followers as they hear him teach and preach.

---

2. John A. T. Robinson, *Jesus and His Coming* (Nashville: Abingdon, 1957), 36–37.

And so we are led to look at the first question the disciples ask in response to Jesus' telling them that the Jerusalem temple will be destroyed (Matt. 24:1–3; Mark 13:1–4; Luke 21:5–7). They are taken aback at the thought of the destruction of the temple, for the former destruction of the temple under Babylonian attack had been a sign of the judgment of God. Jesus' hearers, no doubt, understand that judgment is forthcoming for them as well.

In answer to this first question, or the first part of a two-part question, Jesus is specific. His responses are replete with descriptions of religious and political temptations to go astray from the God of Israel; that wars and rumors of wars will be prevalent; that famine will be rife and earthquakes will shake the very terra firma they find home. There will be a torturing of believers followed by a martyrdom for the name of Jesus Christ. Jesus predicts an apostasy coupled with internal betrayals within the company of the faithful. Endurance will be the key to salvation. Matthew then edits in at 24:14 that the "Gospel of the kingdom" will be proclaimed to the ends of the earth before the end comes. Matthew tips his hand here and shows that when this sentence was said, it was referring to the end of the age and not to the end of Jerusalem. Matthew in his editing process could have believed that the two events, the destruction of Jerusalem's temple and the end of the age, were one and the same. Neither Mark nor Luke so indicate this belief. And Luke, being a Gentile and writing to Gentiles, often sees no use in separating the prophecies since his readers are not particularly interested or invested in the temple at Jerusalem anyway. But here Matthew is the one who coalesces the two future events.

The specificities of Jesus' answer to the first question are clearly found in the historic events of A.D. 64–A.D. 71. In A.D. 64 the Jews revolt against Roman occupation of Judea. The six years following bring severe persecution to Jews and Jewish followers of Jesus alike. When Jesus, in Matthew 24:21 says, "There will be a great tribulation, such as has not occurred since the beginning of the world until now, nor ever shall," he is establishing for his hearers the sheer horror of the Roman destruction of things Jewish. That the temple will be left without one stone on another is utterly unthinkable — yet these hearers believe Jesus. Remember that the audience to which Jesus is speaking is Israel and not the church. "Among the events to occur before the τελοσ, 'end,' spoken of in (24:14) is the 'great tribulation' (v. 21) spoken of in this pericope. As Luke makes very clear in the parallel passage (Luke 21:20), also dependent upon Mark 13, the present passage refers to the imminent destruction of Jerusalem, which was to take place in A.D. 70. This is marked very clearly by the opening reference in Matthew to 'the abomination of desolation.'"[3] Jesus, no doubt, sees this impending war with Rome as cataclysmic, but not as the end of the age. Consequently, he directs that those who hear him do several things. First they are to be sign watchers, and Jesus delineates numerous signs of the end of Jerusalem. They are to watch for the "abomination of desolation" to be set up in the temple (24:15) — which is fulfilled in A.D. 70 when Titus, a Roman general, entered the Holy of Holies, thus desecrating it.[4] Following this act, he burns the temple with the entire city of Jerusalem. If possible, they are to flee Jerusalem. Nothing short of entire desolation and destruction is forthcoming — be prepared.

---

3. Donald A. Hagner, *Word Biblical Commentary: Matthew 14-28* (Dallas: Word Publishers, 1995), 697: "The quotation is from Daniel 9:27. Cf. the idol altar of 1 Maccabees 1:54, 59. With the example of Antiochus Epiphanes in mind, Jesus required neither prescience nor unusual insight to see where the rise of nationalism under Roman occupation would lead. Whether the *abominable sacrilege* refers to idolatry, or to the entrance of Roman imperial eagle standards into the temple area, is immaterial. It was common practice then and for long centuries before, to assert sovereignty over a nation by dethroning its gods and replacing them by those of the conqueror. In the NT writings idolatry of any kind was a warning of distress and judgment to come. Cf. Romans 1:25; 2 Thessalonians 2:3ff.; Revelation 13:4."

4. W. F. Albright and C. S. Mann, *The Anchor Bible: Matthew — Introduction, Translation, and Notes* (New York: Doubleday, 1971), 295.

In light of these warnings concerning the "end of Jerusalem," Jesus also answers the second question (or the second part of the two-part question): "and what will be the sign of your coming and then end of the age?" (Matt. 24:3 et al.). This "end" in the disciples' question may very much have been the same end as the destruction of Jerusalem, though Jesus seems to put a distance between the two, but this is not conclusive. From our vantage point of two thousand years of church history, we can see the distance better than first-century readers would have seen the distance. And though this distancing is what generates the interpretative problems of these discourses, we dare not miss their existence.

And it is here that we are brought back to the self-limiting of Jesus' knowledge in his incarnation. Obviously in his childhood and youth he grew in knowledge and wisdom; evidently in his ministry years (approximately three) he does not know everything as an omniscient God would; and now he owns up to being personally ignorant as to the days and times of the second question asked him. Jesus' precise answer to when the end of the age will come is, frankly, agnostic at best. There is no question *that* it will come; the question remains, *when?* Luke is the only one of the three Gospel writers to omit the statement of Jesus' unknowing. This may very much be because of the Greek value on *"gnosis"* or "knowing," and Luke's unwillingness to submit Jesus to a lack of omniscience in the mind of those who would read his Gospel in an Hellenistic framework. Matthew 24:36 parallels Mark 13:32. They read practically identically, "But about that day or hour no one knows, neither the angels in heaven, nor the Son, but only the Father." The Son (Jesus, the Christ — the one speaking) does not know the day or the hour of the End. This is the essence of what is said about the end of the age.

The great apocalyptic happenings are signs of the destruction coming upon all of Israel — the signs are centered around the fall of the Judea. The agnosticism surrounding the End (notice the capital "E") is met only with Jesus inviting his hearers to be ready — to watch for his (the "bridegroom's") coming or return. It is precisely here that the church has found itself often confused, and such a confusion has brought a curtailment of the emphasis on Second Advent preaching and living. Two thousand years of imprecise exegesis of these scriptures; the repeated appearing of apocalyptic sorcery; and contemporary emphases on "sign-watching," all coalesce to support the curtailment of a Second Advent emphasis. Yet Jesus is simple in this — he does not know, we do not know — therefore watch. We are to live in a period and in an age of watchfulness. And just as there were christophanies (preincarnate appearances of Christ in the Hebrew scriptures) before the Incarnation, so there will be apocalypses before the parousia (the appearing) of Jesus a final time. And the imprecision of when this will occur allows the church to continue to influence the world for Christ. But our curtailment of an emphasis on the End has given paganism a noticeable edge.

Influential Episcopalian lay-theologian William Stringfellow insightfully comments:

> We live now in the United States, in a culture so profoundly pagan that Advent is no longer really noticed, much less observed.... The depletion of a contemporary recognition of the radically political character of Advent is in large measure occasioned by the illiteracy of church folk about the Second Advent, and, in the mainline churches, the persistent quietism of pastors, preachers, and teachers about the Second Coming. That topic has been allowed to be preempted and usurped by astrologers, sectarian quacks, and multifarious

hucksters. Yet it is impossible to apprehend either Advent except through the relationship of both Advents.[5]

Against this backdrop, we are forced to confess that the church, while holding technically to a doctrine of the return of Christ (cf. the Apostles' and Nicene Creeds as well as the memorial acclamations in various rites of Holy Eucharist), has not proclaimed what the apostle Paul calls, "the Blessed Hope." Fanciful interpretations of the book of Revelation, the Antichrist, the number 6-6-6 *ad infinitum* caused many to relegate all of prophecy to completed prophecy (called "realized eschatology"), therefore rendering our emphasis on a Second Advent as nonexistent. The church has consequently had nothing to look forward to.

This, of course, led to apocalyptic sorcery and seeming fictitious paradigms on the one hand, and all sorts of embarrassing apologies on the part of those who could not support such frivolity. All of the date setting, and so on, is to no avail, if we hear Jesus clearly — no one knows, except the Father.

In 1988, pastors, priests, and clergy across America, regardless of their denominational affiliation, received a free copy of a self-published book called *Eighty-Eight Reasons Why Jesus Will Return in Eighty-Eight*. When Jesus didn't return by December 31, 1988, at the stroke of twelve o'clock midnight, the writer returned to his calculations and released the updated version *Eighty-Nine Reasons Why Jesus Will Return in Eighty-Nine*. Well, no further books have followed, thankfully.

Finding in the kenosis of the Christ an allowance for his unknowing, we allow for Christ Jesus to let the "Father only" know the time of the End. It delivers us from finding signs in everything

---

5. From William Stringfellow, "Advent as a Penitential Season," from *A Keeper of the Word*, ed. Bill Wylie Kellermann (Grand Rapids, Mich.: Eerdmans, 1994).

and frees us to expect the person of Jesus Christ and not some impersonal event. The correct reading of the synoptics at this point is crucial and will render us clear in our preaching and teaching that "Christ has died; Christ is risen; *Christ will come again!*"

William Stringfellow captures this poignantly for us as this is applied to our lives in the church today:

> In the first Advent, Christ the Lord comes into the world, in the next Advent Christ the Lord comes as Judge of the world and of all the world's thrones and pretenders, sovereignties and dominions, principalities and authorities, presidents and regimes, in vindication of his lordship and the reign of the Word of God in history. This is the truth, which the world hates, which biblical people (repentant people) bear and by which they live as the church in the world in the time between the two Advents.[6]

---

6. Stringfellow, "Advent as a Penitential Season."

13

To Build the New City
An Eschatological and Secular Hope

JACQUELINE SCHMITT

> Give us, O God, the strength to build
> the city that hath stood
> too long a dream, whose laws are love,
> whose crown is servanthood,
> and where the sun that shineth is
> God's grace for human good.[1]

WALTER RUSSELL BOWIE wrote those words in 1910, part of a hymn commissioned by Henry Sloan Coffin and Ambrose White Vernon. In *Hymns for the Kingdom of God,* Bowie wrote, Dr. Coffin "wanted some new hymns that would express the conviction that our hope of the Kingdom of God is not alone some far off eschatological possibility but in its beginnings, at least, may be prepared for here in our actual earth."[2] Such hymns would contrast with the "by and by" theology of "O mother dear, Jerusalem":

> There lust and lucre cannot dwell;
> There envy bears no sway;

---

1. "O holy city, seen of John," Hymn 582, *The Hymnal 1982* (New York: Church Hymnal Corporation, 1982).
2. *The Hymnal 1982 Companion,* Vol. Three B (New York: Church Hymnal Corporation, 1994), 1075.

> There is no hunger, heat, nor cold,
> But pleasure ev'ry way.³

Bowie, Coffin, and their counterparts in early twentieth-century urban America would have no part of a theology that let the poor suffer now only to receive a reward in heaven. The prayers they set to music called believers to do all they could now to make real the reign of God ushered in by Christ's incarnation. They minced no words as they made their powerful case:

> Hark, how from men whose lives are held
> More cheap than merchandise;
> From women struggling sore for bread,
> From little children's cries,
> There swells the sobbing human plaint
> That bids thy walls arise!⁴

From the 1870s through the First World War, urban America experienced enormous upheaval and congestion. Industry and commerce exploded — with productivity and profit as well as exploitation and violence. Great shifts in population, from farm communities to cities, from cities to suburbs, and from Europe to America, along with great disparities in wealth among those people,⁵ made American society volatile and vulnerable to revolutionary ideas. Some religious people, like Walter Russell Bowie and Henry Sloan Coffin, read these signs of the times and heard God calling them to act. Their readings of scripture's words about the end-times, and especially about what Jesus called the kingdom

---

3. "O mother dear, Jerusalem," Hymn 584, *The Hymnal 1940* (New York: The Church Pension Fund, 1961).
4. "O holy city, seen of John," Hymn 494, *The Hymnal 1940*; this stanza was omitted from the version of the hymn published in *The Hymnal 1982*.
5. "At a time when the national wealth increased 600 percent, the average wage of the workingman decreased by 25 percent." Rosemary Radford Ruether, *The Radical Kingdom* (New York: Paulist Press, 1970), 81–82.

of God, changed. No longer would they preach doctrines that blamed the poor for their plight and advocated voluntary, and meager, benevolence. They were now agents of social reconstruction, recoverers of the prophetic tradition in Jesus' first sermon recorded in the Gospel of Luke:

> The Spirit of the Lord is upon me, because he has anointed me to bring good news to the poor. He has sent me to proclaim release to the captives and recovery of sight to the blind, to let the oppressed go free, to proclaim the year of the Lord's favor.[6]
>
> And he rolled up the scroll, gave it back to the attendant, and sat down. The eyes of all in the synagogue were fixed on him. Then he began to say to them, "Today this scripture has been fulfilled in your hearing." (4:18–21)

Bowie and his contemporaries, following Jesus' example and remembering the words of Isaiah and other Old Testament prophets who believed God was creating a new heaven and a new earth, had no interest in waiting for a just society. Indeed, they believed their words and actions long overdue:

> Already in the mind of God
>   that city riseth fair:
> lo, how its splendor challenges
>   the souls that greatly dare —
> yea, bids us seize the whole of life
>   and build its glory there.

One hundred years later, we live in a similar time of economic disparity, social upheaval, and imperialistic globe-trotting, by nations and by corporations. The social reforms put in place a

---
6. Isa. 61:1–2.

century and a half-century ago do mitigate those disparities and upheavals to a certain extent. A minimum wage, Social Security, child labor laws, occupational health and safety laws, collective bargaining rights, Medicaid, Medicare: These and other reforms from the Progressive and New Deal eras began with the moral outrage and theological change described by Bowie and Coffin and their contemporaries.

Yet the early years of the twenty-first century lack a powerful force which both inspired and repelled Christians one hundred years ago: We no longer have a secular hope for a better world. The revolutionary tradition of socialism offered an eschatological hope to rival those held by religion. "Socialism spoke of a new human personality: the socialist man and woman... the prospect of an inner consciousness formed by communal needs rather than individual aggrandizement...."[7] It was a realized eschatology, with a plan for transforming the cruelties of Western capitalism into a healthier, more equitable society. "Socialism had hoped to place the individual in the midst of a collective setting and purpose, and thereby replace individual, selfish values with those of solidarity. Socialism was the cure for the individual lost in the madness of capitalist civilization."[8] Now, as Rowan Williams points out, in recent books such as *Lost Icons* and in the 2002 Dimbleby Lecture, all we have is the market, with its limitless and crippling choices, and the market state, which exists to ensure the free traffic of capital around the globe.[9]

The challenge to Christians a hundred years ago, then, came from both the right and the left. Conservatives used theology to

---

7. William R. Coats, "The Sunset of Socialism," *Plumbline: A Journal of Ministry in Higher Education* 18, no. 3 (September 1990): 6.
8. William R. Coats, "Awake, Awake to Love and Work," *Plumbline* 18, no. 4 (December 1990): 5.
9. Rowan Williams, *Lost Icons* (Edinburgh: T. & T. Clark, 2002); The Richard Dimbleby Lecture 2002, delivered at the Westminster School, London, December 19, 2002; text courtesy of the Anglican Communion News Service.

uphold the social order of rich and poor. American democracy was a product of the Enlightenment and Protestant traditions which valued the individual and the pursuit of (material and spiritual) happiness. Earlier in the nineteenth century, some Christians were opposed even to benevolence for the poor, believing their downcast station part of God's judgment and will. Yet by the century's waning decades, society was coming apart at the seams. Immigrants from Catholic and Jewish Europe resisted the Protestant view of God's social order — and the great Protestant reform campaigns — just as they resisted the industrialists who kept their wages low and working conditions dangerous. For Irish immigrants, the antislavery crusades and the Civil War were ways the Protestant powerful kept them away from work and economic betterment; their anger erupted in the New York Draft Riots of 1863. For German immigrants, the temperance campaigns were ways they could be stripped of their culture and customs. For workers threatened by death in unsafe factories, kept in virtual slavery in their own homes by the sweating system, living in squalid conditions with little or no sanitation, heat, or privacy, the call to collective action was indeed a call to hope. If that call was carried on revolutionary rhetoric about the overthrow of those monied and propertied classes who were getting rich off their labor, then so much the better, some would say.

These conflicts gave birth to the Social Gospel, a movement of Protestant Christians to rekindle the eschatological tradition in service to social reconstruction. Calvinist notions of sin and depravity, and the evangelical emphasis on personal transformation and salvation, were not up to the task, they realized. Protestantism and the Enlightenment had brought about democracy and progress, but they were promises yet unrealized. A new reformation of heart and mind was now required to bring into being the society God intended. They heard in the socialist revolutionaries a common hope for a new world and a common judgment on greed and injustice. In her 1970 book, *The Radical Kingdom,* Rosemary Radford Ruether shows how Christians troubled by the results of laissez-faire economics embraced the challenge posed by the revolutionaries:

> The analogy between ruthless competition and self-interest and the Christian doctrine of sin as selfishness were drawn. In contrast, democratization and socialization of industry, profit-sharing, and economic cooperation were associated with the Christian ideas of love, community, and brotherhood. The socialist hope for a new cooperative society in the future was readily equated with the Christian hope for the Kingdom of God.... [T]he Holy Spirit was seen at work not simply or even primarily in ecclesiastical institutions but in the struggle for humanity in society at large.[10]

In 1902, Vida Dutton Scudder published a series of four essays in the *Atlantic Monthly.*[11] They were meditations on the challenges to democracy posed by social and labor unrest, as well as the challenges that the unrealized promises of democracy placed on education, social relations, and the church. Scudder was a professor of English literature at Wellesley College, with an academic interest in works about the Middle Ages, such as Tennyson's *Morte d'Arthur* and *Idylls of the King.* In the 1880s, in Oxford studying medieval romantic literature, Scudder heard John Ruskin, art critic and socialist, and her life changed. She recalled her youthful conversion in her 1937 autobiography, *On Journey:*

---

10. Ruether, *The Radical Kingdom,* 82–83.
11. "A Hidden Weakness in Our Democracy," *Atlantic Monthly* (May 1902): 638–44; "Democracy and Education" (June 1902): 816–22; "Democracy and Society" (September 1902): 348–54; "Democracy and the Church" (October 1902): 521–27.

The point of my desire was an intolerable stabbing pain, as Ruskin and the rich delights of [Oxford], forced me to realize for the first time the plethora of privilege in which my lot had been cast. That pain has continued at intervals to stab my spirit broad awake ever since.... [12]

In 1887, Scudder and a group of women college graduates started the College Settlements Association, and opened the first American social settlement based on Toynbee Hall in East London. Jane Addams and Ellen Gates Starr opened Hull House in Chicago just a month later. These young women were the vanguard of the Social Gospel reformers, eager to put their own ideals into practice. They moved into the urban slums to be neighbors to working-class and poor immigrants. Although they shunned explicit attempts to convert their Catholic and Jewish neighbors, they did believe their efforts to bring art, culture, manners, conversation, and cleanliness to the immigrants would uplift, civilize, and Americanize them. These young women felt Scudder's "intolerable stabbing pain" and yearned to be useful in society and to bring meaning to their lives. The great rifts in social relations in urban America could be overcome, they believed, by neighborliness and friendship. The poor would not live in squalor in the slums if they were shown how important it was to live in clean homes and cook healthy and economic meals.

By 1902, the settlement workers had developed a more realistic view of their project. They grew to see that larger social forces caused the poverty and misery of the slums, and they worked for public improvements in sanitation and housing. When their neighbors and friends were threatened with starvation after employers cut their wages, and cut them repeatedly, they saw that perhaps the only recourse these workers had was collective action.

---

12. Vida Dutton Scudder, *On Journey* (New York: E. P. Dutton, 1937), 84.

Some settlement workers made their calling into a profession, becoming the first social workers, occupational health and safety inspectors, and community organizers. For them, all that was needed for social change was for more people to do good; society could be reformed and the immigrants assimilated into productive American citizenship.

Yet there were serious thinkers, Scudder among them, who came to see limitations in the settlement work. In her essay, "Democracy and Society," she wrote, "Our end of social unity will never be reached by establishing special centers wherein the arts of brotherhood shall be practiced."[13] Her criticisms of the settlements echo Jeremiah's prophecy that God intends a new covenant to be written on the human heart:

> The need of our society lies deep. A mere sense of social responsibility, in professions or in daily life, such as one constantly meets in England, is an excellent thing, but it is of limited value. We in America must go beyond that. The motive impelling to wider fellowship must be quite different from the subtle impulse toward the disbursal of spiritual alms, or even from the uneasy sense of a debt to be paid, a justice unfulfilled. It must be borne to us from a future as yet unrealized.[14]

For Scudder, the settlements could offer only a foretaste of the radical reordering of social relationships, in which class differences would be overcome and the settlement ideal of friendship and solidarity would extend across America. This was the unfulfilled promise of democracy.

---

13. "Democracy and Society," 352.
14. Ibid., 353.

> Settlements are means, not ends; they fail unless they foster in the children of their spirit an attitude which will cause each and all to exercise ceaseless, loving, democratic activity in the normal and permanent life. The true center of social unification, the strategic point where the battle of the spiritual democracy will be won or lost, is the ordinary home.[15]

She acknowledges that the reform of all American homes is not likely, especially those of the older generation, but notes that possibilities arise in the new homes formed by "young men and women trained in colleges where the theory of social equality is edging its way, and in settlements where the practice of social equality is attempted." These homes can be places where the new social relations can become a reality.[16]

The goal of democracy is complete social transformation and the eradication of class differences. In her first essay, "A Hidden Weakness in Our Democracy," she writes:

> ...if democracy means anything more than mob rule, it means a moral responsibility on the part of its every member consciously to cooperate in the creation of a noble national life. These things are portentous enough but the end is not yet, and out nation is still in the making.[17]

A personal conversion to this way of thinking is required before one is able to act in solidarity with members of other social classes, and it behooves America's best citizens to lead the way. "Readiness for social sacrifice in the name of democracy [is] the need of the hour,"[18] she writes.

---

15. Ibid., 352.
16. Ibid.
17. "A Hidden Weakness in Our Democracy," 638.
18. "Democracy and Society," 350.

> Three things hold us apart: the mere physical distance which, especially in cities, separates the homes of rich and poor; the tension of American life, keeping us all as busy as we can possibly be, whether the heavy flails we wield thresh wheat or chaff; and our own sense that the physical distance is insuperable, supplemented by the curious instinct to limit our relations to people who like the same books, or art, or manners, as ourselves.... Granted this transformation of our inward and outward life in the likeness of the humanity to be, and all we long for will follow. There is no need of radical theory, no need of violent subversions of the existing order, to overcome the bitterness that holds our producing classes in isolation.[19]

For Scudder and her progressive contemporaries, the prosperity of the Gilded Age and the privileges of their class came at a great cost, personally, spiritually, and to society. Her descriptions of the despair of modernity — the gulfs between rich and poor, the frenzy of enforced busy-ness and overwork afflicting all classes, and the unwillingness to imagine any social relationship with people different from ourselves — echo contemporary discontent with the dictates of modern life. For her, the answer came in an alternative worldview, fed by the two great eschatological themes of the West: from the Hebrew prophets and Jesus, and from Marx and the radical socialists.

Scudder's final essay in the *Atlantic* series is "Democracy and the Church," which she begins by reading into the medieval ideal of the Holy Commonwealth the germs of modern democracy. American guarantees of freedom of religion spare the church here from the associations with aristocracy and tyranny with which it is associated in Europe, yet it is an inheritor of the medieval

---

19. Ibid., 353–54.

church which remained "true to her Master" and "through the religious orders, a home to democratic practice."

> Liberated from hampering temporal control, yet strengthened by the secular ideas that encompass her, she might assuredly approach more nearly than ever before to the apostolic conception.[20]

All citizens must promote democracy, but Christians "bear a double summons to democratic fellowship uttered by their country and by their Lord! Among those who follow the Carpenter of Nazareth should be found the common life we seek."[21]

Yet the church, like political democracy, does not live up to its potential, and damages its reputation by dependence on the privileged classes:

> It leans on them for its support, ministers with primary energy to their spiritual needs, — our millionaires, even when their business methods are open to criticism, are often sincerely pious, — puts up the larger number of its buildings in the quarters inhabited by them, provides the type of worship and preaching most grateful to them, and only as an afterthought establishes those numerous mission chapels, Sunday-schools for the poor, etc., whose very existence marks most clearly the tenacity of the aristocratic principle.[22]

It is inevitable, if this state of affairs continues, that working people will see the church, and all religion, as existing to serve only the privileged, "who, not content with the goods of this world, seek to establish a lien on those of the world to come."[23]

---

20. "Democracy and the Church," 522.
21. Ibid., 527.
22. Ibid., 523.
23. Ibid.

The solution, she posits, is a countercultural change in the human heart,

> an irresistible motive impelling us to deliberate simplicity in that love of our fellows which cannot rejoice in abundance while others go hungry.... [I]n these times of peace, when the desire for luxury or at least for material goods all but dominates our common life, and renders fellowship impossible, the chief call of the church invisible is to an unworldliness manifest to all men.[24]

In the end, she combines the secular and sacred hopes for a better world, which can be built and which Christians especially are called by God to build in the here and now:

> To the church at least, though all else should fail us, we may look with hope unfaltering for the slow but sure realization of that spiritual democracy of which our fathers dreamed, and in the faith of which our republic was founded.[25]

I contend that the movements of the Progressive Era should be viewed as more than dusty, romantic, or impossibly naive ideals. The parallels between our century and theirs, in global and national politics and economics, not to mention in a dominant Christian theology that emphasizes individual feeling and salvation, are too great for us to dismiss the creative and powerful ways Christians a hundred years ago answered the crises of their times. Christians then were both inspired by and feared the secular left. They realized that the socialist critique of social ills sprang from the same eschatological traditions of the Hebrew prophets which inspired Jesus. They rightly recognized that an eschatology divorced from the transcendent power of God would leave people

---

24. Ibid., 525.
25. Ibid., 527.

rootless, just as an eschatology separated from a hope for betterment of human lives in the here and now would be meaningless to those suffering from poverty and oppression. In the matrix of a society exploding from social and economic disparity, Christians in the Progressive Era developed a theology that offered a creative and alternative vision to rapacious and consuming capitalism.

The time is ripe for a new theological synthesis. With the collapse of socialism, the best the secular world can offer is an endless and nauseating round of choices, acquisition, and disposal. Evangelical theology, popular among Anglicans of the middle and upper classes, does little but support market capitalism. Its emphasis on individual feelings toward Jesus or the development of a personal spirituality undercuts any claims to collective action or appeals to the common good. Even Baptist evangelicals, such as sociologist Tony Campolo, denounce the current incarnation of evangelicalism for abandoning Christianity and replacing it with alliance with right-wing politicians and opposition to homosexuality and abortion.[26]

Some theologians, like Rowan Williams, are beginning to see a place for the recovery of the voice of religious traditions in the public square, especially religious traditions that emphasize the common good and the needs of the poor, a moral voice that offers a check on the rampant desires of the unfettered individual (or corporation or nation) to acquire and exploit. As these voices gather force, we would be well to recall the solutions offered by Progressive Christians a hundred years ago. It is worth taking another look at Vida Scudder's appeal to simplicity rather than mindless consumption, and to the common life, in solidarity with people across the class, race, and religious lines that we use to separate ourselves from humanity. Our own hymnal, with

---

26. In a lecture at Northwestern University, October 23, 2002.

prayers drawn from scripture, contains the blueprints for this new theological imagination, capturing the eschatological hope that a hundred years ago changed American society. It is time to go back to those sources, and to give new words for a new hope for this troubled and complex day.

14

An Augustinian Reflection on the Church and Hope

GEORGE H. TAVARD

AS THE EXPECTED FULFILLMENT of the purpose of God for the creation, the eschaton, when the creatures will fulfill their purpose, is the ultimate object of Christian hope. One cannot have faith in God as revealed in Jesus Christ without looking forward to the consummation of all things according to the Creator's will. The early liturgies of both East and West incorporated this perspective in the church's prayer. The "Come, Lord Jesus," of Revelation 22:20, and the *Maranatha* of the *Didachè* (XI, 6) even marked the start of a millenarist perspective which, according to Papias of Hierapolis (second century), was the teaching of presbyters in the Johannine tradition. It was projected, at least in the Epistle of Barnabas, as a reign of Christ on earth on the seventh day, following six days of a thousand years each, that in turn will be followed by the eighth day, eternity in heaven (XV, 5–9). The teaching was accepted by St. Irenaeus,[1] who himself belonged squarely, by his background in Asia Minor, in the Johannine tradition.

The millenarist perspective represented one strand in the expectation of the eschaton in the early church. Another strand

---

1. *Adversus Haereses*, book V, chaps. 34–35.

informed the liturgies of both East and West as they developed in key cities of Palestine, the Levant, Thrace, Egypt, and Italy. This liturgical feature has remained more prominent in the East than in the West. Nonetheless, the theme of the Last Judgment frequently decorated the central porch of gothic cathedrals. As they entered the building the medieval faithful were reminded of the church's expectation of the end and the fulfillment of all the promises, so that the Second Coming was already present, if not always explicitly, in the horizon of worship.

Few authors in the Latin tradition have written about this topic as much as St. Augustine. His mature thought was expressed in the last books of *De civitate Dei*, where he recorded his reflections on the decline of the Roman Empire, symbolic, as he thought, of the future end of the world. It took a long time for Augustine, however, to formulate his views on the City of God and its contrast with the cities of men. There was a development in his thought, and one may wonder if, when he wrote the last books of *The City of God,* he had forgotten some of the points he had made in the *Confessions.*

*

Around the year 400, when the Confessions were composed, Augustine's problem was to figure out philosophically, in line with his recent interest in the books of the Neoplatonists, how the interior world of the soul relates to the outside world. Augustine centered his reflection on a discussion of the nature of memory. Being the repository of past actions, each person's memory is a "vast and infinite sanctuary"[2] that keeps an integral record of the successive interchanges between the soul and its body as together they pursue their human pilgrimage. It is as such "an unknown something frightening, . . . a profound and infinite multiplicity"[3]

---

2. *Confessions*, X, viii, 15.
3. *Confessions*, X, xvii, 26.

of stored experiences, good and bad. What one thus remembers remains, most of the time, unconscious. It lies under the surface, ready to be brought up to mind.

Memory, thus understood, has a direct stake in the future, since it will gather more and more data as long as one remains in this life. At each moment of time "three things are in the soul, and I do not see them elsewhere: the present memory of things past, the present attention to things present, the present expectation of things future."[4] What is yet to come will reach its high point in the final events of the world: the return of Christ for judgment, the judgment itself, and the resurrection of the flesh into eternity. Anticipations of the Second Coming, of the end of this world, and of the "second resurrection" are thus present in the memory of Christian believers, whence they may be called upon to shape new choices and actions. The blessed life in God is not fully present since it is not yet fully shared. A certain foreknowledge of it, however, is gathered from the union with God that is lived in faith, hope, and love, in the communion of the Christian church. As the scholastics would put it later, the current experience of grace gives a hint of eternal glory.

It was in keeping with this conception of memory that Augustine investigated the nature of time at great length in book XI of the *Confessions*. God, the Eternal One, created time as a dimension of matter and, by implication, of the human body, and of human existence that is inseparable from the material world. Now, just as "the sky and the earth" claim that they are not self-made,[5] and point to the divine wisdom and power that are manifest in creation, and hence to the Creator in person, so does time, as a quality of successive existence, claim that it is not itself infinite, and that there must also be eternity, a basic attribute of

---

4. *Confessions*, XI, xx, 26.
5. *Confessions*, XI, iv, 6.

the Creator. Because it is inseparable from the body and its functions, time also affects the soul, which, aware of the passing of minutes, hours, days, and years, aspires to rest in timelessness and desires the Eternal God without being able to satisfy this desire. "You made us for you, and our heart is restless until it finds rest in you," as Augustine exclaimed at the beginning of the *Confessions* (book I, i, 1). Walking today by faith in what is symbolically the sixth day of creation, the believers aspire to the rest of the seventh day: "Lord God, give us peace, — since you have given us all, — the peace of quiet, the peace of the Sabbath, the peace that has no evening."[6]

In the *Confessions* Augustine did not extend this analysis to ecclesial existence. His perspective was restricted to the individual faithful, as was logical for one who, at the time he was writing, still had little experience of the Christian community. It nevertheless implied the conviction that the church does not exist only at the level of spirit or soul since its members are embodied souls. Once the church is seen to be wider and greater than any one of the faithful, the horizon is enlarged immeasurably. At the level of spirit, soul, or mind (the *nous* of the Greeks) the church is as large as the purpose of God for the human creatures.

*

How much wider the church must be as a social entity is evidently another question. Augustine faced it when he argued with the Donatists. He was involved in this controversy from about 393, when he composed a *Psalmus contra partem Donati,* to 412. This led him to equate the church, not with the Christian organization of a given people, nation, or limited geographic area, however "pure" such an institution could be, but with the entire City of God on earth. The church is the *catholica,* the universal

---

6. *Confessions,* XIII, xxxv, 50.

society of the elect. As such it gives a preview of the heavenly kingdom. Its eschatological dimension is manifest in the fullness of grace of the sacraments, which makes it on earth the prophecy and instrument of its own sublimation as the City of God in heaven, the eternal kingdom.

While this horizon was of major importance for later ecclesiological developments, it left questions open regarding the relationship between the present and the eschaton. How does its hold on the past in memory prepare the *ecclesia* for the eternal kingdom? How does the lived and known tradition actively prepare the eschaton?

*

In the years 417–19, Augustine was persistently urged by Hesychius, bishop of Salone, to explain his understanding of the Second Advent of Christ according to the scriptures. Specifically, Hesychius asked for an interpretation of a certain number of specific passages. In his final and longest response (*Epistola* CXCIX), Augustine made clear his opinion that the reading of these texts by Hesychius was excessively literal. He therefore emphasized the spiritual dimension that should inform biblical exegesis and the Christian expectation of the end. Briefly, one should not attempt to find out when the Lord will return to the earth; one should rather prepare for his coming, whenever this may happen, by living in faith, hope, and love.

A hint in the direction of a more precise answer about the relation of the present to the eschaton was given in the brief theology of hope that Augustine formulated, around 421, at the end of the *Enchiridion on faith, hope, and love*. The confession of faith, "considered spiritually, is the food of the strong, from which the good hope of the faithful is born, accompanied by holy charity."[7]

---

7. *Enchiridion*, XXX, 114.

In the thirteenth century Thomas Aquinas, and with him most of the scholastics, would say that living faith must be informed by charity (*Summa Theologiae*, II-II q. 4 a. 3). Aquinas added that the object of hope is *ipsum Deum*, "God as such" (II-II q. 17 a. 1). He also taught that hope bears, primarily, on "the eternal life that consists in the fruition of God" (*in fruitione ipsius Dei:* II-II q. 17 a. 2), and, secondarily, on the graces that will be necessary to reach the blessed life (II-II q. 17 a. 4). Among these graces the Second Advent of Christ and the events of the end of time will be prominent, though Thomas does not make this explicit at this point.

Augustine's perspective was in a sense the reverse: Hope and love are the fruits of faith. Faith affirms the present gifts from God. On this basis hope looks forward to the future, not a temporal future, but the absolute future of the eternal realities that are prayed for in the first three petitions of the Lord's Prayer in the Gospel of Matthew, that is, the sanctification of God's name, the coming of God's kingdom, the fulfillment of God's will "in heaven and on earth, which some have — not absurdly — understood to mean, in the spirit and in the body."[8] I take the sanctification of God's name to imply the acknowledgment and affirmation that God is holy, and indeed the only Holy One. The kingdom to come, in this context, is not an earthly kingdom. It is the heavenly kingdom, which is necessarily associated to the fulfillment of God's will, for in heaven nothing and no one oppose the will of God, but all are its willing instruments.

These three graces "are to be kept without end; begun here below, they increase in us in proportion to our progress; once perfect, which is to be hoped for the other life, they will be possessed forever." Again, "in that eternal life where we always hope

---

8. *Enchiridion*, XXX, 115.

to be, the sanctification of God's name, his kingdom, and his will shall remain in our spirit and our body perfectly and immortally." If, as Augustine notes, the Lord's Prayer in the Gospel of Luke has fewer petitions, this does not change the meaning and scope of hope: "God's name is sanctified in the spirit. God's kingdom will come in the resurrection of the flesh."[9] This reading of Luke seems to confirm the remark that "in heaven and on earth" may mean "in spirit and in body." For each believer the soul and the body will be brought to perfection in the eternal kingdom. The soul will become total adoration of God, and the risen body will itself be a kingdom of God. One may then say that each Christian faithful hopes in a twofold participation in God. The gift of divine participation is the glory to which God destines the believers.

While this is said in relation to the individual faithful it is also open to a broader perspective. Achieved in each person united to God in what the theological tradition will call grace and glory, sanctification and the kingdom of God acquire a collective dimension from the mutual communion of all the faithful. If then the tradition, or transmission of the scriptures and their interpretation, is identified as the church's collective memory, one may ask how the memory of each person is related to the eschaton as the spiritual fulfillment of all in glory.

*

If the decline of the Roman Empire could properly evoke the end of the world, this was in part because it marked the end of the world in which the young Augustine had been brought up and had spent the first years of his career before his conversion in Milan. In a somewhat similar way Augustine himself wrote that death is the end of the world for each individual. It is, however, only the end of this world, not the end of creation. In the general

---

9. *Enchiridion*, XXX, 11, 6.

perspective of book XX of *The City of God,* composed around 426, the chief characteristic of this end, for those who believe in Christ, is that it will bring about the "second resurrection," the rising of soul and body into heaven. This new life will not be entirely new, since all the faithful already experience the "first resurrection," when, by faith and baptism, they rise from sin into life with Christ. The personal question of what happens at death to each believer, however, does not answer the broader question of the eternal destiny of the communion of the church as a whole.

In practice the main point that Augustine discussed in this section of *The City of God* concerns the millennium of Revelation 20:6. Augustine refused to see the thousand years of the Apocalypse as a temporary reign of Christ on earth before the final testing and the end of this world. The number itself, one thousand, stands for an indefinite period of many years, which runs along the entire time of the church (*De Civitate Dei,* XX, ix, 3). In Augustine's providential conception of history this time fits neatly in the history of the world, which he divides in six ages, on the model of the week and of the six ages of human life. This multiple analogy is featured, among other places, at the very end of *The City of God* (XXII, xxx, 5). The first age went from Adam to the deluge, the second from the deluge to Abraham, the third from Abraham to King David, the fourth from David to the Babylonian captivity, the fifth from the Babylonian captivity to the birth of Christ. The sixth will go from Christ to the end of the world. The seventh age will follow. It will not be in time, and will have no successive moments. In eternity "we ourselves" will be this seventh age (*De Civitate Dei,* XXII, xxx, 5).

The Augustinian schema of the ages of the world will persist through the Middle Ages, with one major modification that speaks directly to the question of eschatology. In the theology of St. Bonaventure the seventh age of the world, described as the time of rest, runs concurrently with the sixth.[10] From their place in the continuum of the present world the faithful have access to the world to come, which is not only future but also, as it were, parallel to the present life, though out of time.

The medieval interpretation of the relation of the church to the eschaton was in harmony with Augustine's affirmation of the celestial identity of the church: "Already now the church is the kingdom of Christ and the kingdom of heaven."[11] Similar expressions are frequent. Evidently, if Augustine can refer to "the church, which is the kingdom of Christ,"[12] this is because the church has the same Lord on earth and in heaven. As he announced it in 412, at the start of his long reflection on the City of God, Augustine wished to speak of "the most glorious City of God, whether in the course of time when, living by faith, it is on pilgrimage among the impious, or in the stability of the eternal setting (*aeterna sede*) for which it now waits in patience...."[13] The Lord being the same, the mode of lordship differs. And if, in the medieval schema of the six and seven ages, the church in heaven is parallel to the church on earth before eventually absorbing it, it remains that the Lord does not rule in the same way in heaven and on earth. Augustine himself did not confuse the two reigns. It was to protect the faithful from such confusion that medieval theologians and canonists stressed the distinction between the church militant and the church triumphant.

*

It is easy, however — and this temptation was felt by many medieval spiritual movements — to confuse ecclesial militancy and ecclesial triumph, and to conflate the two realms in one's

---

10. "Secunda aetas concurrit cum sexta, scilicet animarum requies post passioànem Christi" (*Collationes in Hexaëmeron*, XV, 18).
11. "Ergo et nunc ecclesia est regnum Christi et regnum coelorum" (*De Civitate Dei*, XX; ix; 2).
12. "...ecclesia quid est regnum Dei."
13. *De Civitate Dei*, preamble.

mind. When this happens, concern for the eschaton is exposed to opposite perils. On one side, anticipation of the heavenly kingdom can be thought to bring immediate liberation from human precepts and restraints, as though doing the opposite of what laws command could result from the believers' present share in the ultimate freedom of the saints. By reaction, the accusation of immorality was standard against movements that claimed to be especially pure, as happened in the struggles against Priscillian (d. 386) and his followers, or against the Cathars in the early thirteenth century.

On the other side, the confusion of the two realms of heaven and earth can give rise to moral legalism, the assumption that obedience to a system of laws will gain access to the kingdom of heaven, as though human regulations functioned as rules of entry into eternity. Then the commandments are likely to be multiplied or added to by further obligations drawn from customs, conventions, tribal or national prejudices, habits of mind, patriarchal or matriarchal principles, racial prejudices, and irrational taboos. Carried to its logical end, this way leads to an ethical fundamentalism in which laws bear no exception and must be applied literally; with the result that eagerness to ensure uniform and universal justice destroys canonical equity.

A different and more damaging speculation about the kingdom of the saints took shape at the end of the twelfth century, when the very ascetic Joachim of Fiore (d. 1201) announced the dawning of an "age of the Spirit" that would reveal the "eternal gospel." The expected happening would take place around the year 1260. Joachim's eschatology derived largely from a misreading of the Apocalypse, a distortion of Augustine's six ages of the world, and a misunderstanding of the Trinitarian doctrine of God. Following Joachimite conceptions, the Franciscan Order was thrown in turmoil when Giovanni da Borgo San Donnino, in

1254, identified St. Francis as the exemplification of the eternal gospel.

*

In view of these developments one may well wonder if there was something in the heritage of Augustine that allowed such wrong turns to be taken. In fact Augustine's conception of memory as the storehouse of the past provided no criterion for the proper use of the past, though one could be drawn from his systematic practice in the *Confessions* of repenting sins and failures, constantly praying for divine grace, and glorifying God for everything good. Thus the faithful should make good use of their own sinful past. When it comes to the communion of the church and the recourse it should have to its tradition, which naturally looks to the past, in order to prepare the future, a criterion that may be useful to individuals does not work if, as is the case in the Catholic and the Orthodox views, the church is believed to be holy regardless of its members' sinfulness and sins. In this case, what members of the church recover from the tradition can feed notions and actions that will turn out to be heterodox and deleterious. Augustine's City of God on earth needs a tool to control the use of the collective Christian memory.

In the Counter-Reformation, and already in the theologies of Thomas Aquinas and of Bonaventure, this tool is the *magisterium* acting under the assistance of the Holy Spirit. This, however, as the Reformers pointed out, does little more than displace the question, which then becomes: When can the faithful be certain that the Holy Spirit has so assisted the bishops that they should be trusted to teach what is true and command what is right? The need for a more exact criterion led Vatican Council I in 1870 to define the infallibility of pronouncements made by the bishop of Rome under the specific conditions of definitions *ex cathedra*.

And then the question became: When can the faithful be sure that the conditions have been met?

*

There could be another way to face the question that is posited when Augustine's understanding of memory is applied to the church's collective tradition. This way is suggested by what St. John of the Cross wrote around 1584, in *The Ascent of Mount Carmel* (part III, chaps. 1–15), concerning the purification of memory that is necessary for union with God. To put it briefly, memory, the natural faculty of remembering, has to become, under grace, a supernatural faculty of forgetting. It should forget everything from the past that can be an impediment on the way to the heavenly kingdom. The instrument of this forgetting is no other than the virtue of hope, for theological hope looks forward exclusively to the kingdom of God. As such it is radically differently from human expectation, which only looks forward to better things happening tomorrow. Theological hope pays no heed to what the memory has kept that does not promote the kingdom, even if this belongs in the area of holy things or spiritual knowledge. The reason for this radicalism is quite simple: "In the measure that individuals dispossess their memory of forms and objects which are not God they will fix it on God and preserve it empty, so as to expect the fullness of their memory from God."[14]

As he wrote these lines the Carmelite doctor was concerned about the believers' personal holiness. He did not attempt to make this principle a rule for the church as the communion of all who believe in Christ. The long hand of the Spanish Inquisition would presumably have interfered with any presumption to

---

14. *The Ascent of Mount Carmel,* III, chap. 15; 1; *The Collected Works of St. John of the Cross,* trans. Kieran Kavanaugh and Otilio Rodriguez (Washington, D.C.: ICS Publications, 1991), 290.

tell the church's authority what to do. If one pursued this line of thought, however, the whole church should look forward to the Christ to come rather than back to its past. Straining ahead it would see only the Spirit of God leading it through the darkness of faith, through the commitments of love, toward the fulfillment of hope. As I have written elsewhere, "the very heart of the tradition... is the mystery of the future as well as the commemoration of the past and the experience of the present, which demands to be lived as hope as much as faith and love."[15]

One may of course wonder what concrete measures this should mean for the permanent reform of the church for which Vatican Council II called for in the constitution *Lumen gentium,* when it spoke of "the Church,... holy and always to be purified."[16] It would be a contradiction, however, to work out a blueprint of spiritual reformation. One point is nevertheless certain: What a radically Godward orientation will imply in terms of remembering the past, formulating and confessing the creeds in new languages, identifying dogmas, developing spiritualities, building institutions, and determining rules of behavior, may for the time being be left to the Spirit, who can be trusted to unveil it in good time.

---

15. *La tradition au dix-septième siècle en France et en Angleterre* (Paris: Editions du Cerf, 1969), 510.
16. "sancta simul et semper purificanda" (*Lumen gentium,* n. 8).

15

Baptismal Living

Steadfast Covenant of Hope

FREDRICA HARRIS THOMPSETT

BAPTISM IS DEEPLY GROUNDED in the generosity of God. Like all other biblical covenants, whether the Hebraic covenants of Noah, Abraham and Sarah, Moses, Jeremiah, or the New Covenant proclaimed by Paul and others, baptism is a response to God's initiating love. Today we who are called forth by water and the Spirit are, like our biblical ancestors, summoned to lifelong relationship with God. The theological foundation for baptismal living is grounded in the expectant hope that God holds for God's people, pursued in humanity's hope-filled response in seeking God's reign, and expressed in the persistent hopefulness of daily living. As the traditional hymn text asserts: "All our hope on God is founded!"[1]

Two contemporary shifts necessitate renewed critical attention to baptism and to the formative, hope-filled theological foundations of this sacrament. The first shift is liturgical and the second societal. One major perspective for change is evident in the positive ecumenical and denominational achievements of the

---

An earlier version of this essay appeared in the *Anglican Theological Review* 86, no. 1 (Winter 2004): 9–18. Used with permission.

1. See "All my hope on God is founded," Hymn 665, *The Hymnal 1982* (New York: Church Hymnal Corporation, 1982).

modern liturgical renewal movement, which has restored baptism to a central place of liturgical prominence and religious identity. We know that the loving-kindness of God exceeds our responsive sacramental representations. Even so, from time to time in the church's history, we move liturgically closer to the glimpses of covenanting partnership. Liturgical renewal during the second half of the twentieth century offered contemporary Christians the opportunity to renew their theological understanding of baptism. Anglicans, among other Christians, have moved in our worship settings from observance of a sacrament typically focused upon a family's private celebration of a moment in an infant's life to deeper comprehension of promises publicly made, shared, held, and affirmed in gathered community amid individual lifetimes of godly living. We are moving away from patterns that have obscured the fact of God's goodness in creation. Ecumenically, as affirmed in the World Council of Church's text *Baptism, Eucharist, and Ministry*, baptismal theology has shifted from focused emphasis upon the stain of original sin to the promise of new life in Christ. Today, for example, the central question prompted in infant baptism is not, as with many in the past, "What happens if the infant dies?" Whether the candidate for baptism is an infant, a youth, or an adult convert, contemporary pastoral preparation for baptism holds meaning for life. In the situation of infant baptism, we might aptly rephrase the question, "What happens if the infant (or adult) lives?"[2] For all participants — candidates, godparents, sponsors, and the community gathered to witness and support baptismal promises — the gift of baptism extends life-changing implications.

A second shift that impels contemporary reexamination of religious formation in baptism today is occasioned by the context

---

2. Herbert Anderson and Edward Foley, *Mighty Stories, Dangerous Rituals: Weaving Together the Human and the Divine* (San Francisco: Jossey-Bass, 1998), 70.

of violent religious divisions and genocide. The genocidal impact of the Holocaust changed the shape of theology, underscoring the problem for Christians and Jews alike in speaking of God "after Auschwitz."[3] It is a startling fact that 45 million Christians were also martyred during the twentieth century, from those Armenians executed for their faith early in the century up through the 800,000 Tutsis massacred in Rwanda toward the century's end.[4]

In these and other massive outbreaks of ethnic cleansing, religious identity and religious rhetoric have been used to polarize and divide. With such compelling claims upon our attention in communities of faith and within the wider global community, we dare not fantasize or become nostalgic about religious rites of initiation. Nor is it biblically honest to hold privatized religious commitments that are blind to the suffering of others or that are otherworldly. Nor, in this increasingly multifaith world, can people of any faith hoard God's generosity in one religious tradition. In such hard times, attempts to speak honestly about formative religious identity today carry a critical urgency that encompasses multifaith visions of reconciliation.

For Christians, baptism provides an optimistic and hopeful orientation that paradoxically situates us amid human suffering in the world for which Christ died. Anglican liturgical scholar Louis Weil strongly advocates the renewal of baptismal theology as a foundation that will allow us to "coexist with other world religions" and with those who are indifferent to religion.[5] Weil,

---

3. See, for example, Moltmann's autobiographical note on the development of his theology of hope in A. J. Conyers, *God, Hope, and History: Jürgen Moltmann and the Christian Concept of History* (Macon, Ga.: Mercer University Press, 1988), 203-23; and Elie Wiesel, *After the Darkness: Reflections on the Holocaust*, trans. Benjamin Moser (New York: Schocken Books, 2002).

4. See Michael J. McClymond, *Journal of the American Academy of Religion* (December 2002) with statistics drawn from the *World Christian Encyclopedia* (Oxford: Oxford University Press, 2001); and Donald E. Miller, "April Is the Cruelest Month," *Sightings* (May 2, 2003), The Martin Marty Center at the University of Chicago Divinity School.

5. Louis Weil, *A Theology of Worship* (Cambridge, Mass.: Cowley Publications, 2002), 127.

among others, calls for the renewal of a baptismal ecclesiology that is effective liturgically, socially, and globally. This essay theologizes from the standpoint of hope as it is embedded in baptismal living, liturgically represented in covenantal promises, expressed in ministry, directly attentive to evil and suffering, and open to dialogue with people of other faith communities. As a lifelong Episcopalian, I experience and will recount the baptismal story as biblically grounded and liturgically expressed in the Prayer Book service of Holy Baptism. In particular the "baptismal covenant" found in the 1979 Book of Common Prayer sets a hopeful framework for baptismal living. I have shaped the structure of these reflections in accord with the creedal affirmation and the five promises made by those who wish to renew their commitment to Christ in the baptismal covenant.

The theological emphasis in baptism is based on God's action, expresses God's hopeful interest in humanity, and reveals God's generosity in creation. The great neoorthodox theologian Karl Barth is said to have remarked: "God is omnipotent, God is omniscient, and now a few words about baptism." Theologically when we set about to remember baptism, it is important to recall that in baptism, as in creation, we are laden with God's energy and spirit. Baptism is not simply or only an individual decision, it is primarily about God acting and the community of faith responding. It is God's doing that calls forth our responsiveness. Baptism is an expression of God's hope for a people: created, chosen, and adopted anew as God's own. In the earliest Prayer Book services Thomas Cranmer liturgically accentuated, in the promises made and assurances given, that the newly baptized are joyfully received into the arms of Christ.[6] Indeed Anglican theologians from Richard Hooker and F. D. Maurice up to the

---

6. See Stephen Sykes, "Baptisme Doth Represente unto Us Oure Profession," *Unashamed Anglicanism* (Nashville: Abingdon, 1995), 3–23.

present day have emphasized that baptism declares God's goodness to humanity. At one time Maurice, frustrated by the sole emphasis placed on original sin by some of his contemporaries instead of on the promise of baptismal renewal for humanity, is said to have exclaimed, "We are called Christians, not Adamites." Similarly in a nineteenth-century Church of England sermon, a colleague of Maurice described baptism as commencing "with a benediction, and not with a curse."[7] Bill Countryman, a New Testament scholar and Episcopal priest, recently described baptism as interpreting "the gift bestowed in birth." This sacrament reaffirms and renews the holy character of creation. It expresses God's continuing engagement with and hope for humanity.

Appropriately our response to God in the baptismal covenant starts with an affirmation of faith. This covenant begins with the Apostles' Creed recalling Jesus' life, death, and resurrection, and affirming God's triune nature. The 1979 Prayer Book liturgy retains the historical development of creeds as baptismal statements. Moreover, reciting the creed as presented in the contemporary baptismal covenant recalls the early Christian baptismal practice where the creed was spoken by the candidate for baptism in response to three questions. In today's Prayer Book service all present are invited to participate in the creedal affirmation of faith. Each time a baptism takes place, members of the congregation are more than observers, witnesses, or even sponsors; all are able to renew their faith in a God who extends a new covenant of hope to humanity.

From the people's affirmation of faith in the Apostles' Creed, the baptismal covenant proceeds to address what one priest aptly

---

7. J. L. Davies, "Baptism: An Admission to the Privilege of Worship," in *The Worship of God and Fellowship among Men: A Series of Sermons on Public Worship Preached at Christ Church, St. Marylebone* (Cambridge: Macmillan, 1858), 66.

calls "the consequences of faith in daily living."[8] What kind of responses will each of us make in our daily lives? In the baptismal covenant all present are invited to respond to a framework of five questions that move from commitments to continuing formation, to repentance, proclamation, service, and seeking justice and peace. There are several different and appropriate ways to explore the five promises in the baptismal covenant. Ian Douglas, for example, points to this covenant as a charter for the baptized to engage in mission.[9] In *Living Water,* Klara Tammany provides multidimensional pathways for adult formation built around baptismal promises.[10] Deborah Flemister Mullen describes baptism from an African American perspective as a "Sacrament of Struggle."[11] I have chosen to frame these questions as expressing a covenant of hope. This accords biblically with God's overriding purpose in offering humanity a future and a hope. Even in times of serious displacement, as presented again and again by the prophets, God's hope is for the long haul, it is not for a quick fix or a fast "return to normalcy."[12] The First Letter of Peter, sometimes described as a sermon on baptism, proclaims "new birth into a living hope" (1:3).[13] This is an ongoing process. Baptism does not rest alone on a past promise taken by us or for us by others, nor is it a pledge to ensure our future security. Hope is the basis for our present and continuing response,

---

8. Christopher L. Webber, *A User's Guide to Morning Prayer and Baptism* (Harrisburg, Pa.: Morehouse Publishing, 1997), 37.

9. Ian T. Douglas, "Baptized into Mission: Ministry and Holy Orders Reconsidered," *Sewanee Theological Review* 40, no. 4 (1997): 435–36.

10. *Living Water: Baptism as a Way of Life* (New York: Church Publishing Incorporated, 2002).

11. "Baptism as Sacrament of Struggle and Rite of Resistance," in Susan E. Davies and Sister Paul Teresa Hennessey, eds., *Ending Racism in the Church* (Cleveland: United Church Press, 1998), 66–73.

12. Walter Brueggemann, *Hope within History* (Atlanta: John Knox Press, 1987), 87; Brueggemann's insights have repeatedly guided my efforts in this essay.

13. Daniel J. Harrington, *The Church According to the New Testament: What the Wisdom and Witness of Early Christianity Teach Us Today* (Franklin, Wis.: Sheed & Ward, 2001), 74.

our responsibility to God. As such it bears repeating. Sara Maitland, a Christian feminist theologian, underscores the nature of this responsibility:

> Hope lies rather in accepting that God's engagement in the creation gives us not just the right, but the obligation to create and sustain the future.... Hope is the basis for taking responsibility: for claiming our capacity to create, to make a genuinely new thing. It is also the springboard for trying to act justly, and for accepting absolutely our incorporation into each other.[14]

More than participating in a Sunday morning baptism and Eucharist, the baptismal covenant invites each one of us to be daily participants in living hope. Fortunately we are reminded of this responsibility to take hope each time a baptism occurs.

We are not left alone or without resources for this journey in hope. Accordingly and appropriately the first affirmation extended in the baptismal covenant is a commitment to lifelong religious formation through worship, prayer, Bible study, and life together in community. We are asked to recognize this need for ongoing formation when we pledge to "continue in the apostles' teaching and fellowship, in the breaking of bread, and in the prayers."[15] The nourishment that comes through observing the holy routine of the church year and participating in Word and Sacrament are primary ways that Anglicans "continue in the apostles' teaching." Yet just as worship is not the whole of the church's life, regular Sunday attendance is not the whole of religious formation. Sunday school is not just, nor was it ever, only for children; Christian education is not confined to Sunday. Verna

---

14. Sara Maitland, *A Big-Enough God: A Feminist's Search for a Joyful Theology* (New York: Riverhead Books, 1995), 167.
15. For this and all quotations from the Baptismal Covenant that follow see the Book of Common Prayer (New York: Church Hymnal Corporation, 1979), 304–5.

Dozier, one of the most provocative instigators of baptismal ministry, asserts that "religious authority comes with baptism."[16] If the baptized, including laity as well as clergy, are to claim their authority in church and in society, continuing study of scripture and tradition as well as attentive knowledge of contemporary life is required. Baptism signals that God has important work to do. In the baptismal covenant we commit ourselves to replenishing resources for this journey through worship, prayer, and study.

The strong language of the second promise is arresting: "Will you persevere in resisting evil, and, whenever you fall into sin, repent and return to the Lord?" The reality of systemic evil and of individual sinfulness are each directly acknowledged. This pledge reiterates the three renunciations of evil made at the time of baptism: "Satan and all the spiritual forces of evil," "the evil powers of this world," and "all sinful desires."[17] In the baptismal covenant all present recommit themselves to resist external forces of evil as well as to repent personal sins. The baptized, in the early church and in today's perilous times, live in a world marred by violence and suffering. The baptismal covenant actively addresses this condition with hopeful language of forgiveness and resistance. It recognizes starkly that there is no social transformation without personal transformation. Repentance is multidimensional and ongoing. Active, not passive, response is called forth as is perseverance over the long haul.

This lesson applies to biblical times as well as to our own. Prophets and other theologians have long recognized the need for reshaping hope in new situations. This is clear in Jeremiah's response to the exiles: "I know the plans I have for you, says

---

16. *The Calling of the Laity: Verna Dozier's Anthology* (Washington D.C.: Alban Institute, 1988), 115.

17. These three contemporary renunciations from the 1979 Book of Common Prayer, 302, replace and strengthen earlier Prayer Book references presented in a single renunciation.

the Lord, plans for welfare and not for evil, to give you a future and a hope" (29:11).[18] Augustine may have had resistance in mind when he noted that "hope has two lively daughters — courage and anger."[19] In our own day Martin Luther King Jr. often quoted words attributed to Edmund Burke, "The only thing necessary for the triumph of evil is for good men to do nothing."[20] Vincent Harding, African American historian and activist who has recounted the North American freedom movement, hails the "human potential for resistance and hope."[21] Similarly one of my faculty colleagues, Canon Ed Rodman, contends that hope lies in the opportunity to resist. All of this and more is summed up by the injunction to "persevere in resisting evil," and in the call to repent and return to the Lord. This baptismal promise puts the decision to respond to evil and sin in our hands. This is strong religious medicine, just the sort of prescriptive affirmation needed to undergird hope among God's people in times of suffering, violence, and genocide.

Another call extended to the baptized in the baptismal covenant is biblical proclamation. "Will you proclaim by word and example the Good News of God in Christ?" Scripture for Christians is our primary language, our native tongue. Directly encountering the sacred in scripture was at the core of the religious revolution we call the "Reformation." Our Protestant ancestors did not take access to their Bible book for granted; indeed they renewed worship to embrace its wisdom. Thomas Cranmer's sixteenth-century Prayer Book collect summoned his contemporaries to "hear, read, mark, learn, and inwardly digest"

---

18. See also Brueggemann, *Hope within History*, 3, 68.
19. Maitland, *A Big-Enough God*, 167.
20. Cited in Vincent Harding, *Hope and History* (Maryknoll, N.Y.: Orbis Books, 1990), 212.
21. Quoted in *YES!* 24 (Winter 2003). See also his "Letter to Teachers in Religious Communities and Institutions," *Hope and History*, 201–28.

the Bible's teaching. The contemporary version of this Collect omits Cranmer's description that scripture works "by patience and comfort of thy holy Word." Perhaps many today think the Bible should provide quicker answers. Proclamation for early Anglicans involved "patience," sounding a note similar to the call to persevere. It also worked as a "comfort."[22] Although in modern English this word is tamed into soothing images, in the sixteenth century its original meaning implied acting "with strength." The original intent of evangelization, indeed of Jesus' teaching, involved strengthening those who were with him — those called to follow him — in addition to sending out disciples to teach amid new cultures, lands, and peoples. For the baptized, the hope of transformation, the strengthening voice of comforting one another, begins at home. Proclamation, as we "inwardly digest" its strength, extends outward in word and deed. Louis Weil reminds us that a baptismal understanding of the church is "rooted in the real world."[23] Pulpits are important yet secondary way stations of evangelization; the place of proclamation for the baptized is located in everyday settings.

Scripture also tutors the baptized in exemplary living. The challenge, "Will you seek and serve Christ in all persons, loving your neighbor as yourself?" is a decidedly scriptural call to service. The baptized are sent into the world to serve in God's name. Again this baptismal promise is not designed to be tamed or confined to Sundays. The request here is not for volunteers. It is, as God's adopted own, to follow Jesus. Baptismal living does not simply mean "being good volunteers."[24] Verna Dozier bluntly asks, "Do you want to follow Jesus? Or are you content just to worship

---

22. See the 1979 Book of Common Prayer, 184 and 236.
23. Weil, *A Theology of Worship*, 18.
24. I owe this observation to my faculty colleague and state representative, Byron Rushing.

him?"[25] The call to discipleship, to service in the world, is not privatistic or for the faint of heart. It is for the baptized, the collective, steadfast body of Christ sent forth in the power of the Spirit to perform the service set before them. Such service rests on the biblical, hope-filled promise of abundant gifts for ministry, like the many charisms named in the Pauline Epistles.

The call of the baptized to committed service is demanding. Loving our neighbors may well prove costly. As Desmond Tutu repeatedly reminds audiences today, the people of God are meant to be Godlike, which we show in particular by loving our enemies. Dietrich Bonhoeffer summed up the role of the baptized in his book *The Cost of Discipleship*, as a stance that embraces suffering as a universal part of the human condition, in which God is also present. In Hitler's prisons, those who sought and received Bonhoeffer's spiritual guidance were not only fellow inmates but prison guards. Hope comes with the recognition that suffering is part of the human condition and God embraces suffering fully. As in scripture, hope emerges from the perspective of neighborly love amid the powerless and marginalized. Seeking and serving "Christ in all persons" is an all-encompassing promise.

This call to service prepares us for a fifth promise, one that builds upon each of the preceding promises affirmed in the baptism covenant and that lifts up biblical visions of hope. The commitment to "strive for justice and peace among all people, and [to] respect the dignity of every human being" is summative of the high calling of the baptized community. One of the earliest baptismal formulas signified God's promise of freedom and unity in Christ. Paul envisioned baptism as overcoming all that separates human beings from one another and God: "there is no longer Jew or Greek, there is now no longer slave or free,

---

25. *The Dream of God* (Cambridge, Mass.: Cowley Publications, 1991), 142.

there is no longer male and female; for all of you are one in Christ Jesus" (Gal. 3:27–29). An implicit message is that cultural diversity discloses God's creativity. Paul's promise of baptismal unity in Galatians is expansive as well as inclusive. Nineteenth-century theologian Frederick Denison Maurice taught that God's redemptive love was intended for all, including those of other religions. The explicit intention of the fifth baptismal promise respects the dignity of each person and culture, and commits followers of Christ to justice and peace throughout the world. It is a boundless promise.

Today, as in biblical times, religious divisions ostensibly militate against peace and justice among people of different cultures and faiths. Dare we live with hope in today's world? How might a vow to seek "justice and peace among all people" become part of daily living? One story about seeking God's shalom comes via a colleague recently returned from a church-sponsored peace mission among Palestinians. He reported stories of those who insisted that hope was a luxury they could no longer afford. A banner displayed at a massive demonstration for peace poignantly noted, "Due to present circumstances the light at the end of the tunnel has been put out." What happens if hope seems lost? What then is the responsibility of the baptized? The promises of the baptismal covenant do not stand alone. They are supported and upheld in common prayer. "Let not the hope of the poor be taken away" is a daily petition in Morning and Evening Prayer. The psalter offers comfort, as in the opening verse of Psalm 46, "God is our hope and strength, a very present help in trouble."[26]

Each of the promises in the baptismal covenant is saturated with responsive hope in God. This is repeatedly signaled by the reply offered after each of the five promises: "I will, with God's

---

26. The reading is from the 1662 Book of Common Prayer; the 1979 Prayer Book substitutes "help" for "hope."

help." Hope, as presented in this essay, is not a possession or an object. It is a living process, a "bold conviction of an alternative possibility," a promise that the present is provisional and open to change.[27] This is our inheritance, a salvific birthright that we thankfully acknowledge in the postcommunion prayer when we describe ourselves as "heirs, *through hope,* of thy everlasting kingdom."[28] Christians continue to be, as noted in early baptismal testimony from the First Letter of Peter, birthed "into a living hope." Daily we are supported in baptismal living not simply by our good intentions but by a God who stands by her adopted children in countless ways. This covenant, like all biblical covenants, evokes a living partnership, an enduring covenant of hope.

---

27. Brueggemann, *Hope within History,* 69, 80.
28. The 1979 Book of Common Prayer, 339, emphasis added.

16

The Final Reconciliation
Reflections on a Social Dimension of the Eschatological Transition

Miroslav Volf

The Last Judgment — the Final Reconciliation

When asked whether it is true that one day in heaven we will see again our loved ones, Karl Barth is reported to have responded, "Not only the loved ones!" The sting of the great theologian's response — be ready to meet there even those whom you dislike here — is more than just a personal challenge. It contains a serious and, as it turns out, inadequately addressed theological problem. How can those who have disliked or even had good reasons to hate each other here, come to inhabit together what is claimed to be, in Jonathan Edwards's memorable phrase, "a world of love"?[1] The not-loved-ones will have to be transformed into the loved ones and those who do not love will have to begin to do so; enemies will have to become friends.

An earlier version of this essay appeared in *Modern Theology* 16, no. 1 (January 2000), © Blackwell Publishers Ltd 2000, published by Blackwell Publishers Ltd, 108 Cowley Road, Oxford OX4 1JF, U.K., and 350 Main Street, Malden, MA 02148.

    1. The title of Jonathan Edwards's fifteenth sermon in the collection *Charity and Its Fruits* is "Heaven Is a World of Love" (*The Works of Jonathan Edwards*, ed., John E. Smith [New Haven, Conn.: Yale University Press, 1957–], 8:366–97). Cf. Amy Plantinga Pauw, " 'Heaven Is a World of Love': Edwards on Heaven and the Trinity," *Calvin Theological Journal* 30 (1995): 392–401.

A sense that such a social transformation is a condition of "heavenly" existence may lie behind a funeral practice in Germany in which a kind of a post-mortem reconciliation between the deceased and their enemies is enacted in the form of prayer. Participants in the burial service remember before God those whom the deceased may have wronged or who may have wronged them.[2] Popular piety is also aware of the issue. In tightly knit Christian communities one sometimes hears the injunction that their members had better learn to love each other now since they will spend eternity together. Sometime between a shadowy history and eternity bathed in light, somewhere between this world and the coming world of perfect love, a transformation of persons and their complex relationships needs to take place. Without such transformation the world to come would not be a world of perfect love but just a repetition of a world in which, at best, the purest of loves falter and, at worst, cold indifference reigns and deadly hatreds easily flare up.

Traditionally, the last judgment along with the resurrection of the dead was taken to be the site of the eschatological transition from this world to the world to come. But if the need for transformation of persons as well as of their complex relationships is a real one, the question is whether the last judgment, as usually conceived, can carry this weight. Consider Augustine, whose thought is particularly pertinent not only because his eschatology shaped significantly the later tradition[3] but because he uses the

---

2. Professor Jürgen Moltmann has drawn my attention to this custom. In the printed burial service for the prominent Tübingen New Testament scholar Professor Ernst Käsemann, we read: "Wir denken vor Gott in der Stille: an den Verstorbenen, an jene, die eng mit Ernst Käsemann verbunden waren, an jene, denen Ernst Käsemann nicht gerecht geworden ist, an jene, die ihm nicht gerecht geworden sind, und jene, die darauf warten, dass wir uns lossagen von den Herrschern, die ueber uns herrschen..." (*Transparent* 52/98, 19).

3. See Brian E. Daley, *The Hope of the Early Church: A Handbook of Patristic Eschatology* (Cambridge: Cambridge University Press, 1991), 131ff.

metaphor "peace," including social peace,[4] to describe the world to come and contrasts it to the violence of the kingdoms of this world. As he defines it in *The City of God*, the peace of the coming world is "perfectly ordered and harmonious enjoyment of God and of one another in God."[5] Notice, however, how Augustine describes the eschatological transition from the world of violence to the world of peace. "Now, it is through the last judgment that men pass to these ends, the good to the supreme good, the evil to the supreme evil,"[6] writes Augustine. The last judgment is a divine act directed toward individuals which definitively executes the division of humanity into damned and saved and apportions appropriate rewards and punishments. If one operates, however, with a robust notion of social peace at whose center is the enjoyment of one another in God, as Augustine does, then it is easy to see how the last judgment can be indispensable to such a peace but difficult to see how it can be sufficient to usher it in.

According to Augustine, the last judgment concerns primarily matters of justice;[7] it separates "the good" and "the bad"[8] and ensures that "the true and full happiness" be "the lot of none but the good" and "deserved and supreme misery" be "the portion of the wicked, and of them only."[9] Unless, contrary to Augustine's claim, the good are already creatures of perfect love, the execution of such justice will not make them love in the world to come those whom they may not have loved now.[10] Granted, for Augustine the

---

4. On the social character of Augustine's eschatology see Henri Irenée Marrou, *The Resurrection and Saint Augustine's Theology of Human Values*, trans. M. Consolata (Villanova, Pa.: Villanova University Press, 1966), 33.

5. Augustine, *The City of God*, in Whitney J. Oates, ed., *Basic Writings of Saint Augustine* (New York: Random House, 1948), xix, 17.

6. Ibid., xix, 18.
7. Ibid., xx, 1–3.
8. Ibid., xx, 22.
9. Ibid., xx, 1.

10. In his critical engagement with the doctrine of the last judgment, Friedrich Schleiermacher rightly noted that the notion of the last judgment as separation of the believing and unbelieving requires as supplement a notion of the "inner separation" of believers

last judgment is but *one* aspect of the eschatological transition toward heavenly peace. Another is the resurrection — an aspect of the ontological *novum* that a comprehensive *transformatio mundi* represents — which heals the weakness of the flesh and clothes the person in *immortalitas* and *incorruptio*.[11] The last judgment and the *transformatio mundi* together would create sufficient conditions for mutual human enjoyment; together they are meant not only to make perfect love possible, but sin impossible. The two would indeed be all we need if the eschatological transition were a creation of a brand-new world of love, rather than a transformation of the existing world of enmity into a world of love. But the contrary is the case. Unlike the present world, the world to come will not be created *ex nihilo* but *ex vetere*.[12] Hence either only those who are already fully reconciled in this world could be admitted into the coming world or the reconciliation would have to occur as part of the eschatological transition itself. The first option seems excluded by Augustine's belief that one cannot have complete peace in this life.[13] The second, which Augustine does not explore,[14] needs to be developed if the eschatological

---

from "those elements of sinfulness and carnality which still cling to them." Such inner separation, he claimed, "would simply be completed sanctification." *The Christian Faith*, trans. H. R. Mackintosh and J. S. Stewart (Philadelphia: Fortress, 1976), 714 [#162].

11. See Stanislaw Budzik, *Doctor pacis: Theologie des Friedens bei Augustinus* (Innsbruck: Tyrolia Verlag, 1988), 310–22.

12. See John Polkinghorne, *The Faith of a Physicist: Reflections of a Bottom-up Thinker* (Princeton, N.J.: Princeton University Press, 1994), 167; Jürgen Moltmann, *The Coming of God: Christian Eschatology*, trans. Margaret Kohl (Philadelphia: Fortress, 1996), 265.

13. Cf. Augustine, *Basic Writings of Saint Augustine*, xx, 9.

14. Augustine's comments on purgatorial punishments (ibid., xx, 25; xxi, 24) may leave space open for this second option. The later developments of the doctrine of purgatory thematize only the individual's standing before God — and in relation to *that* problem they also speak of the relation of the pilgrim church and the church triumphant to the church suffering. Individuals' standing before one another — the history of their mutual sin and the need for reconciliation — is dealt with at the threshold of purgatory. Though the souls in purgatory "love each other with a supernatural charity which has its source in God," which makes purgatory "a region of that perfect fraternal charity, so easily missed on earth," there nonetheless is "scarcely a soul in Purgatory that is not expiating some faults against charity." Martin Jugie, *Purgatory and the Means to Avoid It*, trans. M. G. Carroll (Westminster, Md.: Newman Press, 1949), 41. But given that they perfectly love each other, nothing needs to change in their relationship while in purgatory; since they

transition is to reorder human relations such that human beings enjoy not only God but also one another.

Whereas justice is central in Augustine's theology of the last judgment, grace is central in Martin Luther's. The thought of judgment according to works is present, but it is integrated into the overarching judgment of grace.[15] For believers, the last judgment is not so much a process by which the moral quality of human deeds is made unmistakably manifest and appropriate rewards and punishments apportioned, but above all an event in which sinners are forgiven and justified. Christ the final judge is none other than Christ the merciful savior. "To me," writes Luther, "he is a physician, helper, and deliverer from death and the devil."[16] The Johannine Jesus says, "anyone who comes to me I will never drive away" (John 6:37). Luther interprets him to mean:

> Let it be your one concern to come to Me and to have the grace to hold, to believe, and to be sure in your heart that I was sent into the world for your sake, that I carried out the will of My Father and was sacrificed for your atonement, righteousness, sanctification, and redemption, and bore all punishment for you. If you believe this, do not fear. I do not want to be your judge, executioner, or jailer, but your Savior and Mediator, yes, your kind, loving Brother and good Friend. But you must abandon your work-righteousness and remain with Me in firm faith.[17]

---

are in purgatory, they are not in need of reconciliation. If former enemies, they are rather eager "to show the sincerity of their reconciliation" (42).

15. See Ole Modalsli, "Luther über die Letzten Dinge," in Helmar Junghans, ed., *Leben und Werk Martin Luthers von 1526 bis 1546: Festgabe zu seinem 500. Geburtstag* (Göttingen: Vandenhoeck & Ruprecht, 1983), 1:334–44.

16. Martin Luther, "Sermon on Luke 7:11–17," in Eugene F. A. Klug, ed. and trans., *Sermons of Martin Luther: The House Postils* (Grand Rapids, Mich.: Baker Books, 1996), iii, 34.

17. Martin Luther, *Luther's Works*, ed. Jaroslav Pelikan, and trans. M. H. Bertram (St. Louis, Mo.: Concordia Publishing House, 1959), xxiii, 58.

Divine judgment at the end of history completes divine justification, grounded in Christ's redemptive work, in the middle of history.[18]

Yet it is not clear how the final justification of the ungodly would *as such* create a world of love — not even if we take it to include what Friedrich Schleiermacher has called "complete sanctification."[19] No doubt, it would ensure that we would meet in the world to come even those whom we have not considered particularly lovable in the present one. But for us to *love* the unlovable, two things would need to happen. First, in a carefully specified sense we ourselves would need to "justify" them, and, given that they may consider us no more lovable than we consider them, they would also need to "justify" us, and we all would need to receive this "justification" from each other.[20] Second, above and beyond giving and receiving justification, we would also need to want to be in communion with one another. To usher in a world of love, the eschatological transition would need to be understood not only as a divine act toward human beings but also as *a social event between human beings,* more precisely, a divine act toward human beings which is also a social event between them. Or so I would like to argue in this essay.

Put in the form of a question about the perpetrator and the victim of the first violence in primal history, the subject I will explore is this: If Cain and Abel were to meet again in the world to come, what will need to have happened between them for Cain

---

18. For a powerful contemporary restatement of this position see, for instance, Eberhard Jüngel, "The Last Judgment as an Act of Grace," *Louvain Studies* 15 (1990): 389–405.

19. Schleiermacher, *The Christian Faith,* 714.

20. The refusal to *receive* "justification" from the other entails a refusal to see oneself as the other sees one and to accept the way the other relates to one. It constitutes therefore refusal of communion, at least until perspectives have been readjusted. This anthropological phenomenon makes plain why soteriologically unbelief, understood as refusal to receive divine justification, constitutes a rejection of communion between God and oneself, especially since, unlike judgments of our human neighbors, God's judgment of us entailed in the offer of justification is, by definition, infallible.

not to keep avoiding Abel's look and for Abel not to want to get out of Cain's way? Put in a form of a thesis, the argument I will develop is this: If the world to come is to be a world of love, then the eschatological transition from the present world to that world, which God will accomplish, must have an interhuman side; the work of the Spirit in the consummation[21] includes not only the resurrection of the dead and the last judgment but also the final social reconciliation.

The thesis is novel, or at least severely underemphasized and underdeveloped. Some contemporary theologians have come close to advocating it, however. Reflecting on the shape of social relations in the world to come, Friedrich Mildenberger suggests in his *Biblische Dogmatik* that we think of the last judgment as an act of purging, in which aspects of human relationships compatible with the perfected world remain and those incompatible burn up. In some ways, this is a contemporary restatement of the notion of judgment as purification rather than punishment, prevalent in the Eastern tradition. Mildenberger understands the eschatological purification, however, against the background of socially constructed identities. Since human identities are shaped by relationships and since relationships can be freighted with evil, for the perfect sociality to emerge evil residues of relationships must be removed.[22] He seems to imply, however, that the removal of sin can take place without the involvement of people who stood in those relationships, a kind of divine readjustment of individual identities structurally comparable to the one expressed in the image of earthly attachments being scraped off the soul as it is

---

21. For a discussion of the eschatological consummation as the work of the Spirit see Wolfhart Pannenberg, *Systematic Theology*, trans. Geoffrey W. Bromiley (Grand Rapids, Mich.: Eerdmans, 1998), 3:550–55.
22. See Friedrich Mildenberger, *Biblische Dogmatik: Eine Biblische Theologie in dogmatischer Perspektive. Band 3. Theologie als Oekonomie* (Stuttgart: Kohlhammer, 1993), 279–80.

drawn to God, which Gregory of Nyssa employs in *On the Soul and the Resurrection*.[23] But to concentrate exclusively on individuals and disregard their relationships is to sacrifice in the account of the way a person is freed from sin the fundamental insight into how the identity of a human being as a person and as a sinner is constructed. If identities are constructed and have been injured in a social process, should then not their healing, too, involve a social process, even if one grants that much of the healing can happen internally to an individual person?

Wolfhart Pannenberg seems implicitly to advocate the equivalent of what I call "the final reconciliation." Exploring how antagonisms between the individual and society will be overcome in the world to come, he writes in *Systematic Theology*, "God is the future of the finite from which it again receives its existence as a whole as that which has been, and at the same time accepts all other creaturely being along with itself."[24] The reception of one's own existence as perfected by God must go hand in hand with the acceptance of others. To be eschatologically fruitful, the notion of acceptance, which Pannenberg only suggests, would need to be unpacked and its full social and temporal dimensions elaborated. But the notion points in the right direction because it implies that before the antagonism between individual and society can be overcome — before the world of love can be created — *relationships* between human beings must be transformed.[25]

---

23. Gregory of Nyssa writes: "Wrapped up as it is in material and earthly attachments, it (the soul) struggles and is stretched, as God draws His own to Himself. What is alien to God has to be scraped off forcibly because it has somehow grown onto the soul." *On the Soul and the Resurrection*, trans. Catharine P. Roth (Crestwood, N.Y.: St. Vladimir's Seminary Press, 1993), 84.
24. Pannenberg, *Systematic Theology*, 607.
25. After I had already argued for the final reconciliation in "Sin, Death, and the Life of the World to Come" (prepared for the consultation on "Eschatology and Science" at the Center of Theological Inquiry, Princeton), I came across an article by Josef Niewiadomski, at the end of which he briefly suggests something like "the final reconciliation" as an interhuman process. He imagines the last judgment as an event in which all victims and all perpetrators will face each other and in which the evil suffered and inflicted will be

My argument that the final social reconciliation is an integral element of the Spirit's work in the consummation will proceed in three simple steps. First, I will examine one notable example of "the final reconciliation" in philosophical literature — Socrates' comments about the last judgment in *Phaedo* — and via an appreciative critique of Socrates lay the groundwork for my own proposal. Second, I will offer positive theological reasons for advocating "the final social reconciliation" by relating it to the nature of human beings, the character of sin, and the shape of salvation. Finally, I will engage two questions which provide critical test cases for the plausibility of the thesis: (1) whether it is compatible with the affirmations that human beings were reconciled with one another in Christ and (2) that the subject of the eschatological transition is God rather than human beings. Before embarking upon my journey I should note that, though a particular notion of the last judgment is central to my arguments, I am able to develop the notion of the last judgment in this text only as it relates directly to the final social reconciliation.

Victims' Mercy — Perpetrators' Salvation

One rare but notable philosophical text which advocates the possibility and the need of a post-mortem reconciliation is the

---

fully manifest to each person. Were it not for God's immeasurable goodness and unlimited willingness to forgive, such an encounter of victims and perpetrators would amount to a day of wrath in which all, prone as human beings are to self-justification and accusation of others, would condemn each other to hell. "Each would insist on his or her own status as a victim, each would demand retaliation and each would seek to place on others the punishment that he or she ought to receive." "Hoffnung im Gericht: Soteriologische Impulse für eine dogmatische Eschatologie," *Zeitschrift für katholische Theologie* 114 (1992): 126. Yet, faced with the radical grace of divine forgiveness, "hardly anyone will withhold forgiveness and continue to insist anachronistically upon his or her own right and revenge" (126). The judgment day will therefore be a day on which divine mercy toward humanity will elicit individuals' mercy toward each other. As will become clear at the end of my essay, my proposal differs from Niewiadomski's in two major respects. First, he does not ground the appropriation of the final judgment of grace pneumatologically, and, second, he fails to make the critical step from forgiveness to reconciliation.

"eschatological myth" in Plato's *Phaedo*. As I will elaborate shortly, many aspects of that myth are theologically problematic. Christian theology will do well, however, to appropriate, reformulate, and develop some of its basic insights. Before engaging the text, I ought to clarify a hermeneutical question. I will eschew the debate of Plato scholars about the proper interpretation of the "mythical" character of the text. It is not clear in the dialogue how precisely the mythic "tale" relates to the preceding arguments. Socrates himself says that, though the tale of "the soul and her mansions" is not "exactly true," "inasmuch as the soul is shown to be immortal," we may "venture to think, not improperly or unworthily, that something of the kind is true."[26] Given that Socrates has *argued* for the immortality of the soul, and therefore for a particular "nature of the pilgrimage" which he was "about to make,"[27] I will take him at his word and interpret the myth as a narratival rendering, made necessary by the limitations of discursive analysis,[28] of a future afterlife, rather than, for example, primarily an image of the present life.[29]

Toward the end of the eschatological myth Socrates, who is about to execute on himself the sentence of death by drinking poison, tells his friends about the sentences the dead will have passed on them when they "arrive at the place to which the genius...conveys them." Of the five groups in which he divides humanity, the sentences for four groups are predictable, more or less. Those "who appear to be incurable by reason of the greatness of their crime" are "hurled into Tartarus" ("a chasm which

---

26. Plato, *Phaedo*, 114d, in *Dialogues of Plato*, trans. B. Jowett (Oxford: Clarendon Press, 1875).
27. Ibid., 61d.
28. See David A. White, *Myth and Metaphysics in Plato's Phaedo* (Selinsgrove, Pa.: Susquehanna University Press, 1989).
29. See Kenneth Dorter, *Plato's Phaedo: An Interpretation* (Toronto: University of Toronto Press, 1982).

pierces right through the whole earth"[30]) "which is their suitable destiny, and they never come out." Those "who appear to have lived neither well nor ill" — the great majority of people[31] — are "purified of their evil deeds" and "receive the rewards of their good deeds according to their deserts." Those "who have been preeminent for holiness of life" are "released from their earthly prison, and go to their pure home which is above, and dwell in the purer earth." Finally, those who "have duly purified themselves with philosophy, live henceforth altogether without the body, in mansions fairer far than these, which may not be described."[32]

Sandwiched between the third and fourth is the last group, whose sentence Socrates expounds most extensively. The group comprises those "who have committed crimes, which, although great, are not irremediable," such as those "who in a moment of anger, for example, have done some violence to a father or a mother and have repented for the remainder of their lives, or, who have taken the life of another under the like extenuating circumstances." Their sentence seems unusual at first sight and questionable in many of its aspects, but is nonetheless in some ways profoundly right. Here is how Socrates describes it:

> ... these are plunged into Tartarus, the pains of which they are compelled to undergo for a year, but at the end of the year the wave casts them forth — mere homicides by way of [the river] Cocytus, parricides and matricides by Pyriphlegethon — and they are borne to the Acherusian lake, and there they lift up their voices and call upon their victims whom they have slain or wronged, to have pity on them, and to be kind to them, and let them come out into the lake. And if they prevail, then they come forth and cease from

---

30. Plato, *Phaedo*, 112a.
31. Cf. ibid., 90a.
32. Ibid., 113c–114c.

their troubles; but if not, they are carried back again into Tartarus and from thence into the rivers unceasingly, until they obtain mercy from those whom they have wronged; for that is the sentence inflicted upon them by their judges.

A possible healing of a particular kind of perpetrator, Socrates suggests, depends not only on the purgatorial pain suffered and on the perpetrator's plea for mercy, but also on the willingness of their victims to show mercy.

It is easy to locate the spots at which Socrates' account of "the last judgment," and in particular of the sentence for curable souls, is problematic,[33] at least from a Christian perspective. I will leave aside here, for instance, his well-known privileging of a bodiless state in which a soul can comprehend Ideas as such, and not as they are immanent in sensible particulars; it does not rhyme with the resurrection of the body. Instead, I will concentrate on issues which concern the general character of the judgment and the specific sentence of curable souls. As will be evident, my perspective is decisively shaped by a theological tradition with some reservations about the traditional notions of purgatory.

---

33. Some critiques of Socrates' account of the curable souls' redemption rest on a misreading, however. Kenneth Dorter, for instance, objects that it presupposes that the victims must be in the Acherusian lake (in whose proximity flow the rivers Cocytus and Pyriphlegethon from which the perpetrators call upon the victims) and that therefore those perpetrators cannot be forgiven whose victims are not in the lake because they have lived a virtuous life or have purified themselves by philosophy, thus standing in no need of purification (Dorter, *Plato's Phaedo*, 172). But the reason why the perpetrators call for the victims in the vicinity of the Acherusian lake need not lie in the fact that the victims are in the lake, but that *the perpetrators need to go into the lake* (to be further purified and then "be born as animals" [Plato, 113a]) if the victims have mercy on them. They call upon the victims, Plato says, "to have pity on them, and to be kind to them, *and let them come out into the lake.*" Even more problematic is the suggestion of Renna Burger, predicated on the same misconception. She argues that "Socrates, who may never have to pay a penalty for injustice in the Acherusian lake, would thus condemn to eternal punishment in Hades the Athenian demos, who condemned him to death in one day and then lived to repent it." *The Phaedo: A Platonic Labyrinth* (New Haven, Conn.: Yale University Press, 1982), 202; similarly Peter J. Ahrensdorf, *The Death of Socrates and the Life of Philosophy: An Interpretation of Plato's Phaedo* (Albany: State University of New York Press, 1995), 192. But Burger fails to note that, according to the myth, the condemnation of Socrates does not qualify as a remediable crime in the first place because involuntariness is an essential feature of such crimes, and therefore does not apply to the case at all.

First, Socrates operates with what might be described as a mirroring relation between pre-mortem and post-mortem life. The soul is judged "on the basis of its degree of goodness while the soul animated the human body"; the task of the judge is simply to "ratify" the soul's moral status.[34] Especially since Luther, in Christian theology, on the other hand, the judgment is fundamentally a saving event, at least for the blessed. Second, Socrates believes that there are crimes so heinous as to render those who committed them incurable and that there are lives so pure as to earn those who led them mansions beyond description. In the Christian tradition no deed is imaginable that would as such hurl a person of necessity (Socrates' "destiny") into damnation, for the simple reason that deeds are not decisive when it comes to afterlife;[35] inversely, no deed and therefore no life is so holy or pure as to qualify a person for entry into heavenly bliss. Finally, when Socrates contemplates betterment for evildoers in the post-mortem state, change always involves pain inflicted from the outside and understood as a form of purification. Though in the traditional Catholic doctrine of purgatory, "physical" pain is seen as a form of purification, Protestant theology has emphasized transformation as a sheer gift of God involving no other suffering than the pain of self-discovery. All three points amount to a fundamental difference in the character of the last judgment.[36] For Socrates, the last judgment is situated in an economy of deserts; in the next life everyone gets what they have deserved in this life. In

---

34. White, *Myth and Metaphysics*, 261.
35. The unpardonable sin — blasphemy against the Holy Spirit — was, following Augustine, taken to refer to the final impenitence, not to an act of sin, however heinous. "This blasphemy," argued Augustine, "cannot be detected in anyone... as long as they are still in this life"; and except for "an impenitent heart against the Holy Spirit, by which sins are cancelled in the Church," he claimed, "all [other] sins are forgiven." Sermon 71, 21, in *The Works of Saint Augustine. Sermons II* I, trans. Edmund Hill, ed. John E. Rotelle (Brooklyn, N.Y.: New City Press, 1991), 259f.
36. For a restatement of the doctrine of purgatory at whose core is "the pain of self-discovery," see David Brown, "No Heaven without Purgatory," *Religious Studies* 21 (1985): 447–56.

Christian theology, the last judgment is situated in an economy of grace — grace, however, which does not negate justice but affirms it precisely in the act of transcending it.[37]

The only place where Socrates seems to step out of the economy of deserts — though with one foot only, so to speak — is in the treatment of curable souls. They, too, suffer so as to be purified, but the suffering is not sufficient to change their lot. The perpetrators need to be shown mercy by the victims to be admitted to further purification and finally "sent back" (admittedly only "to be born as animals").[38] But here a major problem with Socrates' scheme surfaces. As one commentator notes, in Socrates' proposal everything depends on the "chance factors of the victim's sense of mercy and the wrongdoers' powers of rhetoric."[39] Surely something is amiss if two perpetrators commit comparable crimes but the one with a smooth tongue whose victim is merciful gets off the hook while the less eloquent one whose victim is vengeful suffers the consequences!

Part of the problem is that Socrates has arranged things in such a way that the perpetrator and the victim have to sort out *by themselves* the issues between them. A third party, the judges, only defines the process and sets it in motion. The judges' standing on the sidelines is in fact part of the sentence. In the absence of an appropriate third party arbitrariness reigns. It is not clear, for instance, at what point the unwillingness of the victim to offer mercy and deliver the perpetrator from Tartarus turns into vindictiveness. Furthermore, though a "mechanism" is in place by

---

37. See Miroslav Volf, "The Social Meaning of Reconciliation" (forthcoming).
38. Plato, *Phaedo*, 113a.
39. Dorter, *Plato's Phaedo*, 173. Dorter misreads Socrates when he ridicules his position in the following way: "Thus the more spiteful the victim the longer the punishment, in which case one seems best advised to seek out benevolent people as one's victims" (173). The logic is impeccable, the only trouble being that a condition for a crime to qualify as remediable is precisely that it was not premeditated!

which a perpetrator can be purified, Socrates does not even reflect on the possible need for the victim to be transformed, for instance, to be freed from bitterness and vindictiveness.

The problematic character of the judgment as a whole and of the sentence inflicted on curable souls notwithstanding, profound eschatological insights are contained in the sentence. I am thinking of its two central and interrelated features. First, *the action of the third party, though indispensable, is alone not sufficient to deal with the problem.* Socrates is aware of the perverse interpersonal bond that violence suffered creates between the perpetrator and the victim. For the perpetrator to be released, something needs to happen *between* the perpetrator and the victim, not just *in* each of them (for instance, repentance, in the case of the perpetrator, or inner healing, in the case of the victim). Without a particular kind of interaction between them it is difficult to imagine the perpetrator's restoration. Second, *justice understood as desert does not suffice to restore the perpetrator.* Though justice is indispensable, required also are the psychological and interpersonal phenomena of repentance and forgiveness, of a sense of guilt and the offer of mercy.

Socrates seemed concerned primarily with the fate of the perpetrator as an individual; his or her reintegration into community is not so much in view (though if one were to make a somewhat daring hermeneutical leap and read Socrates' statement in *Phaedo* against the backdrop of the Athenian Stranger's laws for dealing with pollution from involuntary murder in Plato's *Laws* — a period of exile and readmission into the society[40] — a vision of reconciliation between the perpetrator and the victim would be implied). If the interaction between the two in the form of a

---

40. Plato, *Laws*, 865ff.

request for forgiveness and offer of mercy is essential for healing of the perpetrator, it is *a fortiori* essential for the *restoration of the relationship between them and the creation of the community of unmarred and unadulterated love*. I propose therefore that we take up Socrates' two basic insights about the healing of curable souls — the indispensability of a social process and the insufficiency of justice conceived as desert — and place them in the context of an economy of grace, which governs Christian soteriology and eschatology. The basic contours of the resulting account of the final reconciliation would look something like this.

First, the reconciling event would not apply to some crimes of some people but to any (social) sin of any person; it would include all injustices, deceptions, and violences, whether minuscule or grand, whether committed intentionally or not, and whether the perpetrators were conscious of them or not.[41] As a result, a clear division between the group of perpetrators and the group of victims would be broken,[42] yet without blunting a sharp condemnation of the evil committed. Second, the judge as the third party would not simply define and set the process in motion but would, in the precise function of a judge who suffered the victim's fate and was judged in the perpetrator's place, be at the very center of their reconciliation. Third, reconciliation between perpetrator and victim would be decoupled from its necessary relation to the pain of the perpetrator, except for the pain of remorse; healing would be ascribed to the power of God's Spirit working

---

41. *All* (social) sins are offenses against others and therefore make those who commit them into perpetrators and those who suffer them into victims. Such a notion of "perpetrators and victims," which is mandated by Christian theology, is at odds with the dominant contemporary construals of perpetrators and victims. It is an important aspect of the public responsibility of Christian theology to problematize these construals.

42. There is no reason to think that in Socrates' account of the post-mortem destiny of curable souls a victim could not also be a perpetrator. However, the principle seems to hold: the greater the sin required to qualify one as a perpetrator, the clearer the division between perpetrators and the rest. A theologically adequate doctrine of sin, whose one characteristic is not to let any evil — not even an evil thought — remain uncondemned, works against a clear division of humanity into perpetrators and victims.

through the display of truth and grace. Fourth, transformation of both perpetrators and victims would be affirmed; perpetrators would be liberated from their sin and (likely?) attempts at self-justification, and victims from their pain and (possible?) bitterness and vindictiveness.

So far have I made two circles of arguments for the final social reconciliation as an aspect of the eschatological transition wrought by God's Spirit. The first centered on a discrepancy between the traditional accounts of the eschatological transition (the last judgment and the resurrection of the dead) and the terminal point to which the transition was leading (the world of love). The second circle consisted of a critical engagement with Socrates' vision how curable perpetrators are saved from the pains of Tartarus. So far my aim was to create a circumference of plausibility for strictly theological arguments. Much will depend on whether *these* arguments, to which I now turn, are persuasive (or, if not, on whether persuasive ones can be found).

Social Reconciliation at the End

In the following I will progress from the background arguments, taken from anthropology and hamartiology, to the central arguments, taken from soteriology and above all eschatology. The constraints of this essay require me to move faster through the territory I need to cover than I would want. I will stop to highlight and argue for only what is absolutely essential for my purposes without situating my claims within an overarching account of the doctrines in question.

The central anthropological question in relation to the final reconciliation concerns the construction of human identity.[43] If

---

43. For recent theological accounts of the construction of identity see Ingolf U. Dalferth and Eberhard Jüngel, "Person and Gottebenbildlichkeit," in F. Boeckle et al., eds.,

identity — not personhood, which I take to be exclusively a gift of God[44] — is constructed in a social process, then one should expect that the transition to a world of love will not circumvent social process. This holds true whether one understands the person as "a structure of response sedimented from a significant history of communication"[45] or if one distinguishes clearly between the "pattern of sedimented communication" and the "organizer of the pattern," as I prefer. In either case, personal *identity* is shaped by how others relate to persons and by how persons internalize others' relation to them; by how persons actively relate to others and by what they do to themselves and with themselves, including their material practices, in relation to others; by narrower and wider public resonances they help shape and are in turn marked by them,[46] by identification with and divergence from others' investments in specific cultural forms broadly conceived, ranging from language and religion to political and economic institutions and activities.[47] The specific identity of persons results from conscious or unconscious complex relations to culturally situated others. Whatever the concrete shape of these relations turns out to be, selfhood, as Paul Ricoeur has argued in *Oneself as Another,* "implies otherness to such an intimate degree that one cannot be thought of without the other."[48] Significantly,

---

Christlicher Glaube in moderner Gesellschaft (Freiburg: Herder, 1981), xxiv, 57-99; Wolfhart Pannenberg, *Anthropology in Theological Perspective,* trans. M. J. O'Connell (Edinburgh: T. & T. Clark, 1985).

44. See Miroslav Volf, *After Our Likeness: The Church as the Image of the Trinity* (Grand Rapids, Mich.: Eerdmans, 1998), 181-89.

45. Alistair I. McFadyen, *The Call to Personhood: A Christian Theory of the Individual in Social Relationships* (Cambridge: Cambridge University Press, 1990), 114.

46. See Michael Welker, *God the Spirit,* trans. J. F. Hoffmeyer (Minneapolis: Fortress, 1994), 312-14. Cf. Niklas Luhmann, *Ecological Communication,* trans. John Bednarz Jr. (Chicago: University of Chicago Press, 1989), 15-21.

47. Cf. Miroslav Volf, "Cultural Identity and Recognition: On Why the Issue Matters," in Michael Welker, ed., *Brenpunkt Diakonie. Rudolph Weth zum 60. Geburtstag* (Neukirchen-Vlyun: Neukirchener Verlag, 1997), 201-18.

48. Paul Ricoeur, *Oneself as Another,* trans. Kathleen Blamey (Chicago: University of Chicago Press, 1992), 3.

given the temporal character of human lives, the shaping of the self in interaction with others has a diachronic and not only a synchronic dimension. Remembered and suppressed past interrelations with others and anticipated future interrelations all flow into one's ever-changing present identity.[49]

The social construction of personal identity correlates with the essentially social character of personal sin.[50] As the preceding anthropological reflection suggests, it would be a mistake to oppose abstractly social sin and personal sin.[51] Personal sin is always socially mediated (though not socially *caused!*); and social sin — evil enshrined in societal institutions, cultural and religious symbols, ideologies which legitimize these institutions and symbols, and collective decisions grounded in ideologies[52] — is as sin always personally embodied (though not reducible to a specific person's attitudes and actions). Though all sin is, by definition, sin against God, most sin is committed in a multidirectional and multilayered interaction between people, an interaction with both

---

49. For a discussion of the temporality of human consciousness in general under the category of "transversality" that reaches forward as well as backward, but from the perspective of a consistent contesting of any notion of a transcendental ego, see Calvin O. Schrag, *The Resources of Rationality: A Response to the Postmodern Challenge* (Bloomington: Indiana University Press, 1992), 148–79.

50. In traditional, broadly Augustinian, hamartiology, sin as *peccatum originale* is also understood as social in the sense of being a socially shared problem on account of the solidarity of the human family. To underscore a different sense in which sin can be seen as social, David Kelsey has introduced the distinction between "social" and "societal," the latter indicating that the social character of sin has to be understood also "in terms of the 'public' realm of actual societies' arrangements of social power." "Whatever Happened to the Doctrine of Sin?" *Theology Today* 50 (1993): 169–78, 170f. The distinction is analytically helpful. I have decided not to use the term "societal" to describe important aspects of sin, however, though not for what the term implies about sin but for what it seems to leave out. It fails to take seriously enough cultural and subcultural social practices and symbols. When speaking of the social character of sin, I will use the term "social" to refer to both societal arrangements of power and narrower social relations, practices, and symbols.

51. On the interrelation between personal and social sin from the perspective of Catholic theology, see Mark O'Keefe, "Social Sin and Fundamental Option," *Irish Theological Quarterly* 58 (1992): 85–94. Cf. also Siegfried Wiedenhofer, "The Main Forms of Contemporary Theology of Original Sin," *Communio* (US) 18 (1991): 514–29.

52. On these elements of social sin, see Gregory Baum, *Religion and Alienation: A Theological Reading of Sociology* (New York: Paulist Press, 1975), 200–203.

diachronic and synchronic dimensions. It manifests itself, for instance, as "the monstrous injustice of generational succession," to use Oliver O'Donovan's formulation in *The Desire of the Nations*,[53] in which later generations both benefit from the sufferings of earlier ones and suffer the consequences of their misdeeds. Or it takes the form of conflict between persons and communities in which violence, injustice, and deception are the order of the day, and in which the weak suffer at the hands of the strong and the rage of today's victims gives birth to tomorrow's perpetrators. Moreover, sin itself creates a bond between persons which goes beyond the bond that their interrelations in and of themselves create. Evil committed and suffered both severs relationships and weaves a thick network of perverted ties that keep victims and perpetrators returning to each other — in thought, in person, in progeny, or in succeeding generations — to commit new offenses in an attempt to rectify the old ones. This partly explains the power of sin, which is located neither simply inside nor simply outside of the person but both in a person and in social relations.

Insofar as a person is involved in a history of sin, the socially constructed identity of a person is a socially constructed identity of a sinner-and-sinned-against-one, an identity that is also temporarily structured through complex interrelations of remembered or suppressed pasts, experienced presents, and anticipated futures. If this is true of the identity of a person in a world of sin, then we can expect the transformation and healing of persons to be socially mediated (an expectation, which, as I will argue shortly, leaves a wide range of possibilities for construing the relation between divine and human action in the process of transformation). And in fact salvation according to Christian soteriology is fundamentally a social reality, whatever else it is

---

53. Oliver O'Donovan, *The Desire of the Nations: Rediscovering the Roots of Political Theology* (Cambridge: Cambridge University Press, 1996), 287-88.

in addition to that. Communion with the Triune God is at the same time communion with all those who have entrusted themselves in faith to that same God. As Eberhard Jüngel argues in *God as the Mystery of the World,* "at the very same time that I discover this new fellowship with God" I also discover others "to be my neighbors, who belong to that same fellowship."[54] Reconciliation with one's estranged neighbors is integral to the reconciliation with God. The divine embrace of both the victim and the perpetrator has, in a sense, not come to completion without their own embrace. But how can people who have transgressed against each other embrace? How can their common past be redeemed so that they can have a new future? If one assumes personal continuity between a person as a sinner and as a recipient of grace and affirms the irreversibility of life, creation of a completely new past is out of the question. Rather, their past must be redeemed through reconciliation between them. Dealing adequately with sins suffered and committed is *a social process,* involving individual persons and their fellow human beings.

As an illustration of the essential sociality of the healing process, consider the story Simon Wiesenthal tells in *The Sunflower* about receiving a deathbed confession from an SS soldier for killing a Jewish family trying to flee a building to which the Nazis had set fire.[55] Plagued by guilt, the perpetrator wants forgiveness from a Jew. Though deeply moved, Wiesenthal leaves him without a word, partly on the grounds that victims alone can forgive the crimes done against them. The perpetrator's request and Wiesenthal's refusal are instructive. The request comes out of a painful awareness that the remorseful perpetrator cannot

---

54. Eberhard Jüngel, *God as the Mystery of the World,* trans. D. L. Guder (Grand Rapids, Mich.: Eerdmans, 1983), 354 (slightly revised translation).
55. Simon Wiesenthal, *The Sunflower* (New York: Schocken Books, 1976), 9–99.

deal with the evil he committed on his own. He needs his victim's mercy so much that, in the absence of his victim, he feels compelled to search for a substitute. Wiesenthal's refusal to show mercy stems from the correct insight that a third party cannot forgive and mend the relations between the offender and the offended.[56] But what about God? Should not God's forgiveness be all that is needed? Though God, being God and therefore not a mere "third party," can forgive, divine forgiveness of sinners would be falsely understood if it was thought that it could substitute for the victim's giving and the perpetrator's receiving of forgiveness. If divine forgiveness could substitute for interhuman forgiveness, it would, in Matthean terms, make it unnecessary for persons who remembered that their brother or sister had something against them to go and be reconciled to them before offering their gifts "at the altar" (Matt. 5:23-24).

If, because of the character of human beings and their sin, salvation includes social reconciliation, then the eschatological consummation of salvation should include it too. The inference gains even more plausibility if we keep in mind that, unlike, for instance, the Marxian vision of a communist revolution, the eschatological consummation is not simply about the future — about the creation of a new future. It is rather about the future of yesterday, today, and tomorrow, about the future of all lived times.[57] If the past suffused with enmity is to be redeemed, then social reconciliation of those who died unreconciled will be included in the eschatological transition. In addition to this more

---

56. Together with Milton Konvitz I wish, however, that Wiesenthal had explained his refusal to the perpetrator and then gone on to offer him solace, See ibid., 160; cf. L. Gregory Jones, "Stumped Repentance," *Christianity Today*, October 26, 1998, 94-97. Indeed, I wish he had offered him even forgiveness, though not for the crime against the family killed but for the injury done to *Wiesenthal* by the crime against the family and the Jewish people. But, of course, it is easier to be wise after the situation than in it.

57. See Miroslav Volf, "After Moltmann: Reflections on the Future of Eschatology," in Richard Bauckham, ed., *God Will Be All in All: The Eschatology of Jürgen Moltmann* (Edinburgh: T. & T. Clark, 1999), 253.

formal eschatological argument, good arguments for the final social reconciliation are inscribed in the three central features of the last judgment. The last judgment is an enactment of God's grace (as well as of justice), it is a social event, and it aims at its own personal appropriation. I will briefly describe each of these features of the last judgment, but expound more extensively its neglected interpersonal character.

First, on the Last Day a judgment of *grace* will be passed — again, grace understood not as excluding justice but as affirming justice in the very act of transcending it. The judge will be none other than the Christ, who died in the place of those who sinned and suffered the fate of those who were sinned against. Since "the judgment day is *his* day (Phil. 1:6; 1 Cor. 1:8)" and "the seat of judgment is *his* seat (2 Cor. 5:10)," the last judgment "cannot, under any circumstances, be perceived as interfering with or rendering problematic the judgment which leads to the justification" of the ungodly,[58] rightly argues Eberhard Jüngel, along with a chorus of other contemporary theologians. It would be a mistake, however, to think of the judgment of grace as a lenient judgment. To the contrary. "There is no more severe judgment possible than that which is effected by grace and measures everything against grace."[59] On the judgment day all persons' sins will be narrated in their full magnitude. But since this will happen in the context of grace,[60] they will be freed from guilt and transformed by that

---

58. Jüngel, "The Last Judgment," 395.
59. Ibid., 397.
60. As Hans Urs von Balthasar notes, it is precisely through the look at the one whom one has "pierced" (Rev. 1:7) that one will realize the magnitude of one's sin. "Die goettliche Gerichte in der Apokalypse," *Internationale katholische Zeitschrift Communio* 14 (1985): 33. For the cross as the site of recognition of sin's magnitude, see Martin Koehler, *Die Wissenschaft der christlichen Lehre von dem evangelischen Grundartikel aus im Abrisse dargestellt* (Leipzig: A. Diechert, 1893), 270: "Am Kreuze Christi ermisst der Gerechtfertigte die Bedeutung der Menschensuende, und erst in und mit dem Verstaendnisse des Heilswerkes vollendet sich die unter dem Gesetze des alten Bundes erwachsende

same Christ who has already become their "righteousness and sanctification" (1 Cor. 1:30).

Second, in Old Testament eschatological prophecies judgment is a *social* event. The Lord will judge between Israel and its oppressive leaders (Ezek. 34:17, 20, 22) and "between many peoples" and "strong nations far away" (Mic. 4:1-3; Isa. 2:4). Behind these prophecies lies a notion of judgment, fixed in the legal formula, "Let Yahweh judge between you and me,"[61] whose goal is "the restoration of *shalom* which prevailed prior to the prevailing strife or dispute."[62] Especially with *shalom* as its goal, judgment cannot simply take place in relation to each of the parties for themselves with the consequence of establishing their guilt or innocence and punishing or rewarding them, but *must also take place with respect to both together with the consequence of redefining their relationship.*

Significantly, the expectation of a "judgment between" seems to be one of the Old Testament sources of the belief in an afterlife, which emerges somewhat tenuously on the margins of its traditions.[63] Arguably, a major reason why this expectation inches itself to the surface in the Old Testament has to do with the experience of injustice (see Ps. 73).[64] To describe the nature of

---

Suendenerkenntnis." For a development of this theme in a broader Christological context, see Karl Barth, *Church Dogmatics*, IV/1, ed. G. W. Bromiley and T. F. Torrance (Edinburgh: T. & T. Clark, 1956), 358-413.

61. See Claus Westermann, *Genesis 12-36: A Commentary*, trans. J. D. Scullion (Minneapolis: Augsburg Press, 1985), 241.

62. Temba L. J. Mafico, "Judge, Judging," in *The Anchor Bible Dictionary*, vol. 3, ed. David Noel Freedman (New York: Doubleday, 1992), 1105.

63. See Joseph Ratzinger, *Eschatology: Death and Eternal Life*, trans. Michael Waldstein (Washington, D.C.: Catholic University of America Press, 1988), 88-90. Cf. Pannenberg, *Systematic Theology*, 3:563-68.

64. On Ps. 73 in relation to eschatology, see Ratzinger, *Eschatology*, 88-90. Cf. Diethelm Michel, "Weisheit und Apokalyptik," in A. S. Van der Woude, ed., *The Book of Daniel in the Light of New Findings* (Leuven: Leuven University Press, 1993), 420-22. For a view contesting an eschatological reading of the Psalm, see Martin Buber, *On the Bible: Eighteen Studies*, ed. Nahum N. Glatzer (New York: Schocken Books, 1968), 199-216.

the injustice in question it is insufficient simply to point to innocent suffering. The social dimension of this suffering needs to be brought clearly into focus. The injustice does not consist only in the fact that the "upright" suffer rather than enjoy good fortunes; more precisely, it consists in the fact that they suffer *whereas* the "arrogant" prosper. In Psalm 73, the statement: "[A]fterward you will receive me to glory," is the response to *this social problem* (Ps. 73:24; cf. Job 21:7-15; Jer. 12:1-4).[65] The expectation of enduring communion with God for the upright (Ps. 73:23-28) is meant not simply as a recompense of sorts for suffering, but also as a response to the injustice that their suffering represents when set over against the good fortunes of the arrogant, especially their oppressors.[66] The emergent notion of the final judgment in the Old Testament concerns relations *between* people.

A compelling account of the last judgment's social character — indeed, of its political and world-historical character — can be found in the thought of Jonathan Edwards. Starting with the presupposition that all human beings through all generations "have moral concerns one with another" because they are "linked together," Edwards argued for the last judgment as a universal public event. The "causes and controversies" between individual persons (such as between a parent and a child), between rulers of nations (such as between Roman emperors and the kings they conquered), between peoples (such as between "the

---

65. In *The City of God* the *social* problem that the suffering of the upright and the prosperity of the arrogant present is an important backdrop for the discussion of the last judgment. Augustine writes: "For that day is properly called the day of judgment, because in it there shall be no room left for the ignorant questioning why this wicked person is happy and that righteous man unhappy. In that day true and full happiness shall be the lot of none but the good, while deserved and supreme misery shall be the portion of the wicked, and of them only" (xx, 1).

66. This eschatological expectation — assuming that it is such — correlates well with the way the Old Testament poses the problem of theodicy. It concerns primarily social rather than strictly individual evil, such as illness. See Walter Brueggemann, *Theology of the Old Testament: Testimony, Dispute, Advocacy* (Minneapolis: Fortress, 1997), 385-99; cf. Walter Brueggemann, "Theodicy in a Social Dimension," *Journal for the Study of the Old Testament* 33 (1985): 3-25.

Spaniards and Portuguese" and "all the nations of South America"), indeed between whole generations (even those which lived "a thousand years" apart) will be settled by God as the lawgiver and judge.[67] As the frequency of the preposition "between" in Edwards's text attests, the last judgment is fundamentally a social event. Given the interconnections between human beings, all have a case against all and each has to receive justice with respect to all.

Third, as a transition to the world of perfect love, the last judgment is unthinkable without its *appropriation* by persons on whom it is effected. The divine judgment will reach its goal when, by the power of the Spirit,[68] all eschew attempts at self-justification, acknowledge their own sin in its full magnitude, experience liberation from guilt and the power of sin, and, finally, when each recognizes that all others have done precisely that — given up on self-justification, acknowledged their sin, and experienced liberation. Having recognized that others have changed — that they have been given their true identity by being freed from sin — one will no longer condemn others but offer them the grace of forgiveness.[69] When that happens, each will see himself or

---

67. Jonathan Edwards, entry #1007, from the forthcoming third volume of the "Miscellanies," Amy Plantinga Pauw, ed., in *The Works of Jonathan Edwards*, ed. Harry S. Stout (New Haven, Conn.: Yale University Press). Cf. Robert W. Jenson, *America's Theologian: A Recommendation of Jonathan Edwards* (New York: Oxford University Press, 1988), 179. It was Robert Jenson who, in a private conversation, originally drew my attention to Edwards's explication of the last judgment as a social event.

68. Behind this formulation, as well as others that thematize the role of the Holy Spirit in the consummation, lies a transposition into the eschatological mode of the Holy Spirit's role in the appropriation of salvation. Cf. Karl Barth, *Church Dogmatics* IV/1, 147ff., including the role as the one who convicts of sin (cf. John 16:8-11).

69. As the above account of the last judgment's appropriation underscores, the social character of the judgment does not stand in opposition to its personal character. The connection of the two is suggested in Rom. 14, where the apostle Paul writes that "all will stand before the judgment seat of God" and that "each of us will be accountable to God" (Rom. 14:10, 12; cf. 2 Cor. 5:10; Eph. 6:8). See von Balthasar, "Die goettliche Gerichte in der Apokalypse," 229. The mention of the eschatological judgmental "all" and "each" in a text which condemns judging others may be significant. Between the lines it suggests that the divine judgment of each includes also a judgment about that person's judgment of others and calls implicitly for an alignment of persons' judgment

herself and all others in relation to himself or herself as does Christ, the judge who was judged in their place and suffered their fate.[70]

In a kind of reversal of the parable of the unforgiving servant at which the parable itself aims (Matt. 18:23-35), at the Last Day the grace truly received by the power of the Spirit will translate itself into an unreserved and irrevocable gift of grace to others and, since one is always both a victim and a perpetrator, the reception of grace by others. Indeed, to accept God's judgment of grace fully means to offer grace to offenders and to receive grace from the offended. For those, however, for whom the judgment day does not become the day of giving and receiving grace, it will become a day of wrath leading to a hellish world of indifference and hate.[71] Seeking to justify themselves as Christ the judge reveals the truth about their lives, they will, in Matthean terms, seize their debtors "by the throat," demand payment, and, since it will not be forthcoming, condemn them "into the prison" until they do pay (Matt. 18:30). They will have thereby shown themselves as not having received divine grace and will therefore be "handed over" by God "to be tortured" until they pay their "entire debt" (Matt. 18:34). To refuse to show grace to the offender

---

of others with God's judgment of them. See James D. G. Dunn, *Romans 9-16*, Word Bible Commentary, 38b (Dallas: Word Books, 1988), 814. Put more generally, the last judgment concerns each person's standing before God, but in such a way that it includes the judgment about what each has done to and suffered from others, and how he or she has integrated relations to others into his or her identity. Hence, to put things personally, when I appropriate God's judgment, I appropriate it as a judgment of me not only in my relation to God but in my multiple and multidirectional relations to all and therefore also as a judgment of all in relation to me.

70. Balthasar introduces the idea of personal appropriation of the judge's perspective when he suggests that the saints will be able to judge "the world" and "angels" (1 Cor. 6:2-3) only when "jeder Einzelne, auch die erwaehnte Heilige, durch seinen Blick auf den Durchgeborenen so gelaeutert ist, dass sein Blick auf die Welt und die Engel sich dem des Menschensohns angeglichen hat." Hans Urs von Balthasar, "Gericht," *Internationale katholische Zeitschrift "Communio"* 9 (1980): 227-35, 231.

71. Cf. Niewiadomski, "Hoffnung im Gericht: Soteriologische Impulse für eine dogmatische Eschatologie," 126.

and to receive grace from the offended is to have rejected God's judgment of grace.

With the personal appropriation of the divine judgment of grace between people we have entered the space in which the last judgment is becoming the social event of the final reconciliation. But just as forgiveness of even those offenses for which true repentance was made is not yet reconciliation between enemies, so appropriation of the divine judgment is not yet social reconciliation. Reconciliation has not yet taken place when individuals have changed in relation to the transgression inflicted and suffered. Though it is indispensable for each to assent to God's truthful and just resolution of all disputes and give to others and receive from others the same grace of forgiveness contained in Christ's judgment of grace, still more is required to enter the world of love. For if nothing more than all this happened, each could still go his or her own way, fully satisfied that justice has been served and mercy shown. Reconciliation will not have taken place until one has *moved toward one's former enemies* and *embraced them* as belonging to the same communion of love.[72] With that mutual embrace, made possible by the Spirit of communion and grounded in God's embrace of sinful humanity on the cross, all will have stepped into a world in which each enjoys the other in the communion of the Triune God and therefore all take part in the dance of love freely given and freely received.

---

72. In the discussion of former enemies entering purgatory, Father Hubert suggests that if the person has not fully forgiven his offenders, on purgatory's threshold "he immediately and completely forgives the injustice. For in purgatory love "does not brood over an injury" even for an instant. His dispositions toward the offender are those of an unfeigned and tender charity and he prays much for him. If during the purgatory of the onetime injured person, the offender himself goes to purgatory, an immediate and perfect mutual friendship between both is effected under the mighty sway of love. Thus do they imitate their Saviour who forgave his enemies." *The Mystery of Purgatory* (Chicago: Franciscan Herald Press, 1975), 32. In my terminology, this immediate effecting of perfect mutual friendship is reconciliation; the change of individuals' dispositions toward the offender is not, at least not *yet*.

Reconciliation — Divine Act and Human Agency

An important test-case for the plausibility of my proposal concerns its compatibility with the affirmations that human beings were reconciled with one another in Christ and that the subject of the eschatological transition is God rather than human beings. The main function of these affirmations in relation to the eschatological transition is to give certainty to its outcome. Everything has already been accomplished *de jure* in Christ (to use Karl Barth's favorite way of putting it), and whatever still remains to be done so that it would be realized also *de facto* is an unfailing divine work. The thesis about the final social reconciliation seems to introduce uncertainty because it presupposes limited and fallible human beings as participants, and that not only in relation to God but in relation to one another. I will argue in the following that this is in fact not the case. In order to develop my argument adequately, I would need to offer a positive account of the relation between the divine act and human agency in the eschatological transition. Since such an account is well beyond the scope of this essay, I will address the issue by indicating minimal requirements with respect to human participation which need to be satisfied for the proposal to work. The advantage of this procedure is that, if successful, it will open a wide space for the proposal's reception by making plausible its compatibility with the most radical assertion that the work of salvation is finished and that the will's turning to God and holding onto God is itself God's work.

One can object to my thesis about the final social reconciliation by arguing that interhuman reconciliation is already included in the *finished* work of Christ. Do we not read in Ephesians that Christ "has made both groups [the Jews and the Gentiles] into one" and that he has abolished the law so as to create "in himself one new humanity" and "reconcile both groups in one body through the cross" (2:14–16)? What room could there be for the eschatological reconciliation, given that one new and fully reconciled humanity is already created in Christ? We can imagine the same objection from the perspective of Karl Barth's powerful restatement of the doctrine of reconciliation — or at least from a particular reading of it. From the side of humanity, reconciliation in Christ, whose history is identical with the history of humanity, means that "we are lifted up, that we are awakened to our own truest being as life and act, that we are set in motion by the fact that in that one man God has made Himself our peacemaker and the giver and gift of our salvation."[73] What other reconciling activity between human beings would need to happen at the end of history that has not already happened in its middle — indeed, before its beginning — by the inclusion of all humanity into the history of Jesus Christ?

Does the objection stand, however? Consider again the Epistle to the Ephesians. It resists a reading that would render reconciling activity of flesh-and-blood people superfluous. One of its main purposes, if not the main purpose, was in fact to encourage the recipients to "make every effort to maintain the unity of the Spirit in the bond of peace" (4:3). As to Karl Barth's doctrine of reconciliation, readings of his thought according to which the force of divine action renders human participation superfluous have proven implausible.[74] The very text I quoted above continues, "What remains to us of life and activity in the face of this actualization of His redemptive will by Himself... is not for us a passive presence as spectators, but our true and highest activation."[75] Barth's affirmation of the reality of the human acting

---

73. Barth, *Church Dogmatics* IV/1, 14.
74. See especially John Webster, *Barth's Ethics of Reconciliation* (Cambridge: Cambridge University Press, 1995); John Webster, *Barth's Moral Theology: Human Action in Barth's Thought* (Edinburgh: T. & T. Clark, 1998).
75. Barth, *Church Dogmatics*, 14f.

subject is robust. He is only "unwilling so to emphasise" this reality "that it becomes detached from its gracious origin and its sustaining energy in the act of God."[76]

Now, one may not wish to state together with Barth that the history of God's act of reconciling us to himself simply *"is* our true history,"[77] without immediately pointing to the obvious ways in which our history has yet to be transformed. One may find, for instance, the implication implausible that a Serb and a Kosovar — to take an example from the war that is raging as I write these lines — now deeply at odds with each other, *have been reconciled to each other* even before they existed, let alone before they had any quarrel with one another. I certainly do. But even if one advocated as radical a position as Barth's, the thesis about the final social reconciliation can stand. Given his stress on sanctification and vocation, on "the resurrection and the Holy Spirit in which the outgoing, self-realizing character of reconciliation is articulated,"[78] Barth cannot let reconciliation simply float above people, disconnected from their concrete relationships. No doctrine of reconciliation can be adequate which denies that an interhuman reconciliation ought to happen that is "in some nontrivial sense... the very own act of the persons in need of mutual reconciliation."[79] If so, then the idea that human beings have been reconciled in Christ to God and one another does not render the notion of the final social reconciliation problematic. It leaves room for an understanding of the final social reconciliation as the Holy Spirit's perfecting of the interhuman reconciliation which God has accomplished in Christ and in which human beings have been involved all along in response to God's call.

---

76. Webster, *Barth's Ethics,* 97 — italics added.
77. Barth, *Church Dogmatics* IV/1, 547 — italics added.
78. Webster, *Barth's Ethics,* 97.
79. George Hunsinger, in a personal communication.

Since reconciliation between two parties requires their involvement because it cannot take place "above" them, the notion of the final social reconciliation leads inevitably to the question of agency. If they are involved, how is their involvement related to divine involvement, which in the tradition so unmistakably and universally dominates the scene of the last judgment? Commenting on the character of the eschatological consummation, Oswald Bayer draws on the prophetic, dominical, and apostolic metaphor of the eschatological feast.[80]

The basic contrast Bayer draws is a familiar one. It is between divine action and human "work." And certainly, if it is anywhere appropriate to stress divine action, it is so with respect to the final consummation. Does the contrast, however, call into question the thesis about the final social reconciliation? It would, if it sufficed simply, negatively, to draw the contrast between divine action and human agency. But it does not suffice. Take, for example, the metaphor of the eschatological feast, on which Bayer's comments lean. If the feast were just about having one's hunger sated, then it would do to highlight only the contrast. If the feast is about celebrating, however, then it is essential also to explore how divine action is positively related to humans coming to enjoy one another's presence. Whatever one's position on synergism may be,[81] it should be uncontested that human beings are not simply passive objects — like blocks of wood — of God's action. That "the sons of the kingdom" are "not preparing the kingdom" but

---

80. Bayer claims: "Solche Gemeinschaft, in der Trennung, Vereinsamung und Isolierung ueberwunden sind, ist nicht erarbeitet und erworben, nicht von der Weltgeschichte erwirtschaftet, sondern von Gott gewaehrt, geschenkt, von ihm zuvor "bereitet," wie es zugespitzt in der Erzaehlung vom Grossen Weltgericht heisst (Mt. 25:34)." Oswald Bayer, "Das Letzte Gericht als religionsphilosophisches Problem," *Neue Zeitschrift für Systematische Theologie* 33 (1991): 209-10.

81. For Oswald Bayer's explication of Luther's position in contrast to Melanchthon, see "Freedom? The Anthropological Concepts in Luther and Melanchthon Compared," *Harvard Theological Review* 91 (1998): 373-78.

"are being prepared" for the kingdom does not in any way, following Luther,[82] undermine the claim that God *"does not work in us without us."*[83] Indeed, no stronger claim regarding the relation between divine action and human agency vis-à-vis final social reconciliation can be found.

Just as God's action of preparing the children for the kingdom is indisputable, so God's "not-acting-in-them-without-them" is indispensable. Contrary to Bayer, the communion cannot be created "before" the actual reconciliation of enemies who belong to the communion. True, in Matthew's account of the judgment of the nations, Jesus does say to those on his right, "Come, you that are blessed by my Father, inherit the kingdom *prepared* for you from the foundation of the world" (25:34). But the kingdom here refers to the "space and time" of the communion and the conditions for the communion, not to the communion of the kingdom's denizens itself. For Jesus refers to something that is not constituted by the entry of persons, whereas the communion is by definition constituted by it. God has prepared "the kingdom" without any human participation, but human beings do participate in the entry into the kingdom. "Enter!" they are told by the judge. Though Matthew does not have the final reconciliation in view, my argument in this essay is that the final reconciliation is an essential dimension of this entry.

Let me conclude by commenting briefly on the import of my endeavor here. Formally, I have attempted to suggest a better fit between the account of the eschatological transition on the one hand and the Christian belief that "heaven" is a world of

---

82. Martin Luther, *Luther's Works*, ed. Helmut T. Lehmann (Philadelphia: Fortress, 1972), xxxiii, 153 (De servo arbitrio).
83. Ibid., xxxiii, 243. To put my claim in Luther's terms but rather abstractly, in the final reconciliation former enemies act in the precise sense in which human beings must act if God is not simply to act upon them but act in them in such a way as not to act without them.

love as well as the beliefs about the construction of identity, the character of human sin, and the shape of salvation on the other hand. If persuasive, the thesis about the final social reconciliation is a modest contribution to greater consistency among Christian doctrines.

Materially, I have highlighted three important and interrelated aspects of the eschatological transition. First, over against an almost exclusive concentration on individual human beings and their destinies in most accounts of the eschatological transition, I have argued that we should also take seriously human beings as social beings, whose personal identities are inextricably bound up with their near and distant neighbors. Second, I have endeavored to move away from the dominance of justice as desert in the eschatological transformation.[84] Concern for justice is absolutely indispensable, of course, but it is salutary and theologically adequate only as a constituent part of the more overarching notion of grace. I take this to be a basic insight about social relations inscribed in the logic of God's treatment of sinful humanity as evident in the doctrines of atonement, of salvation, and of the last judgment. Third, I have attempted to thematize more clearly the character and import of human participation as an interhuman activity within the overarching account of the eschatological transition accomplished by the power of the Spirit.

The combined emphasis on divine grace as the defining origin and sustaining power of the whole process, on human participation as a fruit and indispensable medium of that grace that transforms sinful persons and their relationships, and on the community of love in the Triune God as the goal of the process explains the introduction of the category "social reconciliation"

---

84. A recent notable eschatology which takes seriously social relations and stresses the primacy of grace in the eschatological transition is Moltmann's *The Coming of God* (250-55).

into the transition from a world of sin to the world of perfect love. The final reconciliation is the eschatological side of the vision of social transformation contained in the movement of the Triune God toward sinful humanity to take them up into the circle of divine communal love.[85] The notion of the final reconciliation strengthens that vision and thus shapes social practices.[86]

---

85. As the three combined emphases suggest, my reflection on eschatological transition here is part and parcel of specifying the eschatological side of the ecclesial and broader social reflections expressed in my books *After Our Likeness* and *Exclusion and Embrace: A Theological Exploration of Identity, Otherness, and Reconciliation* (Nashville: Abingdon, 1996), and in the article " 'The Trinity is Our Social Program': The Doctrine of the Trinity and the Shape of Social Engagement," *Modern Theology* 14 (1998): 403–23.

86. This text was presented as part of the 1999 Laidlaw Lectures series at Knox College, Toronto. I am indebted to Ivica Novakovic, my research assistant, for his extraordinary competence and helpfulness. Professors Robert W. Jenson, George Hunsinger, Patrick D. Miller, Amy Plantinga Pauw, Rusty R. Reno, and Judith M. Gundry-Volf offered helpful comments on a previous draft of the text. I wrote this essay as a Pew scholar and member of the Center for Theological Inquiry, Princeton, New Jersey, where I benefited from the comments of my fellow members.

17

The Intolerable Burden of the Past, the Pure Figment of the Present, and the Surpassing Worth of the Future*

PAUL F. M. ZAHL

> Behold, I am coming soon, bringing my recompense, to repay every one for what he has done. I am the Alpha and the Omega, the first and the last, the beginning and the end.
> —Revelation 22:12–17

THIS ESSAY understands the past as entirely determinative of human destiny when the Christian experience of God is factored out of the equation. The essay regards the future as entirely determinative of human destiny when the Christian experience of God is factored into the equation.

The "present," or present moment, on the other hand, is an abstraction. It is a construct that disappears into thin air the moment it is objectified. For the non-Christian, the present is a repetition of the past, a constant being-pulled-backward. For the Christian, the present is a creature of the future, deriving its vibrancy, its meaning, and its value entirely from what lies ahead.

---

*"The Intolerable Burden of the Past": General Confession, 1928 Book of Common Prayer, 75, line 9; Ps. 38:4. "The Pure Figment of the Present": Ps. 90:4–6. "The Surpassing Worth of the Future": Phil. 3:8.

The purpose of my essay is to anchor the present in the future, on the basis of the vitiation of the past's extreme magnetism by virtue of the historic action of God's Son, the Christ from Galilee.

The Past

For every human being, the past carries with it an unendurable weight, crushing the life and vigor from every person who has ever lived. The Psalmist experienced this famously in Psalm 51: "Against thee, thee only, have I sinned, and done that which is evil in thy sight, so that thou art justified in thy sentence and blameless in thy judgment" (v. 4). The past has been lived out before God, *in foro dei*.

In the New Testament, the experience of God's crushing weight upon the misfiring and self-serving human personality is the experience of St. Peter. St. Peter exclaims to the Lord both poignantly and despairingly, "Depart from me, for I am a sinful man" (Luke 5:8). This Big Fisherman flops down at Christ's feet in (humanly) irremediable regret for his faithlessness. Peter's position of self-despair and exhaustion is classic sainthood, for Peter's lay-down-your-arms becomes the Rock on which Christ has built the church. Christian sainthood consists in self-despair brought about by a razor-sharp encounter with the judged past. And this past, the human remembered past, is a chronicle of the things done and the things left undone.

Christian anthropology, which accentuates the intrinsic staining character of sin, original sin's ontological participation in the DNA and thus the destiny of each single human being and thus also of every society of men and women that has ever existed, understands the present as simply the carrying forward of the past's indelible repetition into the next event, into the next scene of life. In Christianity, the child is always father to the man.

The past as burden, the past as a quenching, withering parasite thing is evoked quintessentially in two famous allegories. One is *The Pilgrim's Progress*. The other is *A Christmas Carol*.

The first allegory narrates the universally intended story of one man, the type of the alive conscience, whose name is Christian. This human being with the name Christian awakes one morning with a sack attached to his back. The sack is attached so tightly that he is unable to budge it or undo it to any degree. The reader is supposed to understand that the sack is the burden of Christian's sin. It was always there, but he only became aware that it was there when he came into the hearing of the stirring, alerting Word of God. Christian awakens, like a character in Edgar Allan Poe, with "one loud, long, and final scream of despair."[1] Christian's exclamation is the cry, "What can I do to be saved?"

John Bunyan's allegory then carries Christian on a long and arduous journey. The initial climax of the journey, the end of part one of the *Progress* and also the beginning of part two, is the hero's coming to the Cross of Christ, the instrument of cancellation. In a tersely written encounter, the burden of the man drops effortlessly from his shoulders and fully out of view. The sack actually drops into the emptied tomb in which Christ once lay. Only then does the hero become a pilgrim. Only then does the hero have a future. Only then is Christian able to have his first experience of what joy is. "Great dungeons lay ahead of him. But for the moment he was light as air.... So Christian gave three leaps for joy, and went on singing."[2]

Charles Dickens told the same story two hundred years later, but set it within a different chronology and gave it a different plot mechanism. In *A Christmas Carol*, which also includes a

---

[1] "The Pit and the Pendulum," *The Complete Tales and Poems of Edgar Allan Poe* (New York: Modern Library, 1938), 257.
[2] John Bunyan, *The Pilgrim's Progress* (London: Frowde, 1903), 37.

commentary on time and its intangibility, Ebenezer Scrooge is so frozen up by his past that there is scarcely even a present moment in existence for him. His clockwork habits and schedule, the chill imparted to absolutely everything he touches, convey a man frozen in the present because of decisions taken and grievances borne within the past.

The tight glacier of time gone by, which his former (and dead) business partner compares to chains, "the chains you wrought in life," must be broken by the means of repentance. Scrooge's past, which he visits in compact detail, is unbearably poignant and evocative of tears. His repentance, within the first "visitation" of the book (i.e., by the Ghost of Christmas Past) consists in tears shed over... himself. But it's a beginning, the first, narcissistic step on the road to a future.

Scrooge's present life, the accusatory, pathetic, and even menacing present to which he is exposed through the second visitation, becomes what people today term a "wake-up call." The consequences of Scrooge's past behavior and persona are written out in torturing images and painful situations of which he has been completely unaware and of which he is the cause. It is the portrait of Christian, in the *Progress, before* he observed the looming sack cutting into his neck.

Toward the end of the book, Scrooge is escorted into his future, a future completely determined by the past. The future is a predictable state, and a horrible one. But Dickens sees the man awaken! The phantastic specter of his future state electrifies his present, which becomes transformed into a new future. Scrooge becomes awake, fully alert to the true facts and consequences of human self-damage. These facts and consequences can only be reversed from the vantage of hope. "Must these things be?" he asks. "Or can they be changed?" They can be.

A *Christmas Carol* is one of the best allegories of the Christian view of time that has ever been given. Its unquenchable appeal down the years is evidence that human persons understand at some level, maybe even universally, that the child is father to the man; that unless the child be refathered, there is no grounds for hope; and that the past faced, in the context of an external love that is the grace of God, is able to re-create the future. The present is nothing. The past is everything — unless it be forgiven. Then the present can be reconfigured, for it becomes the alpha to the omega of a good future.

> Scrooge was better than his word. He did it all, and infinitely more; and to Tiny Tim, who did not die, he was a second father. He became as good a friend, as good a master, and as good a man as the good old City knew. . . . Some people laughed to see the alteration in him, but he let them laugh. . . . His own heart laughed, and that was quite enough for him.[3]

The intolerable burden of the past is a fact of life which parish clergy observe almost every day. We see it in others partly because we see it in ourselves. And we see it everywhere because it is also written into our profession, which is the profession of a confessing and also an absolving Word. I see it in fathers and sons. I see it in mothers and daughters. I see it at funerals, where there is almost always someone who is *not* there who should be or who would have been had there not been a rupture. I see it at weddings, and almost every Friday evening, at the psychically tense rehearsals for weddings. The big question on Friday evenings is this one: Where will the woman sit for whom the groom's father left the groom's mother? What shall we do

---

3. Charles Dickens, *A Christmas Carol* (New York: Washington Square Press, 1963), 218.

with the stepfather? What if he was once the bride's uncle? I see this played out almost every Friday. The names change, but the faces remain the same. These are the faces of guilt and malice, bitterness and treasured-up hurt, rejectedness and contempt. Parish ministers observe such scenes at weddings, at christenings, at memorial services, and in the study, hour after hour, "tomorrow, and tomorrow and tomorrow" (*Macbeth,* Act V, Scene 5).

I began this first section of my essay, which concerns the past, with a citation from the Revelation to St. John. "I am the Alpha...the first...the beginning" (22:12-17). These three nouns constitute an extremely important attribute of God. He is the Beginning. He was there at the beginning. Each of these nouns expresses scripture's conviction, found throughout the Bible, that God lives at the initial moment of everything and everyone that has ever been. Therefore he is able to meet us in our pasts. This is stated in a surpassingly comforting way in the 139th Psalm: "For thou didst form my inward parts, thou didst knit me together in my mother's womb.... My frame was not hidden from thee, when I was being made in secret.... Thy eyes beheld my unformed substance; in thy book were written, every one of them, the days that were formed for me, when as yet there was none of them" (vv. 13, 15, 16).

Christian reconciliation with an obtruding past — and all past experience, being linked to human sin, is inherently obtrusive — is possible. It consists in the retrojection of past negativities by means of the Cross of Christ which is found at the deepest and most submerged point of all missed opportunities and all spite and all bitterness and everything that has ever caused bitterness. Forgiveness, the result of an appalling death writ large by the magnified decree of divine action in one historic willed event acquiesced in by its Subject (who was also its Object), is read into our innumerable pasts by the Gospel confession of the Christian Church. No one is beyond the reach of what the Prayer Book calls "His saving embrace."

In our worst yesterday, He was there.

The Figment of the Present

There was a poster to be seen on the walls of almost every main-line church office in America during the early 1970s. It read, "Today is the first day of the rest of your life." The saying was usually credited to a Roman Catholic nun, Sister Mary Corita.

The poster became popular at the same time that Hollywood produced a memorable, now kitschy science-fiction film called *Logan's Run* (1973). In the world of *Logan's Run,* every day was known as Lastday. This was because everyone who reached his and her thirtieth birthday in the futuristic (nightmare) world depicted in the movie was incinerated in a rite of supposed "renewal." Lastday was a way, *the* way, of keeping the population down. Every day was somebody's Lastday.

These two notions of the present, which were exactly simultaneous in the popular landscape of the early 1970s, were exactly opposite. In the poster, the present moment inaugurated the future. In *Logan's Run,* the present moment was your last.

The present is an abstraction. It is empirically unverifiable save when it is over. Its weight, or value, depends completely on its relation to what preceded it and what follows it. The moment the present is examined, or reflected on, it ceases being the present. The present is notoriously — I would say impregnably — hard to describe or pin down or even qualify.

Isaac Watts's hymn text for Psalm 90 is apt, both philosophically and theologically:

> A thousand ages in thy sight
> are like an evening gone;
> short as the watch that ends the night
> before the rising sun.
>
> Time, like an ever-rolling stream,
> bears all our years away;
> they fly, forgotten, as a dream
> dies at the opening day.[4]

The present, an infinitesimal point in time situated on the boundary between the past and the future, is not concrete. It is formless. It is entirely and practically elusive. Even if it did exist in some conceptual sense, it would exist in no felt sense. It dies, like a dream, at the next instant.

In Reformation terms, the present moment is under the domination of the Law. This is because the past, which is a weighed and thus a judged and guilty thing the moment it is reviewed or scrutinized, or even reflected on, owns the present. *The past owns the present.* Because the past is under the rule of sin, the present moment is also. In keeping with Galatians 3:22, every present moment in time is the creature of sin. "The Scripture consigned all things to sin [i.e., the past], that what was promised to faith in Jesus Christ [i.e., the future] might be given to those who believe [i.e., at the present]." The present without faith knows no future other than death (Rom. 6:23). To put it a different way, the present is the result of whatever has preceded it. Without a remedy, which is some sort of acquittal, the present is the invariable aggregate of a judged past.

---

4. See "O God our help in ages past," Hymn 680, verses 3–4, in *The Hymnal 1982* (New York: Church Hymnal Corporation, 1982, 1985).

The Worth of the Future

A diagnosis of the vacuous present, defined only, centrally, by an unbearable burden of past sin (ontological) and sins (ethical), is bad business.

But it is the case. As Alfred Mollegen used to say, "Original sin is the only empirically verifiable Christian doctrine." The present exists under a Damocles sword — judgment day, unrenewing Lastday for the past. Therefore, the only relevant question for the human present is this one: What shall I do to be saved? "For the sting of death is sin, and the power of sin is the Law" (1 Cor. 15:56).

Christian faith, however, understands a massive disconnect to have been brought into being by means of the historic coming of Christ. In the New Testament, by which I mean the New Testament of life, not just the distinctively Christian written scriptures, the Lastday character of the present (*Logan's Run*) is, in fact, converted into an entirely fresh character: that "first day of the rest of your life." In Christianity, today *is* the first day of endless following days.

Without the vitiating, depressing stress of the Law's every-pound-of-flesh demand, the present turns into something completely different. The present becomes the creature of the future. The newness of the present is derived from the God-judged *Emeritierung* of the tainted past. If the Atonement is true, and forgiveness has been effected on behalf of every one who calls on the Lord to be saved — like Bunyan's hero Christian — then we are now under grace and not law. The Narnian freeze has turned to spring (C. S. Lewis).

This is why St. Paul took such pains to declare, and repeat, "If any one is in Christ, he is a new creation. The old has passed away. Behold, the new has come" (2 Cor. 5:17).

The question now becomes this: of what does our (Christian) future consist? If the *mortmain* of the past is abreacted through the death of Christ and through one's emotional catharsis when one engages with that death, what takes its place? What exists from God's gift to take the place of the old, dead hand?

As in most Christian theology, there is a proper symmetry to theological thinking. Just as the Old Testament represents the Alpha of God's judging and legal presence with his people, so the New Testament expresses the Omega of God's forgiving and graceful present with them. The forgiving, graceful presence of God is affirmed — expected — in the anticipation of death as nonwrathful. It is also affirmed in the anticipation of the completed community, after death, of the City of God.

Life in the matrix of New Testament hope, both individual and collective, is sustained by fearlessness in respect to death and by confidence in the great society of an eternal Christian family. I am uncomfortable with timetables and with any specific orientation to human history that tries to synchronize concrete events with Salvation History (Acts 1:7). But we are on solid ground in respect to our personal eschatology, that is, the courage we may evince before finality — which is not finality at all for Christians — and in respect to the shared kingdom to come (Rev. 21:2f).

When will the New Jerusalem be constructed and dedicated? Nobody knows.[5] When will my personal New Jerusalem, that incorruptible, continuous, and beloved identity, be inaugurated? At the moment of my death. That is enough.

---

5. Everyone should see the last ten minutes of D. W. Griffith's 1916 masterpiece of Christian eschatology entitled *Intolerance*. The prisons are opened, the fighting men throw down their rifles, and the family of man is one on the great plain of ended conflict under the dazzling chariot of Christ come in glory. Griffith, a devout Christian, pulled it off visually. He portrayed on film the consummation of Christian hope. We shall always be in his debt.

18

Heaven as a State of Mind
Peter Abelard's "O quanta qualia"

WANDA ZEMLER-CIZEWSKI

1   O what their joy and their glory must be,
    those endless Sabbaths the blessèd ones see;
    crown for the valiant, to weary ones rest:
    God shall be All, and in all ever blest.

2   Truly, "Jerusalem" name we that shore,
    city of peace that brings joy evermore;
    wish and fulfillment are not severed there,
    nor do things prayed for come short of the prayer.

3   What are the Monarch, his court and his throne?
    What are the peace and the joy that they own?
    O that the blest ones, who in it have share,
    all that they feel could as fully declare!

4   Now, in the meantime, with hearts raised on high,
    we for that country must yearn and must sigh,
    seeking Jerusalem, dear native land,
    through our long exile on Babylon's strand.

5   There, where no troubles distraction can bring,
    we the sweet anthems of Zion shall sing;

while for thy grace, Lord, their voices of praise
thy blessèd people eternally raise.

6 There dawns no Sabbath, no Sabbath is o'er,
Those Sabbath keepers have one evermore;
One and unending is that triumph song
Which to the angels and us shall belong.

7 Low before him with our praises we fall,
of whom and in whom and through whom are all;
of whom, the Father; and in whom, the Son;
and through whom, the Spirit, with them ever One.[1]

Peter Abelard is not generally known as a hymnodist, and yet, paradoxically, one of the most widely used hymns of Christian hope is his composition for Saturday vespers, "O quanta qualia." It is one of the few medieval religious poems to have survived with its original tune, and can be found in Roman Catholic, Episcopal, Lutheran, and other Protestant collections of church music. My intention in what follows is to look back into the first half of the twelfth century and to locate the hymn in its original historical, liturgical, and theological contexts. These may prove surprisingly relevant to our own times and to the question of Christian hope in the twenty-first century.

The Historical Setting

Born in 1079, Peter Abelard was sixteen years old when the first Crusade was launched at the Council of Claremont. The eldest

---

1. *Peter Abelard's Hymnarius Paraclitensis*, An Annotated Edition with Introduction, by Joseph Szövérffy. II. The Hymnarius Paraclitensis Text and Notes (Albany, N.Y.: Classical Folia Editions, 1975), 76–78; Sister Jane Patricia, *The Hymns of Abelard in English Verse* (Lanham, Md.: University Press of America, 1986), 54–55. "O what their joy and their glory must be," Hymn 623, *The Hymnal 1982*, words by Peter Abelard (1079–1142), altered translation by John Mason Neale (1818–66) (New York: Church Hymnal Corporation, 1982, 1985).

son of a Breton knight, he might conceivably have joined other members of the French military aristocracy in their expedition to recapture Jerusalem from the Seljuk Turks. Instead, he chose to give up his inheritance so as to become, in his own words, "a free-lance knight of Minerva,"[2] traveling from one cathedral school to another to study first logic, then theology with the most distinguished scholars in France.

Brilliant and pugnacious, Abelard rapidly made enemies with his relentless critiques of his teachers' language theories and theological methods. Before long, his reputation attracted so many students that he was able to set up as master of his own school, first at Corbeil and Melun, then in Paris, on the Left Bank.

Abelard was in his late thirties when he discovered Heloise, the niece of Fulbert, a canon of Notre Dame cathedral. The brief account of their affair in the *Historia calamitatum*[3] presents the reader with a sordid little seduction in which Abelard appears to have taken advantage both of the uncle's gullibility to gain access to the girl, and of Heloise's appetite for learning to bring her into his grasp. After Heloise found herself to be pregnant, the couple were secretly married, although their arrangement seems soon to have been revealed by the triumphant Fulbert. When Abelard settled his unhappy young wife at the convent of Argenteuil, where she had been educated, rather than leave her with her unreliable uncle, the latter became convinced that he had been duped, and that Abelard was attempting to dissolve the marriage. Fulbert therefore sought revenge by bribing Abelard's servant to admit a pair of hired toughs into his master's rooms, where they castrated him, and fled.

---

2. *Abélard: Historia Calamitatum:* texte critique avec une introduction publié par J. Monfrin (Paris: Vrin, 1967), 63.
3. Ibid., 71–75.

But for the extraordinary devotion and tenacity of Heloise, the story might have ended in disgrace and obscurity. Instead, the fame of Abelard and Heloise would grow all the greater after the end of their marriage. Heloise took vows at Argenteuil, and Abelard entered the Benedictine order at the royal abbey of St. Denis. Within a few years, she had become abbess of her community, while Abelard continued to study and write on the doctrine of the Trinity. In 1121, however, he suffered the condemnation of his first theological treatise at the council of Soissons, and with his abbot's permission withdrew from the community of St. Denis to a hermitage on the river Seine, which he named the Paraclete, in honor of the Holy Spirit. He was recalled in 1125 from this retreat when the monks of St. Gildas in his native Brittany elected him to be their abbot.[4] Unfortunately, both parties soon found the situation unendurable, so much so that in 1132, Abelard fled back to France in fear for his life.

In the interval, St. Denis had come under the authority of a new abbot, Suger (1081–1151), whose ambitious plans for the community included an extensive building program and the accumulation of an unprecedented wealth of art objects, liturgical vessels, vestments, and books.[5] In the course of realizing his ambitions, he reclaimed for St. Denis the property of Argenteuil, expelling its community of nuns, thereby rendering Heloise and her associates homeless. However, it became possible for Abelard to have them settled at the Paraclete, and in 1131 to have it dedicated for their use with the blessing of Pope Innocent II. Throughout the remaining years of the 1130s, Abelard

---

4. Ibid., 98–101.
5. Constant J. Mews, "Peter Abelard," in *Authors of the Middle Ages*, vol. 2, nos. 5–6, *Historical and Religious Writers of the Latin West*, ed. Patrick J. Geary (Aldershot, Hants., U.K., and Brookfield, Vt.: Variorum, 1995), 14–16. See also *Abbot Suger on the Abbey Church of St.-Denis and Its Art Treasures*, ed. and trans. Erwin Panofsky, 2nd ed. by Gerda Panofsky-Soergel (Princeton, N.J.: Princeton University Press, 1979).

and Heloise would work together to establish at the convent of the Paraclete a community of Benedictine nuns dedicated to the study of scripture, and especially to correction of the existing text of the Latin Vulgate, through knowledge of Greek and Hebrew.[6] At the request of Heloise, Abelard composed a *Rule* for the community and 133 hymns for use in their liturgy, including "O quanta qualia." He also maintained a correspondence with Heloise and the community in general, composed a number of sermons for them, and, at Heloise's request, wrote a commentary on the first two chapters of Genesis, as well as the brief responses to exegetical questions that are contained in the *Problemata Heloissae*. In short, their partnership survived both personal tragedy and professional catastrophes to found a brilliant and durable monastic legacy.

The Liturgical Context

Foremost among the activities of a monastic community, whether of men or women, is celebration of the divine office. Each day at the Paraclete would have begun with the office of Matins, sung before daylight. At daybreak, the office of Lauds would be sung, followed by Prime, Terce, Sext, and None, so called from the first, third, sixth, and ninth hours of the day. Vespers would have been sung before dark, and Compline would conclude the day's activities just after nightfall. Of these liturgical hours, Matins, Lauds, and Vespers are the longest. In addition to the regular cycle of offices for each day of the week, there are special observances for the Sunday liturgies; for Christmas, Holy Week, and major

---

6. Mews, "Peter Abelard," 16; Wanda Cizewski, " 'In saeculo quondam cara, nunc in Christo carissima' — Heloise and Spiritual Formation at the Convent of the Paraclete," *Proceedings of the PMR Conference* 8 (1984): 69–76.

feast days of the church year; and for commemorations of major saints' days.

Of the 133 hymns composed by Peter Abelard for Heloise's community,[7] the first 29 were designed for use in the daily offices of Matins, Lauds, and Vespers. A second collection of 46 hymns were composed for Christmas, Epiphany, the Presentation, Holy Week, Ascension, Pentecost, and the dedication of a church. Lastly, a collection of 56 additional hymns were composed in honor of apostles, evangelists, and other saints whose commemorations were part of the calendar of feast days observed at the Paraclete. Each set of hymns was preceded by a preface in which Abelard makes it clear that Heloise and her associates are the instigators at whose insistence he ventures to compose both words and music for the enhancement of their liturgical celebrations.

"O quanta qualia" is the final hymn of Abelard's first collection, and it forms part of a remarkably innovative cycle of hymns celebrating the hexaemeron, or six days of Creation. Although Latin hymns in praise of the Creator and Creation of the world had been written by Ambrose of Milan, the Venerable Bede, and others,[8] Abelard's cycle is the most extensive and theologically complex of all, including hymns on the creative work of each day according to both the literal and the allegorical senses of the text. As such, the hymn cycle connects closely to the commentary on Genesis that Heloise had also commissioned, and restates a number of themes developed in detail in Abelard's exposition of the Genesis text. At the same time, the hymns touch on theological and ethical issues developed elsewhere in Abelard's writings.

---

7. Szövérffy, I. Introduction to Peter Abelard's Hymns, 59–82.
8. Ibid., 33.

The Theological Content

"O quanta qualia" is the last word in a complex, week-long meditation upon the creation of the material world and the allegorical interpretation by which each day of Creation represents an age or stage in the history of humankind, from Noah through the patriarchs and kings of the Old Testament to the New Testament and Christ's saving work.[9] Thus, the hymns for Saturday Matins, Lauds, and Vespers celebrate the conclusion of a week's work for the sisters of the Paraclete, the conclusion and benediction of God's primordial Creation week, and not least of all the conclusion of time and history with the Sabbath of eternal rest at peace in the life to come.

The theological content of the hymn for Vespers is expressed by means of three Old Testament motifs, namely, the city of Jerusalem, the Sabbath day of rest, and Babylon the place of exile. Abelard provides the key to unlocking the full range of meaning implied in these motifs in hymn 10, for Sunday Lauds. Sunday, as the first day of the week, corresponds to the first day of Creation, on which God said, "Let there be light." Building an allegorical interpretation of the day, Abelard combines several allusions in a single metaphor, the transition from evening to dawn. As the sisters of the Paraclete would have known, he had reversed Augustine's reading of "evening" and "morning" light in his commentary on Genesis 1:1–3,[10] interpreting the evening with which each day of Creation week begins as the obscure and mysterious truth of things in the mind of God before creation, contrasted with their utterance into created reality or "day" as God speaks them into existence by his creative Word. At the same

---

9. Ibid., 60–63, summarizes contents and motifs; for full Latin text, see vol. 2, 15–78.
10. Peter Abelard, *Expositio in Hexaemeron*, in *Patrologia Latina* 178.740CD; compare Augustine, *De Genesi ad Litteram libri duodecim*, 5.18, ed. J. Zucha, in Corpus scriptorum ecclesiasticorum latinorum 28.3.2 (Vienna: Tempsky, 1894), 161.

time, Abelard contrasts the obscurity of the Mosaic covenant, symbolized by the veil (*velamen*) that covers Moses' face when he descends from Mount Sinai (cf. 2 Cor. 3:7–8), with Christ the incarnate Truth (*Est in re Veritas*) who fulfills the prophecies of the Old Testament. Finally, "evening" light is compared with death, especially the death of Christ crucified and of the saints, while "morning" light is the light of Christ's Easter Sunday resurrection, which casts its radiance forward through time to the general resurrection of all the people of God.

With these contrasting allusions established as his interpretive framework, Abelard's three hymns for the Sabbath can be seen to express a deepening sense of the believer's participation in God's creative work and also God's eternal, mystical repose. Briefly stated, the theme of hymn 9, for Saturday Matins, is the power by which the Creator in six days brings order to unformed, primordial chaos, so as to sanctify on the seventh a day of repose. In this day is symbolized, for the believer, an eternal Sabbath of rest after the chaos and struggles of earthly life. At Lauds, in hymn 28, the grace and gifts of the Holy Spirit are shown to be the means by which the believer, as member, is united to the head, who is Christ. Secure, finally, in the vision of this grace-filled union with their Lord, the community then concludes their day and their week with hymn 29, and its praise of the heavenly Jerusalem. It is not only the resurrection and life to come, but also a present serenity of thought and affect, to which they journey from the Babylonian exile of unfulfilled desire, imperfect logic, sorrow, labor, and pain.

Conclusion

As a career theologian, Peter Abelard was resoundingly unsuccessful in his own time. His *theologiae* were condemned not only at Soissons, but also at Sens in 1142. He did not live to pursue an appeal to Rome, which, in any event, he would have lost.[11] As abbot of St. Gildas, he was unable to impose discipline on his community, and came into conflict not only with the monks but also with the local feudal lord, who took protection fees from the monastery.[12] To say that he was well acquainted with chaos, unfulfilled desire, pain, and sorrow is no exaggeration. Nevertheless, he made two choices in life that secured his immortality both in the popular legends of the Middle Ages, and as the author of "O quanta qualia."

First, he chose to set aside his inheritance as the firstborn son of a knight, and in so doing relinquished the legacy of violence and pride that characterized the feudal aristocracy of early twelfth-century Europe. By that same decision, he also rejected the violent quest for recapture of the earthly Jerusalem, which would occupy the fighting men of Europe for almost two centuries. Second, Abelard chose to remain loyal to a woman he had wronged, and in finding a home for Heloise and her associates, chose to right the wrong done to them by men of his own religious community. In a sense, he turned his back on the Babylonian splendors of St. Denis as Abbot Suger envisioned it, to cast his lot with the poor and the supposedly useless, a band of homeless women. In short, Peter Abelard not only wrote, but also lived the vision of Christian hope that his hymn continues to recall to mind from generation to generation.

---

11. Mews, "Peter Abelard," 18–19.
12. *Historia Calamitatum*, 98–99.

19

Heavenly Hope
How the Book of Revelation Sings to My Chronic Pain

John D. Zemler

As a disabled person I get two things that most people do not have. First, I get excellent parking. Second, I get knocked down in shopping malls by self-styled "health walkers." I suffer from chronic pain and mobility problems. On a good day I have near-full use of my right arm and hand. We won't go into what a bad day is like. All of this is a far cry from the young Eagle Scout I was once, who ran, swam, and camped, and who was later a U.S. Army officer with service overseas. When I later lost the command of my body and dealt with chronic fatigue and pain, there were times that the despair set in and I seriously considered suicide.

Yet, looking past the despair, I have found that my condition has had its advantages. I can now appreciate John of Patmos's Revelation in ways that I never could before. There is emphasis on endurable suffering in Revelation, and it continues to strike me. Being a Christian has no material guarantees, no new car, no seats in the front row. Revelation is a text that is intended to encourage me beyond the material life. As a Christian who suffers, I read Revelation as a text of hope. It is a text which teaches me that God is in charge, a text which teaches me to take the long view. All in all, Revelation has made it easier to withstand despair and even look beyond the pain. In Revelation one learns to suffer in a Christian way. Christianized suffering allows me more fully to explore the words attributed to John the Baptist: "He must increase, but I must decrease" (John 3:30). Revelation allows me a framework of hope within my suffering.

This essay seeks better to appreciate Revelation through its articulation of hope for the suffering Christian. Interestingly, Revelation does not even contain the word "hope" in its text.[1] Nevertheless, Revelation offered the Christian auditors of its initial communities a reason to do more than simply endure their suffering. The readers of later Christian communities[2] have not always appreciated this real-world value of Revelation, its encouragement to hope. For the Christian within a liturgical tradition, Revelation instills hope in those who are in an otherwise hopeless situation. This hope, simply stated, is conveyed through the choirs of heaven.

The Book of Revelation and the Problem of Its Genre

The book of Revelation was most likely written while the emperor Domitian ruled (81–96). Raymond Brown dates it between 92

---

1. Within the New Testament, six writings do not contain the word "hope" in either its verbal (ἐλπίζω; *elpizō*; to hope) or nominal (ἐλπίς; *elpis*; hope) forms. These books are Mark, 2 Timothy, James, 2 Peter, Jude, and Revelation. Except for Mark, each of these books is considered to be a later writing. The referenced Greek text is the United Bible Society, third (corrected) edition. All scripture passages in this essay are quoted from the Revised Standard Version.

2. Given the letters to the seven churches (Rev. 2:1–3:22), I presume that there are actual Christian communities — a nascent diocese? — that lie behind this text. For current discussion on the use of the term "community" and its application to Christian writings, see Philip Sellew, "Thomas Christianity: Scholars in Quest of a Community," in *The Apocryphal Acts of Thomas*, Studies on Early Christian Apocrypha 3, ed. Jan N. Bremmer (Leuven: Peeters, 2001), 11–35.

and 96, and its audience was the "Churches in the western sector of Asia Minor,"[3] which is today's western Turkey.

The genre of the Revelation is that of apocalyptic literature. This is an insider's genre, for members only. References to then-current events are made by symbols which are intelligible only to those within a particular community.[4] This use of coded speech, while at times frustrating to the modern reader, serves as a life preserver to the text's original community. The Romans would not have taken kindly to the circulation of a text that explicitly said that Rome would be destroyed. The coded language allows the explicit to be spoken and yet concealed.[5]

The community that produces/receives an apocalyptic text understands itself to be under persecution. They are suffering as a group and as individuals. The persecution may be real or only perceived, but either way the sense of being under siege is reflected in this genre. Additionally, apocalyptic texts reveal hidden information that can only be made manifest by a supernatural messenger. The messenger then takes the writer on an instructive journey through a supernatural abode, typically heaven or hell.[6]

---

3. "Revelation (The Apocalypse)," in *An Introduction to the New Testament* (New York: Doubleday, 1997), 774, 805–8.

4. See Bruce M. Metzger, *Breaking the Code: Understanding the Book of Revelation* (Nashville: Abingdon, 1993); Austin Madison Farrer, *Rebirth of Images* (Boston: Beacon Press, 1963).

5. This is similar to the description of why Jesus spoke in parables in Mark 4:10–12: "And when he was alone, those who were about him with the twelve asked him concerning the parables. And he said to them, "To you has been given the secret of the kingdom of God, but for those outside everything is in parables; so that they may indeed see but not perceive, and may indeed hear but not understand; lest they should turn again, and be forgiven." Indeed, the phrase "He who has ears to hear, let him hear," associated with parables, is used by John of Patmos in his interpretation of a vision of the beast, "If any one has an ear, let him hear..." (Rev. 13:9). This parabolic phrase is also found at (or near) the end of each of the letters to the seven churches.

6. These places can be multiple heavens/hells or a single heaven/hell. See Martha Himmelfarb, *Ascent to Heaven in Jewish and Christian Apocalypses* (New York: Oxford University Press, 1993), and *Tours of Hell: An Apocalyptic Form in Jewish and Christian Literature* (Philadelphia: University of Pennsylvania Press, 1983).

For a fuller discussion of Christian apocalyptic literature, see Adela Yarbro Collins, "Apocalypses and Apocalypticism: Early Christian," *Anchor Bible Dictionary*, 1:288–92; also by Collins, "Revelation. Book of," *Anchor Bible Dictionary*, 5:694–708; James C.

The writer then conveys to the rest of the community the contents and (perhaps) the meaning of the vision(s).

The difficulty with apocalyptic literature is that the further in time one gets from the original community, the more difficult it becomes to interpret and understand the text. The references, already coded and obscure, become less easy to interpret. The more difficult it becomes to interpret the symbols as originally intended, the easier it becomes to misinterpret them literally. Given that the original community felt itself under persecution, these symbols are then most easily interpreted through a lens of violence and suffering, and not one of hope.

Almost immediately after its writing and distribution, the book of Revelation became less and less accessible to its subsequent readers. Referents to the symbols are lost because the symbols were not updated with the experience of each new set of readers. This must have been especially so after the Edict of Milan made Christianity a legal religion in the Roman Empire in the year 313. By the year 400 Christianity was the state religion of the Roman Empire. An image-filled text written for those under Roman persecution would be less understandable

---

VanderKam and William Adler, eds., *The Jewish Apocalyptic Heritage in Early Christianity* (Assen, Netherlands: Van Gorcum; Minneapolis: Fortress, 1996); Paul S. Minear, *New Testament Apocalyptic* (Nashville: Abingdon, 1981).

For additional discussion on the book of Revelation, see Bruce J. Malina and John J. Pilch, *Social-Science Commentary on the Book of Revelation* (Minneapolis: Fortress, 2000); Columba Graham Flegg, *An Introduction to Reading the Apocalypse* (Crestwood, N.Y.: St. Vladimir's Seminary Press, 1999); James L. Resseguie, *Revelation Unsealed: A Narrative Critical Approach to John's Apocalypse* (Leiden and Boston: Brill, 1998); Raymond E. Brown, "Revelation (The Apocalypse)," in *An Introduction to the New Testament* (New York: Doubleday, 1997); Wilfrid J. Harrington, *Revelation*, Sacra Pagina 16, ed. Daniel J. Harrington (Collegeville, Minn.: Liturgical Press, 1993); Richard Bauckham, *The Theology of the Book of Revelation* (Cambridge and New York: Cambridge University Press, 1993); Elisabeth Schüssler Fiorenza, *The Book of Revelation* (Philadelphia: Fortress, 1985); John J. Pilch, *What Are They Saying About the Book of Revelation?* (New York and Ramsey, N.J.: Paulist, 1978). I use the text by Harrington for teaching my undergraduates.

to those who were themselves later members of the official state religion.

Except for Revelation, Christians could still readily engage the rest of the New Testament regardless of their situation of persecution and state citizenship. One might say that the "shelf life" of the symbols and images employed in the Gospels and Epistles are longer lasting than those of Revelation. Canonical decisions were made much later than the year of the composition of Revelation. It is not surprising that this particular apocalyptic text was not as quickly accepted into the Christian canon as most of the other canonical texts.[7] While quickly accepted in the western church, Revelation was disputed in the eastern church as late as the tenth century.[8]

Given Revelation's apocalyptic genre, one is not surprised to find symbolic imagery within it. This vivid imagery can distract the reader from the hopeful message of the text. The message is that no matter how bad things get, God is still in charge. This message is distorted, if not lost, by some modern efforts to make Revelation into scary conversion propaganda. Unfortunately, today the text is often employed to frighten people into becoming Christian.[9] In this misguided effort to terrorize people into Christianity, the message of Christian hope, as well as love and forgiveness, is fully lost.

---

7. Several other Christian apocalyptic texts did not enter the New Testament, e.g., the Apocalypse of Peter, the Apocalypse of Thomas.

8. For a concise history of the acceptance of Revelation into the canon, see Collins, "Revelation, Book of," 695.

9. I have never understood this use of Revelation. To scare one to become a Christian by teaching "become a Christian or God will inflict all of these plagues and disasters on you" seems at odds with the understanding that "God is love" (1 John 4:7). What happens when one quits being scared? Does one quit being a Christian? The ministry of Jesus focused on healing, forgiveness, and teaching, and it did not engage a "convert or die" mentality.

Patient Endurance and Hope

The word "hope" does not appear in the book of Revelation.[10] "Patient endurance" in Revelation has been equated with hope in the rest of the New Testament.[11] It has also been interpreted as requiring that those of the original audience should accept persecution, so as to endure it. This endurance of persecution has been understood to include "sharing in the passion of Christ."[12]

In the Greek text of Revelation, one reads "patient endurance" in seven instances.[13] Four of these occurrences are in the letters to the seven churches (Rev. 2–3).[14] In these cases "patient endurance" is understood to refer to their "staying power,"[15] the way in which they hold up under the challenges referenced in their respective letters. Yet, the occurrences of "patient endurance" in these instances are there to praise endurance; they are not illustrations or calls to hope.[16]

The other three occurrences of this term are part of the authorial commentary delivered by John of Patmos and are not actually part of the visions. The first use of "patient endurance" occurs as John begins to tell how he received the visions. "I John, your brother, who share with you in Jesus the tribulation and the kingdom and the patient endurance, was on the island called Patmos

---

10. A fascinating comparison between the idea of hope in George Orwell's *1984* and Revelation is found in George Lea Harper Jr., "Winston Smith, Meet John of Patmos: Reflections on Orwell's *1984* and the Book of Revelation," *Religion and Intellectual Life* 2, no. 1 (1984): 60–68. In Orwell, hope is "the oblivion of death" (64). In Revelation, hope "affirms that the faithful are never really alone" (67). This is to say that the suffering Christian has no need to despair.
11. Terrence Prendergast, "Hope (NT)," *Anchor Bible Dictionary*, 3:285.
12. Harrington, *Revelation*, 140–41; see also 50 and 201.
13. Patient endurance (ὑπομονή).
14. Ephesus twice, and Thyatira and Philadelphia once each.
15. Schüssler Fiorenza, *The Book of Revelation*, 191.
16. For a different view on this use of *hupomonē* in Rev. 3:10, see Theodore Mueller, "'The Word of My Patience,' in Revelation 3:10," *Concordia Theological Quarterly* 46, nos. 2–3 (1982). Mueller translates it as "the word of my patience." Although I prefer the translation of "patient endurance," neither translation diminishes my emphasis on the hope found in Revelation.

on account of the word of God and the testimony of Jesus" (Rev. 1:9). In this case John does not speak toward any particular hope, but to his solidarity with his co-sufferers who also suffer on behalf of their faith.

The second and third cases are instances where John offers commentary after two visions. In Rev. 13:1–8, John sees the "Beast" and relates its authority over all the world except those whose names are written in the book of life. John then parabolically states:

> If any one has an ear to hear, let him hear: If any one is to be taken captive, to captivity he goes; if any one slays with the sword, with the sword must he be slain. Here is a call for the endurance and faith of the saints.

John then continues with the vision of the Beast and concludes with another interpretive summary which calls for understanding, but not endurance. The understanding refers to the number and sign of the Beast. The visions of chapter 14 are bisected in verse 12 by another interpretive summary. John inserts:

> Here is a call for the endurance of the saints, those who keep the commandments of God and the faith of Jesus.

The persecuted Christians are being encouraged to put up with the persecutions and avoid the mark of the beast lest they receive God's judgment.

In each of the cases where John adds commentary to the visions and mentions "endurance," it is in the context of withstanding the present moment, but not in a sense of the hope for the future. While the message of perseverance in suffering is a necessary one, it is not a message of hope. What shows the sense of hope to be missing in these calls to endurance is the lack of any reflection that the suffering of the Christians is just and that their future will be spent with God. This *lacuna* is rectified by the presence of the choirs in heaven.

Choirs Singing Hope

If read incorrectly, God in Revelation can be determined to have a self-esteem problem. Time and again the inhabitants of heaven burst out in choruses of just how great God really is. This percolates throughout the text after the seven letters to the churches have been read. I assume that God does not suffer from low self-esteem and that these choirs must be there for another reason. The first encounter of the heavenly choirs are in chapter 4 as heaven is depicted in imagery related to Isaiah 6 and Ezekiel 1. Here the 24 Elders (24E) and the Four Living Things (4LT) first sing God's praises. Usually one encounters angels singing and at times they are joined by the 4LT and the 12E.

If God does not suffer from low self-esteem, nor needs to hear how great he is repeated over and over, then what are all these praises for? They are for us, the first auditors and the subsequent readers of Revelation. We look over the shoulders of these praising choirs and learn about God through their songs and exclamations. Thus, these hymns and acclamations are for the benefit of the auditor/reader. Furthermore, these lessons and affirmations of God are for whoever hears them, both at the time of their composition and today. Then and now, they teach about God.

The choirs tend to focus on three statements about God and/or the Lamb. First, they make ontological statements that correspond to Alpha-Omega statements about Jesus encountered elsewhere in Revelation. Second, they make Creator statements. Third, they make statements about justice.

The 4LT and 24E sing their first songs independently of one another. The 4LT "...never cease to sing: Holy, holy, holy is the Lord God Almighty, who was and is and is to come" (4.8). This song makes an ontological statement on the eternity of God. It teaches the Christian that anything one may suffer is transitory, while the God one serves is eternal.

By teaching this ontology, Revelation builds on the statement from Hebrews 13:8: "Jesus Christ is the same yesterday and today and for ever." Several times this sentiment is expressed in Revelation in terms of the 4LT's song, "who was and is and is to come." It is also expressed in the Alpha-Omega statements that precede (1:8) and conclude (22:13) the visions presented to John of Patmos. The acknowledgment that the Lord for whom they suffer is truly eternal offers hope to the suffering Christian. Indeed, the cycle of visions is effectively bracketed by these declarations of God's eternality. For a suffering person, the assurance is that anything they encounter is further encompassed by Jesus the Christ. Christ is more than their suffering, not the other way around. Grounded in my own personal experience with pain and despair is the knowledge that Christ supersedes them. This is hopeful and comforting to me. It does not eliminate the pain, but it makes the pain easier to bear. Perhaps most importantly, it wards off despair.

The second song comes from the 24E as "they cast their crowns before the throne, singing, 'Worthy art thou, our Lord and God, to receive glory and honor and power, for thou didst create all things, and by thy will they existed and were created.'" This song exemplifies the aspects of justice and creation. The aspect of justice is seen in the understanding of God as "worthy." More on this aspect will be brought up later on, but note that the worthiness of God is based upon the lesson that God is worthy because God created all things, even those which are suffering. This is reminiscent of the creation imagery in Job 38:1–42:6, where God persuades Job that as the Creator he does not owe Job special explanations beyond the fact that he is the Creator of everything. As the Creator of everything, God is ultimately in charge, whether an explanation is offered or not. While I would like to have an explanation of my suffering, I am not only satisfied, but sated, knowing that God is ultimately in charge. As a former troop commander, I am grateful that someone else is taking care of things, including me.

Revelation goes beyond the theodicy of God as the Creator is depicted in Job. Revelation includes a promise of consolation as one of the elders explains to John regarding those who have been martyred for the Lamb:

> Therefore they are before the throne of God
>   and serve him day and night within his temple;
>   and he who sits upon the throne will shelter them with
>   his presence
> They shall hunger no more, neither thirst any more;
>   the sun shall not strike them,
>   nor any scorching heat.
> For the Lamb in the midst of the throne will be their
>   shepherd.
>   and he will guide them to springs of living water;
> and God will wipe away every tear from their eyes.
>   (Rev. 7:15–17)

The elder states that they shall have no more needs, wants, or sorrows. This goes well beyond the theodicy of Job to a theodicy of "it is all worth it," not only because God created everything, but because God will comfort and shelter one in the afterlife. Suffering Christians have the promise of an afterlife where God will shelter; they shall dwell in his presence. This is more than "pie-in-the-sky-when-you die." It is the assurance that the Lamb will console us.

Note the Lamb guiding us " ... to living streams of water.... " While the terms "water" and "living" are significant in the Johannine writings, the phrasing also deliberately echoes Psalm 1:

> Blessed is the man ... his delight is in the law of the Lord, and on his law he meditates day and night. He is like a tree planted by streams of water, that yields its fruit in its season, and its leaf does not wither. In all that he does he prospers.

The scene depicted in Revelation 7:15–17, with its living water, is one where the sufferer will meditate on God day and night as in Psalm 1. Yielding fruit in season means that we may not be able to achieve or physically do what we would like to do just now, but that with the Lamb of God we will be firmly planted with God and without tears, able to yield fruit in *our* season. In *our* season — whether in time or in eternity — God knows! Learning — meditating — on the Law/Word of God day and night, for eternity. Is this not heaven, to be in the vision of God?

In Revelation 5:1–5 there is the question of who is worthy to open the seven-sealed scroll. The 24E and the 4LT all sing the "new song," singing of the Lamb: "Worthy art thou to take the scroll and to open its seals ... " (Rev. 5:9). The lesson we are assured of is that the Lamb is worthy. If the Lamb is worthy, then those who are martyred for the Lamb know that they suffer and die for a just cause. A few verses later they are joined by the host of angels: "Worthy is the Lamb who was slain, to receive power and wealth and wisdom and might and honor and glory and blessing!" This is followed by every living creature throughout the entire creation offering praise to the Lamb (Rev. 5:13–14).

Again, the Lamb is worthy. If what you suffer and die for is worthy, then that suffering has meaning and the sufferer has hope.

The songs and exclamations by the 24E and the 4LT are punctuated with the teaching that the Lamb is worthy. This reinforces the idea that God is just, and instills hope in the sufferer.

This essay focuses on the aspect of justice in worthiness from the perspective of the sufferer. There are two dimensions of the justness of God in Revelation. As we have seen, the choirs of heaven teach us that God is just and this offers hope to those who suffer for his sake. Second, Revelation also contains another aspect of God's worthiness. We learn that the punishments inflicted on the enemies of God are also just. An example of this is in 16:5–7. The third bowl has been poured and the angel exclaims that God's judgments are "just." This aspect of God's justice is to emphasize that those who receive his wrath have earned it. The exclamations of God's judgments against them as "just" are meant to assuage the auditor/reader from thinking that God is too heavy-handed against those who are causing the suffering.

An additional aspect of the justness of God's wrath is the observation that God does not ask us to help punish others physically. The Christian call is not a call to violence. Jesus does employ violence in John 2:13–22 as he cleanses the Temple. He does not call his disciples to engage in violence; nor at Gethsemane, when Jesus is arrested and on the verge of humiliation, suffering, and death, does he call the disciples to help him with violence. Christians may be called to endure violence and personal suffering, but they are not called to inflict violence and personal suffering. This realization from Revelation and elsewhere is a moment of hope and liberation. The killing of people, no matter how "bad" they have been, is not in the Christian's job description. There is no Christian call to violence: not in the Gospels, not in the Epistles, nor even in Revelation (where one might expect to find it, given the scenes of God's justice).

The song to God is liturgical. There is comfort in knowing that as the heavenly host worships God, so we worship in our liturgy. As we worship God in our liturgy, and as we look over the shoulders of the heavenly host worshiping God in Revelation, we learn about the goodness and justice of God. As we worship God we learn about God. And since the book of "Revelation is proclamation, not prediction"[17] we gain comfort from that knowledge.

The aspects of God expressed in the heavenly liturgy and the songs praising God provide hope to the suffering Christian of the first century and to those of the twenty-first. This particular Christian knows that the pain will not go away. I can only walk so many steps in a day and use my hands for so many effective minutes in a day (and for these steps and minutes I am grateful). For the soldier turned academic, pain and physical limitations are indeed frustrating. Yet the frustration does not end in despair, nor in isolation from God. My frustrations and my pain are bracketed by the eternality of God. Christ was there before the pain, is here just now as I am typing with the pain, and he will continue to be with me after the pain is gone and the tears are wiped away. This is truly the message of hope in the book of Revelation.

---

17. Wendell W. Frerichs, "God's Song of Revelation: from Easter to Pentecost in the Apocalypse," *Word and World* 6, no. 2 (1986): 217.

Contributors

Robert M. Cooper is priest at Good Shepherd Episcopal Church in Little Rock, Arkansas, and a docent at the Arkansas Arts Center in the same city. Previously, he has served as a college chaplain, a university and seminary professor, a pastoral psychologist, and poetry editor for the *Anglican Theological Review*. He is author of numerous journal and magazine articles and many poems. Most recently, his articles have appeared in the *Sewanee Theological Review* and in the volume of essays *Engaging the Spirit: Essays on the Life and Theology of the Holy Spirit*.

Ralph Del Colle is an associate professor in the Department of Theology at Marquette University, Milwaukee. His areas of concentration are christology, pneumatology, trinitarian theology, and the theology of grace. He is the author of *Christ and the Spirit: Spirit-Christology in Trinitarian Perspective* and contributed a chapter on the "Triune God" to the *Cambridge Companion to Christian Doctrine*. He is co-editor of the *International Journal of Systematic Theology* and served as president of the Society for Pentecostal Studies, 2002–2003. His interests in research and scholarship include trinitarian theology and the question of time and eternity in God as well as explorations of the doctrine of grace in an ecumenical perspective. He has served on a number of ecumenical dialogues for the Roman Catholic Church, including the international dialogue with classical Pentecostals, the international consultation with Seventh-Day Adventists, the United States dialogue with Reformed Churches, and a regional dialogue with United Methodists. He was a member of the Roman Catholic delegation to the World Council of Churches Assembly in Harare, Zimbabwe, in 1998.

The Rev. Travis Du Priest is vice president of the DeKoven Foundation for Church Work and executive director of the DeKoven Center in Racine, Wisconsin. For over twenty-five years he taught Humanities at Carthage College and was active on a national level with collegiate honors education. Past president of the National Huguenot Society, he has written and spoken widely on colonial Huguenot history and spirituality. He has twice received awards for outstanding papers at conferences as well as the Distinguished Teacher Award from Carthage. He has published books on seventeenth-century writers Jeremy Taylor and Katherine Philips, as well as numerous articles of literary criticism, over two hundred essays on spirituality, and five chapbooks of poetry.

Reginald H. Fuller was Molly Laird Downs Professor of New Testament at the Virginia Theological Seminary, 1972–1985. He also served as Baldwin Professor of Sacred Literature at Union Theological Seminary, New York, 1966–1972, professor of New Testament languages and literature, Seabury-Western Theological Seminary, 1955–1966, and professor of theology, St. David's College, Lampeter, Wales, 1950–1955. He participated in the national Lutheran-Episcopal dialogues (I–II), and the international Anglican-Lutheran dialogue. He is the author of *Foundations of New Testament Christology* and *Preaching the Lectionary.*

Alexander Golitzin, hieromonk (priest-monk) of the Orthodox Church of America, is associate professor in the Department of

Theology at Marquette University in Milwaukee, Wisconsin. He has also served as a visiting professor at St. Vladimir's Seminary in Crestwood, New York, and as a visiting lecturer at the Graduate Theological Union, Berkeley, the University of California at Berkeley, and Stanford. He was tonsured monk at the Monastery of Simonos Petras, Mt. Athos. His publications include *Et Introibo ad Altare Dei: The Mystagogy of Dionysius Areopagita with Special Reference to Its Predecessors in the Eastern Christian Tradition; St. Symeon the New Theologian on the Mystical Life: The Ethical Discourses;* and *The Living Witness of the Holy Mountain: Contemporary Voices from Mount Athos.* He was a co-editor of the *Historical Dictionary of the Orthodox Church.*

Charles Hefling is a professor of systematic theology at Boston College in Chestnut Hill, Massachusetts, and instructor in theology for the vocational diaconate program of the Episcopal Diocese of Massachusetts, of which he is a presbyter. He is currently at work on *The Meaning of God Incarnate: Christology for the Time Being,* and in 2002 became editor-in-chief of the *Anglican Theological Review.*

Robert D. Hughes III is the Norma and Olan Mills Professor of Divinity and Professor of Systematic Theology, the School of Theology, University of the South, Sewanee, Tennessee. He has taught at Sewanee since 1977, after serving parishes in Southern Ohio and Toronto. He has been secretary-treasurer and president of the Conference of Anglican Theologians, now the Society of Anglican and Lutheran Theologians. Hughes is a Fellow of the Episcopal Church Foundation. He has served as Tennessee State Conference president and member of the National Council of the American Association of University Professors. He was also a Kent Fellow of the Danforth Foundation and a Visiting Scholar at the Divinity Faculty, Cambridge.

Thomas Hughson, S.J., is an associate professor in the Department of Theology at Marquette University, Milwaukee. He specializes in the social context of Roman Catholic systematic theology. The work of John Courtney Murray has been a main research interest. He edited John Courtney Murray's dissertation, *Matthias Scheeben on Faith: The Doctoral Dissertation of John Courtney Murray*, and published *The Believer as Citizen: John Courtney Murray in a New Context*. A project with the Communications Group in the Catholic Theological Society of America focuses on the potential for renewal in diocesan structures of communication. At present he serves on the steering committee of the Church-State Studies Group in the American Academy of Religion and is a convenor of the Society for the Study of Anglicanism, recently launched at the annual meeting of the American Academy of Religion.

Alan Jones is dean of Grace Episcopal Cathedral in San Francisco and an honorary canon of the Cathedral of Our Lady of Chartres. He was the Stephen F. Bayne Professor of Ascetical Theology at General Theological Seminary from 1972 to 1985. He was also the director and founder of the Center for Christian Spirituality at General Theological Seminary. He is the author of *The Soul's Journey: Exploring the Three Passages of Spiritual Life with Dante as a Guide; Sacrifice and Delight; Passion for Pilgrimage;* and *Living the Truth*.

Harold T. Lewis is rector of Calvary Episcopal Church, Pittsburgh, Pennsylvania. He has taught at Pittsburgh Theological Seminary, the George Mercer School of Theology, and the Institut

Anglican de Theologie in Bukavu, Congo. He has served parishes in the United States., Honduras, and England, and also spent a decade on the presiding bishop's staff. Among his publications are *Christian Social Witness* (in the New Church's Teaching Series) and *Elijah's Mantle: Pilgrimage, Politics, and Proclamation.* His article "By Schisms Rent Asunder? American Anglicanism on the Eve of the Millennium" was the first chapter of *A New Conversation: Essays on the Future of Theology in the Episcopal Church,* edited by Robert Slocum. His poetry has appeared in the *Anglican Theological Review.*

Jeffrey Allen Mackey is an Episcopal priest, currently the interim rector of St. John's Episcopal Church, Kingston, New York, and is academic dean and associate professor of Bible and pastoral ministry at Nyack College, New York City. He is a trustee of the Cathedral Church of St. John the Divine in New York City, and is Master of the Order of Preachers Anglican (Dominicans).

Jacqueline Schmitt has been the Episcopal chaplain at Northwestern University since 1994. She served a variety of parishes in the Diocese of Central New York. She worked with the Episcopal chaplain at Columbia University while attending seminary. She later served as chaplain at Syracuse University and North Carolina State University. She has served as editor of *Plumbline,* a journal of ministry in higher education. She is a member of the corporation of the *Anglican Theological Review,* elected at large, and a member of the *ATR* executive committee.

Robert Boak Slocum is a lecturer in the Department of Theology at Marquette University, Milwaukee. He has served parishes in the Dioceses of Milwaukee and Louisiana. He is the author of *The Theology of William Porcher DuBose: Life, Movement,* *and Being;* editor of *Engaging the Spirit: Essays on the Life and Theology of the Holy Spirit;* and co-editor of *An Episcopal Dictionary of the Church.* He has been a visiting professor at Nashotah House and a visiting assistant professor at Carthage College, Kenosha, Wisconsin. He is the review articles editor of the *Anglican Theological Review.*

George H. Tavard is professor emeritus of theology, Methodist Theological School in Ohio. He was a *peritus* at Vatican Council II and has has been involved in the ecumenical dialogues of the Roman Catholic Church with Anglicans, Lutherans, and Methodists. His publications include *The Church, Community of Salvation: An Ecumenical Ecclesiology; The Thousand Faces of the Virgin Mary;* and *The Spiritual Way of St. Jeanne D'Arc.*

Fredrica Harris Thompsett is the Mary Wolfe Professor of Historical Theology at the Episcopal Divinity School, Cambridge, Massachusetts. She is a scholar of the English Reformation. She is the author of *Courageous Incarnation: In Intimacy, Work, Childhood, and Aging* and *Living with History.* She is a member of the corporation of the *Anglican Theological Review,* representing the Episcopal Divinity School.

Miroslav Volf is Henry B. Wright Professor of Theology at Yale Divinity School. He taught at Evangelical Theological Seminary and Fuller Theological Seminary before joining the Yale faculty in 1998. His scholarly contributions have focused on systematic and ecumenical theology as well as on issues at the intersection of theology and broader culture. In addition to numerous articles, his publications include *Zukunft der Arbeit – Arbeit der Zukunft: Der Arbeitsbegriff bei Karl Marx und seine theologische Wertung* (translated into Croatian and Korean); *Work in the Spirit:*

Toward a Theology of Work; After Our Likeness: The Church as the Image of the Trinity (translation of the German edition); and *Exclusion and Embrace: A Theological Exploration of Identity, Otherness, and Reconciliation* (translated into Hungarian, Croatian, and Spanish). He has edited or co-edited *The Future of Theology: Essays in Honor of Jürgen Moltmann; A Passion for God's Reign;* and *Practicing Theology*. He has had extensive experience in ecumenical work, including dialogues with the Pontifical Council for Promoting Christian Unity. He is a member of the American Academy of Religion and American Theological Association and has held fellowships from the Alexander von Humboldt Foundation (Germany) and the Pew Foundation. He is currently working on a manuscript that explores suffering, memory, and redemption, and is engaged in research on the logic of grace as well as on trinitarian theology.

Paul F. M. Zahl is dean of the Cathedral Church of the Advent in Birmingham, Alabama. He has also served as rector of Episcopal churches in Scarborough, New York, and Charleston, South Carolina, and was curate of Grace Church in New York City. His publications include *Who Will Deliver Us?; The Protestant Face of Anglicanism;* and *A Short Systematic Theology*. He is a member of the corporation of the *Anglican Theological Review,* elected at large.

John D. Zemler is a visiting assistant professor at the Marquette University Department of Theology. He is a former artillery captain in the U.S. Army and is now a teacher of scripture. He teaches courses in the Old and New Testaments, Biblical Folklore, Christology, and the Theology of Nonviolence. In Biblical Folklore, he illustrates how folklore conveys theology. In the Theology of Nonviolence, he emphasizes that violence can almost always be avoided in individual, economic, and military situations if people are willing to set aside their egos and humanize one another.

Wanda Zemler-Cizewski is an associate professor in the Department of Theology at Marquette University, Milwaukee. She specializes in the history and theology of the Middle Ages, especially the theology of the twelfth century. She is currently working on a book-length study of the medieval exegesis of Genesis 2:18–25 (the creation of Eve). She has published numerous articles on theology in the twelfth and thirteenth centuries.

www.ingramcontent.com/pod-product-compliance
Lightning Source LLC
Chambersburg PA
CBHW070232230426
43664CB00014B/2275